DATE DUE

ORNETTE COLEMAN

Also by John Litweiler

The Freedom Principle: Jazz After 1958

ORNETTE COLEMAN

A Harmolodic Life

JOHN LITWEILER

WILLIAM MORROW AND COMPANY, INC.
New York

Library of Congress Cataloging-in-Publication Data

Litweiler, John.
    Ornette Coleman : a harmolodic life / John Litweiler.
        p.   cm.
    Includes bibliographical references and index.
    ISBN 0-688-07212-7
    1. Coleman, Ornette. 2. Jazz musicians—United States—Biography.
I Title.
ML419.C63L6   1993
788.7′165′092—dc20
    [B]   92-22969
                                                                      CIP
                                                                       MN

Printed in the United States of America

First U.S. Edition

1   2   3   4   5   6   7   8   9   10

BOOK DESIGN BY PAUL CHEVANNES

Acknowledgments

Surely the major research published to date on the subject of Ornette Coleman has been *Ornette Coleman 1958–1979: a Discography* by David Wild and Michael Cuscuna, supplemented with updated material in three issues of Wild's magazine *disc'ribe* in the early 1980s; all are published by Wildmusic, GPO 362566, San Juan, Puerto Rico 00936, U.S.A. David Wild not only gave permission to base this book's condensed discography on his own and Cuscuna's much more detailed and inclusive work, he offered editorial suggestions, transcribed Ornette's saxophone solo on the classic "Free," transcribed my 1981 interview with Ornette, and shared a tape of his own unpublished interview. Even today, when schools of jazz proliferate, so much of the most valuable scholarship takes place outside academy walls, the work of knowledgeable, tireless music devotees; among them, the work of David Wild certainly stands out.

So many people graciously provided information and answered my questions about Ornette Coleman's life and career. Truvenza Coleman Leach, in particular, told me about her brother's early years in Fort Worth; thanks also to Bobby Bradford, John Carter—even now, I can't believe the loss of this very important artist—

Charles Moffett, Dewey Redman, Charlie Haden, Gunther Schuller, James "Blood" Ulmer, and Kathelin Hoffman. Further thanks to John Snyder for the interview with him and for sharing a copy of his as-yet unpublished essay on Ornette Coleman; and to Marilyn Lewis, Frances Blackwell, Paul Jeffrey, Pierre Dorge, Richard Wang, John Koenig, Michael Cuscuna, Kunle Mwanga, Joel Dorn, and especially Denardo Coleman for clarifying matters and helping me over rough spots.

Jerry DeMuth, Max Harrison, Kevin Whitehead, Martin Williams, John Szwed, and Larry Kart shared material from their files; Whitehead and Bob Blumenthal also shared tapes of their interviews with Dewey Redman and Ornette Coleman; and also thanks to Art Lange, Howard Mandel, Michael Cuscuna, and Terry Martin for important leads and information. This book would have been impossible to write without the resources of the Chicago Jazz Archives, based at the University of Chicago's Regenstein Library, and without the help of Hans Lenneberg and Chris Carr there. Shawn Kennedy of *The New York Times* did detective work at a critical juncture; thanks also to Cameron Poulter, Charlcea Bullard of the *Fort Worth Star-Telegram*, Don Moye, Thurman Barker, Kay McCarty, Ann Campbell, and several Litweilers for many kinds of aid.

This book began as a project of Quartet Books in London, with preliminary work done by Richard Williams, yet another dedicated scribe; in America, editor Jim Landis, who himself once played Ornette Coleman-inspired saxophone, brought the project to William Morrow and Company. I'm grateful to my agent, Jane Jordan Browne, to Landis, Michael Goodman, Paul Bresnick, and Elisa Petrini of Morrow, and to Chris Parker, Richard Cook, and especially Eliza Pakenham of Quartet for aid, encouragement, and, above all else, saintly patience.

I can well remember the excitement over Ornette Coleman when his first records began to appear, and my own wonder and delight at the rich, blues-crying saxophone solos of *Tomorrow Is the Question!* thirty-two years ago—for me, as for so many others, the power of that first experience of his music has multiplied many times in the years since; his art has been an ongoing, fundamental element of beauty and vision in our lives. So thanks above all else to Ornette Coleman for his music—thanks also for his interviews with me in 1981, in New York City, and with

Lawrence Rocke and me (broadcast on WHPK-FM, Chicago) in 1986. Probably no other jazz artist of our time has been as often interviewed as Ornette Coleman, yet the most intimate story has yet to be told, so the reports that he is writing his autobiography are tantalizing indeed.

John Litweiler

Contents

ORNETTE COLEMAN

Prologue

There are four artists whose music and presence were major turning points in the course of jazz history: Buddy Bolden, Louis Armstrong, Charlie Parker, and Ornette Coleman. Bolden, the legendary first player of jazz, may be only a legend; his playing career ended years before the first jazz recordings were made, and we know of him only through his contemporaries' memories and Bunk Johnson's imitations of a Bolden performance, three to four decades after the event. We know, however, that Armstrong's late-1920s masterpieces virtually defined the word *jazz* for all time, separating this young and fragile music from the American popular musics that surrounded it—musics that had the potential to wholly absorb it, in the way ragtime was absorbed. Nearly two decades later, in the decline of the Swing Era that Armstrong had inspired, Parker climaxed a generation's harmonic and structural discoveries with a matching rhythmic genius, all as elements of a lyricism whose purity and exaltation are almost unrivaled in the art's history. Three years after Parker's death, and slightly over a dozen years since he had led his first recording session, Ornette Coleman emerged on record, with a musical principle—"the pattern for the tune will be forgotten, and the tune itself will be the pattern"[1]—to

15

overturn the very foundations of jazz for its entire previous existence.

Is it true that Coleman, as critic Max Harrison has suggested, is the most far-reaching innovator in jazz's history? Certainly the upheaval his music inspired has had the longest-lasting consequences: In the thirty-odd years since his first album *Something Else!* appeared, no other jazz artist's work has had anything approaching equal resonance. Of the four other main inspirations to today's jazz, one, Albert Ayler, was clearly a successor to Coleman who pushed aspects of Coleman's discoveries to extremes. Two others, Miles Davis and Bill Evans, simply extended the evolution of the bop era to its lingering final stages, Evans with his highly refined sensibility, Davis with modal jazz and fusion music that were, in a way, equally refined; John Coltrane, like Davis, passed through bop and modes and then, after his early hearing of and brief study with Ornette Coleman, arrived at the most radical phases of his steady evolution. To varying degrees the musics of all four were influenced by Ornette Coleman's music, and each in turn exerted great influence himself—but without Coleman's breadth and depth.

In fact, it's fair to call the years since *Something Else!* was released the Ornette Coleman era. What have been the main directions of jazz development in this era? First, and very soon after Coleman's first recordings, there emerged mature, fully developed musics by Cecil Taylor, John Coltrane, and Eric Dolphy, all highly distinctive and, to a large extent, mutually exclusive improvisers. A generation of young musicians who had worked with and/or been encouraged by these three and Coleman constituted a lively New York City underground, culminating in Albert Ayler's extraordinary attempt to reinvent jazz altogether, using its very source materials but, in light of Coleman-inspired concepts of musical freedom. Eight hundred miles away, Chicago improvisers and composers evolved distinctive new concepts of sound, rhythm, form, and structure from ideas germinated in Coleman's work, while across the Atlantic, Coleman's freedom led to free improvisation, and his example led to a European jazz tradition that, while yet quite young, is evolving separately from America's jazz traditions and includes some authentically major artists. Meanwhile, amid all this activity two more idioms evolved: unaccompanied solo improvisations on instruments other than traditional rhythm section instruments, and third stream music—deliberate attempts to fuse jazz and separate, distinctive traditions from around the world—both composed and improvised.

Simultaneously, bop's successor, hard bop, entered its lingering modal period and progressed to various varieties of electric and anti-electric fusion musics, or to black and white fusion musics, as critic Bob Blumenthal once called them. In the 1980s and 1990s a number of young musicians have revived middle and late stages of hard bop, with something of the attitudes of the 1940s traditional jazz revival, to much critical and popular success; as for fusion music, it has produced quite the most popular kind of jazz since the Swing Era.

To all of these, add the separate and distinct directions of Ornette Coleman's own career: after his early small groups, his composing, his violin improvising, and his Free fusion music. Then contrast all of these lines of development with the situation in 1958, when *Something Else!* was recorded, when cool and West Coast jazz lingered, third stream composition was appearing, a few underground or near-underground musicians such as Cecil Taylor, Charles Mingus, and Herbie Nichols were discovering their own voices, and the bop-to-hard-bop succession was the principal line of jazz development. There's no doubt about it—Ornette Coleman was the catalyst for a veritable explosion of activity and of originality.

His impact was not only upon the music itself, it was on the ways jazz artists perceived themselves and their careers. By no means was he the first jazz musician to produce himself in concert and to record himself—but his self-recorded, self-promoted concert at New York City's Town Hall in December 1962 came in the midst of a nationwide jazz recession, and left an important message to a great many younger players who were his successors: If you want your music to be heard, present it yourself. Again, he was hardly the first jazz artist to reject nightclub performing in favor of concert and festival appearances, but because an endless round of nightclub appearances had constituted most jazz musicians' careers since World War II, Ornette Coleman's selectivity about where and when he would perform and the high fees he demanded were still radical. More than bop, swing, or traditional jazz, Free jazz made unique demands on its listeners' attention; it was, therefore, less serviceable as a stimulus to the purchasing of alcohol, and thus a less viable nightclub commodity than earlier kinds of jazz. The natural alternative, for Free musicians, was a career of concerts and festivals. Ideally, an artist should have time and opportunity to care for his own creative needs to compose, meet and recruit musicians, and rehearse, a care implicit in Coleman's decision to pursue a selective performance career. In this way, again, he became a model for any number of musicians who came after him.

A great many people of the over-forty generations can well remember the first time they heard Ornette Coleman's music, usually on the radio or on record. His first impact was enormous—yet listening again to *Something Else!* after over three decades of the Coleman era, it is hard to recall just why this music sounded so absolutely special. Was it the horn solos that intermittently clashed with the pianist's chord changes? Was it the distinctive sounds of the two horns, both in their solos and when they played his original themes? The controversy that arose over Ornette in late 1959, when he first played in New York, is another matter. One of the aspects of the bop revolution was extramusical: A good many jazz musicians and their audiences, conscious of their intellectual and emotional distances from middle-class society and values, nevertheless were themselves exclusive in their attitudes—witness the early rejection of the New York underground players. The young Coleman, too, was an outsider. While in Los Angeles he'd never been part of the largely white West Coast school, which engaged in occasional experimentation but which was largely centered around former big band sidemen (especially from the Woody Herman and Stan Kenton bands) and studio musicians. The black mainstream jazz modernists in Los Angeles were at least as conservative, and they, too, rejected Coleman. Most important, playing bop and hard bop is a discipline that demands extreme involvement in its own forms, harmonies, and rhythms. A musician such as Ornette, whose musical principles called for a far different discipline, was, *ipso facto*, not part of the New York hard bop crowd. More than that, given the publicity attending his New York debut, he was an economic rival of the hard bop players: An audience listening to him in a club or on a record is, obviously, not listening to an older musical idiom. Though his early New York appearances came in a period when hard-core, straightforward jazz was at its peak of postwar popularity, competition for engagements among even outstanding musicians was still keen, and Ornette Coleman's sudden success was resented.

In any case, he prevailed. He persisted in his art at a time when the most significant social movement of twentieth-century America, the African-American drive for equal opportunity and freedom of choice, was gaining momentum. Society was being transformed; apart from the new, widespread black self-awareness, an alternative society of young people with creative values was beginning to emerge. In this atmosphere of openness to new art and new insights, Ornette Coleman's music, after its years of development in California, finally found acceptance—even direct influence—and the opportunity to expand.

"The thing that I have always felt—I think I got it from my mother—is patience," Ornette has said.[2] His persistence came from a unique way of viewing a jazz artist's relation to the conventions of jazz careerdom, and that in itself was the result of a unique way of perceiving that was already evident in his youth. It is no accident that the words *free* and *freedom* have for so long been linked with his career and music. Freedom from conventional modes of thought and conclusions abut every aspect of life is, after all, born with every mortal child; one's circumstances may betray that freedom, but an individual with a strong sense of his own values will again and again exercise freedom of choice, belief, and expression throughout life. The most valuable aspect of freedom, of course, is the freedom to assert your own perceptions in the face of received attitudes and dogma. Ornette Coleman's choices in music and life—his progress to a personal musical voice; his travails in Texas, the South, and Los Angeles; his long periods of silence; his attitudes toward money and creature comforts, toward art and his fellow beings—certainly bespeak persistence in the pursuit of freedom.

It would be understandable if Ornette Coleman, having experienced success after long years of rejection, incomprehension, hostility, and even what appeared to be betrayal, reacted with bitterness and resentment. They have never perverted him, though—quite the contrary, his natural inclination is to great patience with his associates and his fellow mortals, and to an attitude of high tolerance and unjudgmental acceptance. On the other hand, the extent of his success, the realization that he is the major jazz artist of the present time, has left him with a sense of leadership and attendant responsibility. "Ornette carries a great weight," says his friend John Snyder.

"Born, work, sad and happy and etc."[3] is how Ornette Coleman once summarized his life, and those who know him add terms like kind, stubborn, generous, loyal, gregarious, shy, serious, frivolous, a bad businessman, infinitely curious about a wide range of subjects, and so on, features and contradictions that constitute a sane life. A soft-spoken individual with whom others often quickly find resonating chords of openness and interest, he is also wary of being misunderstood. Seeking to express himself in his art, he became, incidentally, a prophet of the jazz and an icon of modern art. More to the point, once the revolutionary surface is forgotten and his music's idiom becomes familiar, he is the sort of person his recordings reveal him to be: happy, sad, confident, fearful, and all the rest.

"Do you know what freedom is? The right to die *your way*," he once said.[4] Substitute the word *live* for *die* and you have the meaning of his art and life.

Randolph Denard Ornette Coleman was born in Fort Worth, Texas, and already an element of confusion about his life enters his story. Most references give his birthdate as March 19, 1930, while his sister, Truvenza Coleman Leach, gives it as March 9, 1931. Their parents, Randolph and Rosa Coleman, came from Robertson County, Texas, a little past halfway from Fort Worth, in northern Texas, to Houston, near the Gulf of Mexico. Randolph was from Calvert, according to Truvenza, who believes her mother came from there too. Randolph and Rosa Coleman married when young and raised two sons and two daughters. The oldest was Allen Coleman, who left home to live in California, where he worked in an aircraft company. He died in the 1940s. The second was Vera Coleman, who was only a seventeen-year-old high school student when she died, having been struck by a cattle truck. Truvenza, born a year before Ornette, says that her father served in the U.S. Army at about the time of World War I, and worked in Fort Worth as a cook and as a mechanic. A cousin named Charles Brown, born in Hearne, Texas, eight miles from Calvert, was a singer, states Truvenza, but it is not likely that this was the same Charles Brown who plays piano, sings, and recorded 1940s and 1950s hits such as

"Drifting Blues," "Merry Christmas, Baby," and "Black Night." That Charles Brown was born in Texas City. Asked in 1988 if he was related to the Fort Worth Colemans, his reply was noncommittal: "Could be. I have relatives all over Texas." Truvenza also refers to the great guitarist-singer T-Bone Walker as her uncle; Walker lived in Fort Worth, where he met his wife in the early 1930s and, says Truvenza, "He started me with piano. I'd sit in his lap and he tried to teach me."

Like her brother Ornette, the youngest in the family, Truvenza Coleman Leach has had a musical career. Using the professional name Trudy Coleman, she first worked as a trombonist and bandleader, and then one night during an engagement, "the man wanted a vocalist. So one of the guys said, 'Well, the money he's going to pay us, you'd better try it,' and I started that night." Trudy sang standards, songs from the repertoires of Billie Holiday, Sarah Vaughan, and other jazz singers. Her six-piece band also played rock and roll, country and western, blues, and whatever other kinds of music would entertain an audience over the years. She made a handful of 45 rpm records for short-lived Forth Worth–area labels, and about 1969, in a period when the major jazz-recording producer John Hammond was recording music "on spec" with the anticipation of releasing it on the Columbia label, Trudy Coleman did an album for him. At the time Trudy was living in New York City on Prince Street with her brother and performing in the Catskills, where she was accompanied by a band led by tenor saxophonist Paul Jeffrey that included pianist Paul Bley, among others. Trudy's Columbia album included sidemen such as Don Cherry, Dewey Redman, and Charles Moffett, but the record company did not release it. She has been retired since the late 1970s.

"My mother started us in music—all four of us," Trudy recalls. "And my father sang. Not professionally, but I guess that's where we got it from." Rosa Coleman had a piano in the house, Randolph Coleman sang in a quartet, and friends would come over to the house to sing and play: "This one man, Bill Kennard, played drums, and Wiley Brown—he was blind—and Mr. Jesse Hooker, he played clarinet. Ornette was very small. So small, our mother made us go to bed when they would have a party, or were having company or rehearsal or something. I don't know where Daddy would perform—we were not allowed to go hear him. 'Love in

Bloom,' that's an old number, my daddy used to sing all of those numbers."

The Colemans were a religious family. Randolph sang in church, Rosa did clerical work there, and Ornette was baptized a Methodist. The family lived in a small house by the railroad tracks, on the east side of Fort Worth where the trains carried cattle to the stockyards not far away, and Ornette's parents worried about him, as a boy, playing too near the trains. Disobedience would bring him swift punishment. "We had a strict upbringing," Trudy remembers. She and Ornette were children during the Depression, and "we didn't have a whole lot of money—we didn't have money to throw away or something like that, but I don't remember going without anything. I might have had to, but I didn't realize it. We had so much love in our family, maybe we were poor and didn't know it. There's a song: 'We ate every night, and the roof stayed on tight.' "

Ornette's memories are rather different, as he told critic Whitney Balliett. He didn't know his father very well. The only photo he's seen of Randolph Coleman showed him in a baseball uniform, when he played on an amateur team. "My mother told me that he was a singer—that he had a very good voice. . . . I remember sitting on his lap. He was tall and very dark. I've heard since . . . that he was a construction worker and a cook. . . . My mother was tall and dark and very strict. She was religious-like, and she didn't smoke or drink or go to night clubs or movies. . . . I think she did something like selling Avon products. . . ."[1] Trudy recalls that her mother worked as a clerk in a funeral home. Rosa Coleman only heard her son play once, in a concert by the Ornette Coleman Trio (Ornette, alto saxophone, trumpet, violin; David Izenzon, bass; Charles Moffett, drums) that Trudy Coleman promoted in Fort Worth in 1966. Ornette used to send her copies of his recordings, and when he returned to visit her in Fort Worth he'd find them in unopened mailing cartons in her home.

Ornette remembers "my sister taking me to a black woman's house in the ghetto. She had a school in her house, and I played with blocks. I was about two, and it cost twenty-five cents a day. But often we didn't have any money, and I'd go without food." (Contrast this with Trudy's memories of growing up during the Depression.) "I went to two different schools—both black, and both very good and strict. A teacher spanked me once because I told her she was wrong. But I was right, and I believe that to this day. I learned quickly in school that all you had to know was the answers. I also learned that once you found out what you should know you didn't have to be there every day. I had to walk about three miles over a lot of train tracks to my first school, and I'd get tired, and some days I'd never make it. When my mother found out, she near beat me to death."[2] At one point, Ornette played hooky for six weeks, "and when my mother found out, she beat me for days." Nevertheless, Ornette maintains, "I never was bad. I just didn't understand what adults were doing."[3]

Is there a trace, perhaps, of disingenuousness in that remark? Because a statement like his earlier "I learned quickly in school that all you had to know was the answers" shows a sharp early sensitivity to a system in which education, in the sense of acquiring sensitivity and proficiency in various disciplines, is less important than the simple amassing of answers. Another event that was more significant to Ornette's developing self-awareness occurred in childhood: "Well, I lost my father when I was seven, and I remember my mother telling me that I would have to be the one that would do the job he would have done if he was still alive—the breadwinner." Perhaps it was remembering the changes in his life that occurred after his father's death, a time when Ornette, his mother, and two sisters lived together (Allen had married and left home), that led him to say, "I didn't come from a poor family, I came from a *po'* family. Poorer than poor."[4]

Outside of home, there was plenty of other music for Ornette to hear on the east side of Fort Worth: "As little kids, my friends and I used to play on kazoos and imitate bands. There were three churches right on my block, and I remember all the time going from one church to the other listening to gospel music."[5] This was the time of the Swing Era, and there was, along with a vast amount of ephemeral music, a higher proportion of genuinely valuable popular music—swing music—than America has enjoyed at any other time in the twentieth century. Ornette recalls hearing big band music by Glenn Miller, Tommy Dorsey, Lucky Millinder, and Les Brown's "Sentimental Journey." Dewey Redman, who also grew up in Fort Worth during those years, recalls that Forth Worth had a black radio station that played music—"They called it race music." When Ornette was in the seventh or eighth grade, Fort Worth bandleader Sonny Strain brought his band to play at a school assembly. Ornette says, "I just really discovered how instruments looked. I asked them, 'What is that? And what is that?' and found out that the instrument that I'd heard that I'd gotten really excited about was the saxophone.

"I asked my mother for a horn, and she said that if I went out and worked, I could have it. I went out and worked, around 1944–45—shining shoes, busboying in hotels, doing summer jobs like scraping paint, all kinds of little jobs. Finally, after saving up my money, my mother told me to look under the couch, and there was a horn, a gold-plated Conn." He took to this alto saxophone right away, teaching himself to play songs he'd heard on the radio and attempting to learn music without the aid of a teacher that he couldn't afford. "I remember thinking, as the book said, the first seven letters of the alphabet were the first seven letters of music, ABC-DEFG."

But the standard concert scale is CDEFGAB.

"So I thought my C that I was playing on the saxophone was A, like that, right? Later on I found that it did exist thataway only because the E-flat alto, when you play C natural, it is [concert] A [transposed]. So I was right in one way and wrong in another—I mean, sound, I was right. Then I started analyzing why it exists thataway, and to this very day I realize more and more that all things that are designed with a strict logic only apply against something: It is not the only way it's done. In other words, if you take an instrument and you happen to feel it a way you can express yourself, it becomes its own law."

Very soon, then, Ornette was exploring the variety of sounds his alto could make, "when I realized that you could play sharp or flat in tune. That came very early in my saxophone interest. I used to play one note all day, and I used to try to find how many different sounds I could get out of the mouthpiece (I'm still looking for the magic mouthpiece). That just came about from, I'd hear so many different tones and sounds. . . ."

He continued to study the saxophone by himself. The only formal instruction he had came when, as a fifteen-year-old, he took a trip to New York City, to visit an aunt who was married to the excellent, Louis Armstrong–inspired trumpeter Doc Cheatham. It was Cheatham who brought young Ornette to saxophone teacher Walter "Foots" Thomas, a former, longtime Cab Calloway sideman. "It seems I made a lot of faces when I played," Ornette remembered. "Thomas had me look into the mirror and play for an hour. That was my lesson."[6]

Learning to play the saxophone without instruction had serious drawbacks. Joining a church band, for instance, he played his misinterpretation of a scale, to the bandleader's derision: "Look at this boy. Playing the instrument wrong for two years. He'll never be a saxophone player."[7] There was some help at hand, though, from Ornette's cousin, James Jordan. He was slightly older than Ornette, played alto and baritone saxes himself, and even gave music lessons on the saxophones. Ornette recalled that the formally trained Jordan "had to know exactly what a thing was all about before he did it. . . . I always wanted to earn respect from Jordan because he went to school and I didn't."[8]

For all the disadvantages of his musical education, Ornette was a fast learner. In his midteens, he began to meet other Fort Worth musicians, both young ones like himself and the older musicians they looked up to. One night a highly admired local saxophonist whom Ornette had never heard showed up at the Coleman house at three o'clock in the morning; he knew that Ornette had a horn, and he wanted to borrow it for a gig. Rosa Coleman didn't like the idea, but Ornette convinced her that he was going to get paid ten dollars for the loan, and anyway he'd go along with the musician to the honky-tonk where he played to retrieve the sax at closing time.

Fort Worth, Texas, lies virtually on the margin between East and West. Originally a frontier town, it is located on the legendary Chisholm Trail, a resting place on the great cattle drives of the nineteenth century. The city retained something of its frontier spirit well into the twentieth century. Fifteen miles west of Fort Worth the cattle ranches begin; oil fortunes are also based there because Fort Worth has also long been a main supply center for the oil industry to the north and west. Some of this lingering frontier spirit is by now admittedly ersatz: In the 1980s, when oil prices dropped, oil people in the flat land and rolling hills near Fort Worth began stocking their vast lands with antelope, lions, and other nonnative game, and charged wealthy "sportsmen" for hunting privileges.

Fort Worth was a segregated city where the black population has long been around 10 percent of the total. Black communities were scattered throughout Fort Worth; one, the east side area where Ornette grew up, is considered, even today, "the wrong side of the tracks." The city's one black high school, I. M. Terrell, was situated near the center of town. There Ornette attended high school, three miles from home, and got to meet other young musicians, students like himself: trumpeter Charles Moffett and woodwind players John Carter, Prince Lasha, King Curtis, and Dewey Redman among them. He played in the high school band until he was kicked out for indulging in some improvising in the midst of John Philip Sousa's "Washington Post March"—Ornette claimed innocence, though he had on other occasions slipped jazz into the band's music without being caught. He'd also begun to play in a church band that was twenty to twenty-five musicians strong, and performed in area churches and at conventions. He was listening hard to local and touring musicians in those days: "Jazz bands, rhythm-and-blues bands would come through Fort Worth and stay a week or two—sometimes they would get stranded. There was a very famous black hotel called the Jim Hotel in Fort Worth, and these musicians would stay there and have jam sessions. I heard Lester Young and lots of other people. He was playing with a guy I thought played much better named Red Connors. There was also a very very beautiful saxophone player named Weldon Haggen—I hadn't had a chance to listen to him but once or twice, but he was unbelievable. I think that's where Red Connors got his information from."

The younger generation of Fort Worth musicians all admired Thomas "Red" Connors in the late 1940s. Prince Lasha called him "the greatest inspiration in the South-West."[9] Moffett, while yet in high school, played trumpet in Connors's combo. Redman says, "There's no way to describe what he did, but I would say he was the John Coltrane of that time. The first time I heard him play, he completely knocked me out because of his command of the instrument, his phrasing, his tone, his playing. I'd say that his tone was a Gene Ammons-Wardell-Dexterish kind of sound—that would be close." Connors played tenor and alto saxes; Ornette says,

He was four or five years older than me. He did make some records, and I know someone made tapes of him, but I don't know where they are. During the time when I had met him, bebop had just become very popular, and he was playing all bebop—solos, songs, everything. But he was also holding down a regular Lawrence Welk–type job. He would usually get the best musicians in the city to play

in his own bands. In fact, there weren't a lot of musicians in Fort
Worth—there might have been lots of white musicians, but I didn't
know them because the law wouldn't allow you to seek them out, to
integrate.

The one possible recording credit that I'm aware of reads, "Possibly: . . . Red Conner, [sic] *Tenor Sax*"—one of three tenor saxophonists in a 1948 Jimmy Liggins recording session in Los Angeles.
The tenor solos at the session were almost certainly by Maxwell
Davis, and sound nothing like Ornette's and Redman's descriptions.[10]

There was plenty of give and take between Ornette and his jazz-
inclined schoolmates. Some, like William "Prince" Lasha—originally pronounced "La-*shay*," rhyming with Bechet—practiced at the
Coleman house because their own families objected to their playing
in their own homes. Moffett, who lived two blocks away from the
Colemans, remembered that Ornette's family were "very sweet, you
could always go around to his house and play."[11] Ornette remembers giving King Curtis some instruction about chords and chord
changes ("he always had a beautiful sound"), and Ornette himself
was studying records by swing musicians such as altoist Jimmy Dorsey—"his sound was so round"—altoists Louis Jordan and Pete
Brown, tenorist Lester Young, and by bebop musicians, too.

On that visit to his aunt in New York City as a fifteen-year-old,
Ornette had heard bebop for the first time in concert, by Dizzy
Gillespie's first big band. Before long Ornette was not only playing
bebop, he was playing it so well that Dewey Redman maintains,
"By this time, instead of sounding like Louis Jordan, Ornette
sounded like Bird, now, you dig? I've heard a lot of players, and
Ornette can play closest to Bird of anybody I've ever heard. You
don't hear him doing that any more, 'cause he plays like Ornette
Coleman now, but at that time . . . and I heard him do it again
when we were in Europe, too." When Ornette took up the tenor
saxophone in slightly later teenage years, he reportedly could play
very much like Allen Eager when he chose to.

Ornette has said that he was playing music for money in the year
after he first began studying the alto saxophone. There were honky-
tonks to play in, where the typical bands were two or three horns
plus a rhythm section, and John Carter has pointed out that there
were plenty of dance dates, even society dances to play:

By the midforties—see, during the Second World War a good many young men who would have been out there playing were in the service. High school–age boys could go out and get work at what would ordinarily be a man's job—that was true in every area of society, and it was true in music. We would play, not so many clubs that high school boys couldn't go into, but a lot of country towns all around Fort Worth, as far as El Paso. We made a lot of money in high school because of that.

Ornette says,

So when I found out I could play music, I really approached the thought that music was the thing that I was going to support my family with and eventually achieve the things that I wished to possess—use music to make money. And it wasn't until I had finished high school and got into an instrumental music per se like bebop—just into the saxophone, since I was a saxophone player—that I started thinking less and less of making money through one specific goal that I had musically. . . .

Ornette's playing music to make money left his family in a dilemma: The income was definitely needed at home, but the places where Ornette often played were the lowest kind of dives. Rosa Coleman solved the problem by deciding that older sister Truvenza should chaperone Ornette to the jobs and collect his pay at evening's end—and so she did.

"In Fort Worth there was lots of segregation," Ornette says. "I know myself, I'd go and play in a white nightclub, and two nights I'd go over and play in a black nightclub, then go over and play in a Spanish, Mexican place. Usually you could play what was popular on the radio everywhere. You could play pop songs in any style, anywhere." And, of course, he learned the appropriate repertoires unique to each of his separate white, black, and Mexican audiences ("white people liked 'Stardust,' black people like 'Flying Home' "[12]). He stayed with the alto saxophone for two years. But then one day, while playing football with some friends in an empty lot, Ornette broke his collarbone. The injury was serious enough that he had to leave school, at least temporarily. Ornette saw to it that something good came from his injury: "I told my mother that the doctor told me that the alto was too hard to play and I needed another instrument—but it wasn't true. I just wanted to get a tenor, because it was easy to get jobs on a tenor in rhythm-and-blues bands. I was playing alto mostly in pop bands, like 'Stardust' and all those kinds of pop songs. In rhythm and blues, I was playing more riffs and more rhythmic things. And so my mother changed my horn, got a tenor, and I started playing tenor around there, '46, '47. I played it about two or three years."

The tenor saxophone proved a real stimulus to Ornette's teenage musical career. He and some gifted young fellow students at I. M. Terrell formed a band, the Jam Jivers, that played high school assemblies and also—managed by Trudy Coleman—dances and engagements. "It was a little jazz group," says Charles Moffett, who played trumpet with the Jam Jivers. "We were playing things like from Louis Jordan recordings. Prince Lasha was singing. As a matter of fact, we played some Charlie Parker tunes, too—Prince Lasha was trying to play alto saxophone like Bird." Dewey Redman remembers a trumpet player named Wannell Goodley as one of the Jam Jivers, and Moffett, even then, playing drums, alternating with another young percussionist. Louis Jordan was an immensely popular figure in the 1940s. With his jump band, the Tympany Five, he made film shorts and recordings and toured the country north and south, playing a simplified post–Johnny Hodges swing style on alto sax with a tone sometimes hard, sometimes lush, and, most popularly, wrote and sang jivy songs like "Choo Choo Ch'Boogie" and "Ain't Nobody Here but Us Chickens." "Guys would be on tour, would make the southern circuit and come through Fort Worth," says Dewey Redman. "Louis Jordan would draw a big crowd—it was always a dance, never like a concert—Illinois Jacquet, Big Jay McNeely—Buddy Johnson was a *big* draw—T-Bone Walker, Joe Liggins, Jimmy Liggins, Pee Wee Crayton, Arnett Cobb. . . ." Ornette recalls hearing Roy Brown, Charles Brown, Lonnie Johnson, and Gatemouth Moore in Fort Worth. It's important to note that the music played by most of these musicians was the sophisticated kind that marked the intersection of the jazz and blues traditions. Bebop musicians may have played in the Jacquet and Cobb bands, but these and the others that Redman and Ornette name were rooted in the Swing Era, both harmonically and rhythmically.

It has been speculated that the older Texas blues tradition, as exemplified by artists such as guitarist-singer Lightnin' Hopkins and the quite remarkable pianist Alex Moore, was an influence on

Ornette Coleman's evolving music. These older players' attitudes to musical line, rhythm, and harmony had surrealistic results, including impulsive compressings and stretching of harmonic structures—with them, a chorus of a twelve-bar blues might last fifteen bars, or ten and a half bars, with anticipated or delayed or dropped chord changes. Ornette says that he never heard the older kinds of blues in youth, so he could not have been influenced by them. Instead, as a young professional tenor saxophonist, he studied the likes of Jacquet, Cobb—both originally Texans—Lynn Hope, and especially Big Jay McNeely, whose one-note riffing and antics won him several years of postwar fame. "I was more like a honker," Ornette reveals. "I have always been able to play very freely rhythmically—if I knew the key, I could do that very well, and easily. That's one reason why I'd gotten lots of jobs, because I could please the crowd, you know." With a big saxophone sound? "Yeah, and Illinois Jacquet had put out 'Flying Home,' and then I'd heard a lot of tenor players in Texas that I'd really liked, and they were influencing me. . . . I never thought about being called [a jazz saxophone player]—I was just playing the saxophone, you know. It wasn't until I got to California and New York that the word *jazz* started being more constrictingly applied to what I was doing than anything else."

Playing tenor saxophone and doing his Big Jay McNeely contortions—aiming his horn at the ceiling, lying on the floor or jumping on tables as he played—Ornette thrived. "Yes, at the club he was dancing quite a bit—he was moving and dancing with that tenor saxophone, on top of tables and everything else—he was having a good time," says Moffett. "He was enjoying himself and making everyone else enjoy themselves. . . . As a matter of fact, I think at the time Ornette and Prince Lasha used to brag that they were making as much money as the schoolteachers that were teaching them." "In most of my playing in Texas, I was backing up a vocalist," says Ornette, with some modesty; for instance, Trudy Coleman, who was the Jam Jivers' manager, got them a gig backing up the great blues singer Joe Turner during a Fort Worth stay that, according to Ornette, lasted a couple of months.

Ornette was making a hundred dollars a week by playing the saxophone. In the late 1940s that was a healthy middle-class income, and the Coleman family surely could use the money. What was wrong about it was the kind of places that Ornette often had to play in to make his living. "Most of the places I worked, the music was just a cover for gambling. Whenever there was a raid, people would grab a girl and start dancing to look legitimate while the Texas Rangers chopped up the gambling table with an ax. I'd be playing some real honky-tonk, and before I knew it, people would be fighting and cutting each other up."[13] It happened that Ornette's high school girlfriend was going to graduate a year before him, and he was looking forward to taking her to the prom. He rented a tuxedo, but then on prom night he received a call to work at a notorious bustout joint, "playing for gangsters and lowlifes."[14] That night "was very rough even for that place. A couple of guys got cut up and one was shot and killed. So there I was sitting up in this place in my tuxedo, crying my heart out thinking that the music I was playing was causing these people to cut each other up. . . ."[15] Ornette never did get to the prom. But if he was to support his family by playing music, there was no alternative to playing in the joints. To his mother, he said, "I don't want to play this kind of music anymore. I think I'm influencing these people to kill each other." Rosa Coleman's reply went to the heart of the problem: "What's wrong with you? You want these people to pay you for your soul?" His mother's words made a big impression.

"Ever since she told me that, I learned what being an adult was," says Ornette. "I was still a young person, and I didn't know about being paid for your soul. I was only thinking about doing something moral."[16]

For by this time Ornette's heart was in bebop. There were his jobs with the Jam Jivers and the engagements with other bands, and there was the music he played after hours. Red Connors had become a friend and was showing Ornette some of the intricacies of playing the tenor saxophone. Late at night, after the rest of the clubs in Fort Worth had closed down for the night, there were sessions at the Jim Hotel where Connors, Coleman, and their friends played the latest Charlie Parker songs. On occasion Ornette played bebop material in Connors's band, and claimed that Connors played "every bebop tune that was recorded between 1943 and 1950." Although the band played head arrangements when it played bebop, Connors impressed upon Ornette the importance of reading music fluently. It's part of jazz lore that Charlie Parker discovered his innovatory harmonic extensions while jamming on standard chord changes in a New York City chicken restaurant;

there was a similarly crucial discovery in Ornette's own development. It happened in 1948 while he was playing alto saxophone in Red Connors's band for an all-white dance. The band was playing "some standard theme like 'Stardust,' and it was my turn to solo on the chord changes of the tune. In that situation, it's like having to know the results of all the changes before you even play them, compacting them all in your mind. So once I did that, and once I had it all compacted in my head I just literally *removed* it all and just *played*."[17] It was the beginning of Ornette's investigation into how to improvise without following the patterns of chord changes. Ornette was fired that night, after the band's employer told him, "Give 'em vanilla! Give 'em vanilla!" Ornette says the dancers stopped dancing and started listening, even though "I was still playing with a dance feeling, a dance beat. . . ."[18] As early as 1949, then, according to John Carter, Ornette was studying substitute chords and asking questions like "Why does this have to be here?" while Moffett went so far as to say "Ornette was sounding like Ornette by the time he was 17."[19]

Essentially, the bebop that Ornette liked to play best was a fugitive music in Fort Worth in the late 1940s. The dives where he so often performed were certainly one nasty part of his initiation into the business of being a professional musician; another nasty part is typified by the club owner who offered him three dollars a night to play from 9:00 P.M. to 2:00 A.M.—"I got enough money to burn a wet elephant, but I ain't gonna give it away."[20] Of another occasion, when he was playing in a white club, Ornette said, "During intermission, I'd have to go in the back and sit down like I was a porter. One night a drunken woman came right up in front of me and raised her dress over her head, and I was frightened."[21] With good reason, says A. B. Spellman in *Four Lives in the Bebop Business*: If a white man had happened by at the time, Ornette would have been murdered.

Truly, for Ornette Coleman, Fort Worth had become

where the West begins and where life ends. I was playing in a white place, I had a beard and my hair was thicker than it is now, and this fellow came up to me and says, "Say, boy, you can really play saxophone. I imagine where you come from they call you Mister, don't they?" He couldn't see me with my hair and beard coming from Texas, Negroes don't go around looking like that. So I said,

"No, this is my home." "I want to shake your hand," he says, "it's an honor to shake your hand because you're really a saxophone player, but you're still a nigger to me." That's how sick he was. There's no answer for that. That's insanity. Playing in a white place, I couldn't tell him what I wanted to tell him, because I would have been jeopardizing my life.[22]

The hell of it was that in Fort Worth Ornette found it impossible to ignore the perversions of life that resulted from a society's racism:

People in Texas, they're so wealthy, it's still like slavery. You had to be a servant. You had to be serving somebody to make some money. When I finished high school, all the kids I knew who'd been to college and came back, they had porter jobs. What's the reason of going to college? That's the reason I didn't go. You got to try to get a job teaching in the colored school system, or that's it. People have been teaching there for fifty years, you have to wait for them to die. . . . Even the principal where I went to school worked in the summer at the hotel where I worked as a busboy. I saw him doing some things, I didn't have respect for him.[23]

When Ornette graduated from high school he got scholarship offers to black colleges, and even went to a meeting at Samuel Houston College in Austin because he'd heard they had a good band. He did not choose to go to school there, however—"They were too snobby for me," he told Whitney Balliett.[24] That decision left him in his hometown, a place that increasingly evidently was a dead end for his talents and self-aware freedom of spirit. "Ornette was very cooperative with me—he played the music we *had* to play here, but he didn't enjoy it," says Truvenza Coleman Leach. "Well, one reason, we had a very strict mother, and to get away, we played the music because we knew how to do it, see. That's why he said, 'I would rather leave.' . . . At that particular time, there was a restriction on us down here, you know what I mean. He had to play one type or style of music and live one type or style of life to stay here, and he just wasn't ready for it, he just wouldn't do it." Of these constraints, Ornette has said, "In the South, you don't think about who you are and what you want. You only think about surviving. So when I found out that being poor and surviving didn't have anything to do with who you were, I said, 'Oh, wait a minute.'

Then I decided that if I'm going to be poor and black and all, the least thing I'm going to do is to try to find out who I am. I created everything about me."[25]

His objective, then, was not merely to escape the distortions of racism, but to realize the freedom of choice that he needed to mature: "What I mean by adult: if you get to a certain age you can be drafted into the Army or you can buy liquor. They have a certain number that tells you you have these rights. But when you want to be an individual there's no age for that. There's not anything to tell you you can now do this. At some point you just start realizing it."[26]

There were times when Ornette sat in with touring bands that had come to Fort Worth, but the opportunity to escape the city, came not from a jazz or a blues band, but from a traveling tent show: Silas Green from New Orleans. Silas Green was a minstrel show, and thus a survivor of a much earlier era of American show business. At separate times early in the twentieth century, both Ma Rainey and Bessie Smith, the most moving and powerful of all blues artists, had performed in the Silas Green troupe. While the original minstrel shows, in the decades before the Civil War, had been white performers' often racist impressions of black music, comedy, and dance, after Emancipation black minstrel shows began to proliferate. By the turn of the century, states historian Eileen Southern, "the minstrel show offered the only profitable vocation for black creative talent."[27] It was in a minstrel show that a young singer, Gertrude "Ma" Rainey, in 1902, introduced blues to the American stage. During the black minstrel shows' glory years, they performed on international stages as well as in the tents in small towns and cities where they played for black audiences in the American South.

Vaudeville—the variety shows that evolved from minstrel shows—sound movies, and finally television have almost finished off the small carnivals and minstrel shows that were so much a part of small-town American life for so much of this century. By 1949, when Ornette Coleman joined Silas Green from New Orleans, the venerable old black company was a badly deteriorating relic. The entertainment was considered low-down; drinking, gambling, and fighting among the audiences had given minstrel shows a bad reputation. To join the show, Ornette had to once again lie to his mother: He told her that he was joining a band that was going to go to Dallas, twenty-eight miles away. Instead, while Ornette was a member, the Silas Green troupe went to Oklahoma and then through the Deep South as far east as Georgia, around eight hundred miles away. "The comedians were like Uncle Tom–type minstrels," Ornette told A. B. Spellman. The music Ornette played in the show's band, like "Nagasaki" and "Twelfth Street Rag," was old, often of pre–World War I vintage—hardly inspiring to a young bebop saxophonist, but just the thing for the show's half-naked shake dancers. It was a lonely tour for Ornette, the only Texan in the band. "I went to some places, man, and saw some scenes that I hate to even talk about. I thought I played in some rough places in Fort Worth, those gambling joints and all that, but the scenes we had in that minstrel group were something else. It was the worst job I ever had. I was miserable."[28]

The minstrel-show band did play a little bit of blues, and Ornette did get to solo in one of the blues. By the time they got to Natchez, Mississippi, Ornette's fellow musicians actively disliked him. While there, he tried to teach some musical ideas to the band's other tenor saxophonist—"Shit, I was tired of doing all of my practicing alone"[29]—who told the bandleader that Ornette had been trying to make him play bebop. That angered the bandleader, who fired Ornette.

Natchez is a small city, and it was a stroke of blind luck that blues singer Clarence Samuels happened to be there and needed a tenor player in his band. Samuels was touring the South, having had some modest success with his recent recordings. After "like two or three days" in Natchez with the Samuels band, Ornette was eating in a restaurant where he met a man who ran a record company that may have been named Imperial, which in turn may have been the same New Orleans–based Imperial Records that very soon would become a highly successful rhythm-and-blues and then a rock label. The man told Ornette that "someone hadn't shown up or something—he was wondering if I could write songs, make up some songs. And I said 'sure' and I went out there, and I must have made up about eight or nine songs. And before I heard them, I was ran out of town. I mean, I don't know what happened to them." In all likelihood the recordings were never issued, a real loss to listeners of a later generation who wonder what Ornette sounded like at this early stage of his musical development. Given the circumstances of the session—a hastily arranged date with a rhythm section probably composed of rhythm-and-blues musicians like those in the Samuels band—they may well show Ornette's conventional R&B phase, with possibly even some bebop phrasing.

It is important that Ornette appeared to be anything but a conventional nineteen-year-old musician. A skinny youth with a long beard and straightened hair, he was a vegetarian with a "Jesus-type image," which in itself was enough to attract the attention of racist cops. They rousted Ornette, who told them that he was a musician; that won him the cops' curses, after which they ran him out of Natchez, apparently for nothing more than appearing unique. The incident did not prevent his staying with the Samuels band, which continued to tour the South well into the autumn of 1949. The music that Samuels played may have been more up-to-date than the music Ornette had been playing with the tent show, but it was still the kind of music favored in bustout joints.

In a dance hall in Baton Rouge, Louisiana, Ornette, in the middle of his blues tenor solo, interjected some of his modern ideas. Not only did the solo make the tough crowd unhappy—it actually stopped the dance. The band played on after Ornette stopped,

and all of a sudden a guy came in and said some musicians wanted to meet me outside, so I went outside and there were these really big guys, six or seven of them. I said, "How you doin'?" And one of them said, "Where you from?" And I said, "Oh, I'm from Fort Worth." And they were all black guys. . . . They started using "nigger" and all this, and "You're not from Texas with your beard like that and your long hair. You must be one of those Yankee kind of niggers!" And all of a sudden a guy kicked me in my stomach and then he kicked me in the ass and I had my horn cradled in my arms and I blacked out cause blood was everywhere . . . They were just beating me to death. One guy took my tenor and threw it down the street. Then Melvin [Lastie] and the band came out and discovered I was beat up and they took me to the police department. The cops said, "What you doing with that long hair?" And they started calling me nigger and they told me that if them other niggers didn't finish me, *they* were *gonna*.[30]

Now without an instrument, Ornette continued to travel with the Samuels band until it reached New Orleans the next week. Trumpeter Melvin Lastie had met Ornette back when Ornette had joined Clarence Samuels in Natchez, and in New Orleans, near the

end of 1949, Ornette moved in with the Lastie family. Melvin's
father, Frank Lastie, was a drummer in church, and David Lastie,
Melvin's younger brother, played alto saxophone. Ornette attended
church with the Lastie family, and borrowed David's horn to play
in church. Ornette recalls, "Melvin could play his heart out. . . .
He seemed to have been—how can I say it?—very spiritual, but
such an individual. He had a unique sound."

After spending two seasons touring with the shabby tent-show
band and being beaten and abused while on the road with Clarence Samuels, Ornette's time with the Lasties, who were friends
with many New Orleans musicians, must have seemed like the
return of normalcy. He stayed with them six months, supporting
himself by doing yard work and odd jobs. "I never went out
much, socializing, because I wasn't that financially equipped to go
out. So when I did go out and play, I would go somewhere and
hear some guys playing, and they were playing Dixieland. . . . I
didn't do much jamming." When he did, he played David Lastie's
alto saxophone. Modern jazz wasn't plentiful in New Orleans yet,
but Ornette says, "They had a big band at the Pentagon and they
had sessions on Sunday—a guy named Joe Bostic had the band
there. I met Edward [Blackwell] I think through the Johnson
brothers, a couple of brothers that were playing saxophone." In-
terestingly, though both pianist Ellis Marsalis and clarinetist
Alvin Batiste were on the New Orleans modern jazz scene at the
time, neither recalls meeting Ornette until several years later.
The friendship with Blackwell, however, definitely dates back to
1949–1950. Although Plas Johnson, Frank Sinatra's tenor saxophonist and a longtime regular in California studio bands, has
maintained that Blackwell was among the New Orleans musicians
who had refused to play with Ornette because he was "out of
time," both Blackwell and Ornette remember their initial meeting
differently. Says the drummer, "When I heard Ornette for the
first time, I felt the happiness he generates. That was one of the
main things that I loved about his playing. It was so free, although he had so many terrible experiences behind him because
of the way he played. I couldn't understand why people couldn't
hear it."[31]

Ornette was testing bebop's limits, playing with a kind of tuning
and occasional free phrasing that the New Orleans modernists
heard as a distortion of Charlie Parker. Ornette recalls the experi-

ence of returning to the alto saxophone after two or three years of concentrating on the tenor, and becoming very aware that "the things that I was playing on the tenor, when I played the alto I thought I didn't have to change keys: The things I played on tenor worked on alto. . . . I mean, because the tenor is the tonic of the alto—that's when I first started getting into harmolodics, as I call it now." Already, in a city in which modern jazz musicians were a decidedly underground group—traditional jazz and R&B were, as usual, very much the dominant New Orleans musics in 1950—there were modern jazz musicians who rejected Ornette Coleman's music.

By this time the Korean War was going on. While in New Orleans Ornette received his draft notice; at his physical examination the doctors discovered that his broken collarbone hadn't healed properly, and rejected him for the army. It was after that that he pulled up stakes and returned to Fort Worth, where his fortunes suddenly took a turn for the better. A club owner from Amarillo named Carter came to Fort Worth looking for a saxophonist to play in his house band. Charles Moffett recalls,

> It was a pretty big, regular club where black people went nightly for entertainment. We were playing there four or five nights a week, and he would book us in other clubs in surrounding cities that were close to Amarillo on the other nights. That's what kept us working full time. When he came to Fort Worth after Ornette, I had just come back from the Navy in 1950. Ornette came around to my house—we were playing on my back porch at that time—and Ornette only went with him provided I would go, too. At that time, for some reason I didn't even have a set of my own drums any more—I don't know what happened to them. So the man had to buy me a set of drums as well as take me.
>
> When we got there, it was a guitar player named Rudy Green that was singing, that was really over the band. He just needed some backup guys. But as that band developed, it ended up being a Fort Worth band, and I don't know what happened, but after about a week Rudy Green disappeared. We had a guy named Junior who played piano there and a guy who played tenor named Red, from Wichita Falls. Finally, Ornette sent for his cousin, James Jordan, who played baritone sax, from Fort Worth. Then he sent for a guy named Aurelius Hemphill, who played bass—Aurelius was a famous playwright in New York, later. So it really made it like a Fort Worth group.

For all practical purposes, then, it was Ornette's band, a jazzy rhythm-and-blues group, that played for four months in Amarillo and lived in quarters that club-owner Carter provided. By autumn Jordan had returned to Houston-Tillotson College in Austin, and it was through his encouragement that Moffett, who had studied at the U.S. Navy's music school and had also been a boxer—the welterweight champion of the Navy's Pacific Fleet—sought and won a scholarship at Houston-Tillotson, too.

Life seemed hopeful to James Jordan and Charles Moffett as they prepared for college in mid-1950. Ornette Coleman, though, was going back to Fort Worth, the city that he had tried to escape—only to find himself in worse places—the year before.

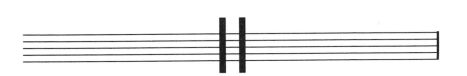

At one time in Ornette's earlier years in Fort Worth he had worked
for a blues singer-guitarist named Connie Curtis "Pee Wee" Crayton, who was originally a Texan himself. When Ornette returned
to Forth Worth in 1950, he discovered that Pee Wee Crayton was
there and "trying to pick up a band, and this guy that had the most
advanced band in Fort Worth became his backup band. They
needed an alto player, and I told my mother that."

It was, of course, Red Connors whose band Crayton had recruited; Ornette had played in the Connors band after the demise
of the Jam Jivers, around 1948. The job with Crayton looked promising—Connors was still playing tenor and directing the band,
Crayton's guitar solo "Blues After Hours" was a hit record that
would become a longtime juke-box standard and would attract audiences, and most important, the Crayton band was going on the
road for a series of one-nighters that would take it to Los Angeles—
fourteen hundred miles west of Fort Worth—"where life ends."

The promise of the Crayton engagements was, for Ornette, not
exactly fulfilled. After some one-night stands, perhaps as few as
two, perhaps as many as ten, "actually it got to the point where he
was paying me not to play. He would sing the regular twelve-bar

blues form and then I would take a solo, and then all of a sudden the people would stop and start listening to me play, they wouldn't dance any more. I guess that was not the proper thing to do, since he was the leader of the band." Crayton, who remembered Ornette as a vegetarian, a "dark, brownskin boy with hair long," remembered the situation differently: "He could play the blues, but he didn't want to. I *made* him play the blues and I paid him *to* play."[1] The band went directly from Texas to California, via autos, and it is possible that Crayton attempted to keep his musicians on a payroll without their playing, since they arrived in Los Angeles to find some dates they were to play had fallen through. "I went with them to California, and when we got out there, there was nothing to do. We were stranded. All of a sudden those guys got drafted into the army—everybody in the band got draft notices—and I was left there in California by myself."

He moved into the Morris Hotel on Fifth Avenue in Los Angeles. It had once been a rather elegant hotel, but by the time Ornette moved in there it was rather run-down, and the neighborhood around it had become dreary, too; he called the area of skid row. It was a hotel where a number of jazz musicians lived, which meant it was a place where he could make musical contacts. They proved to be the wrong sort of contacts, though: Seeing the thin, bearded, long-haired alto saxophonist and hearing him play, they scorned him. Worse, Ornette was unable to find either a playing job or a day gig at the time. The situation was so desperate, in fact, that he had to rely on shipments of canned food and bread in the mail from his mother in order to eat. When his own saxophone broke down completely, he lacked the money to buy a new one and had to rent a horn to play; eventually he had to return it. Drummer Edward Blackwell, who himself moved from New Orleans to Los Angeles at that time, also lived at the Morris, which at least made for some congenial company, and some of the more sophisticated modern jazz musicians in Los Angeles, younger men such as Hampton Hawes and Teddy Edwards, let Ornette sit in with them and even encouraged him. One incident dramatizes the despair Ornette felt in his first Los Angeles period. Rosa Coleman baked him a birthday cake and sent it to him at the Morris. On previous occasions he had shared food with his fellow musicians there; this time they crowded around him and devoured the cake before Ornette, hungry himself, had a chance to eat it.

It was in this period that "a wonderful middle-aged lady let me rent out the back part of a converted garage. There was no heat, but at least it was a place to stay. I took care of the kids—she ran a little nursery—cleaned the kitchen and did other odd jobs."[2] In those days Ornette would walk miles to the black section of Los Angeles, where he attempted to sit in at sessions. In one instance, says Ornette, a popular leader "made me stop playing. I had no money left, so I walked all the way home again in the rain. That sort of thing happened a lot. Some musicians would promise me I could play, but they'd keep me waiting all night. Then, with the place due to close at two in the morning, they'd put me on at three minutes to two. I was getting discouraged. They said I didn't know the changes and was out of tune, but I knew that wasn't so." Lonely, hurt at other musicians' rejection of his own music, Ornette telegraphed his mother to send enough money for him to return to Fort Worth.

Back home, the friends with whom Ornette had played were dispersed in 1952. James Jordan and Charles Moffett were seniors in college, William Lasha had left Fort Worth and was on the move, but Red Connors was back leading a band in the Dallas–Fort Worth area, and Ornette did some playing with him. Also, Ornette recalls,

> I used to play lots of jam sessions. I remember Stan Kenton's band coming through Fort Worth and playing for an all-black sorority dance . . . and the people that was putting on the sorority [dance] took me up to the bandstand and asked him if they would let me sit in with the band. . . . He was very shocked because I had written a melody, a bebop line to fit the changes of "Out of Nowhere," and I asked him to play his arrangement of "Out of Nowhere," and it fit like a glove. He thought I had gotten stranded, he didn't think I was from Fort Worth, and he wanted to offer me a job and help me. I told him, no, that was my home and that I wasn't stranded. . . . I had very long hair and a beard, and I was doing a bebop kind of outfit. Wearing beards and goatees was their style, so I had grown a beard and my hair was—the way the Beatles finally came to America, I was wearing my hair like that in the early fifties. . . . I was more religious—I had just decided to be like that.

Once again Ornette dealt with the Forth Worth dilemma: He wanted to play bebop, for which there was little local market. (Bobby Bradford, who grew up in nearby Dallas, recalls the early-fifties music scene there: "There was an audience for bebop to this extent: When you were playing around town, a band that played for black people, you were going to hear a mixture of bebop and rhythm and blues. A guy could double-time a chorus when we were playing 'Stardust,' but there was no club where you could go hear a band just play *jazz*.") Ornette, in his return to Forth Worth, had not been forgotten by listeners who had heard him during his teenage years there. Bobby Bradford, three or four years younger than Ornette, had heard him play R&B tenor—"His hair was long and he played kind of screaming tenor saxophone. I think he even got on his back [to play]—that was not considered uncouth." Then, in 1953, while a freshman at Houston-Tillotson College in Austin, Bradford attended the wedding of Charles Moffett, and Ornette was Charles's best man at the wedding.

> So after the wedding, part of the reception and buffet dinner was a session of music. Ornette played, [alto saxophonist] Leo Wright, a tenor player from San Antonio named Marcus Adams—all the heavies. All the hams like myself were sitting in the front row. That's the first time I'd heard Ornette play the alto saxophone at length. There were already marks in my mind about where he was going. They played standards, and Ornette was already doing things that nobody could associate with. He was tampering with things in an investigative kind of way. He was playing things that were totally in conflict with the changes—what *appeared* to be in conflict—so the answer to a lot of cats would be, "Well, he's not playing the changes." The chorus after that he probably did, or the chorus before that he played some, in quotes, "strange stuff."

Even though Ornette had formed his own band and was playing for dancers in Fort Worth, he felt he was only marking time there. In 1953 he decided to give jazz, and Los Angeles, another chance. When he returned there, he found that his old friend from New Orleans, Edward Blackwell, who still remained, and he and Blackwell found a house to live in in Watts, at the south end of the city. There they practiced together daily; it was a poverty-stricken period for both of them. Master New Orleans drummer Paul Barbarin, one of the stars of Luis Russell's marvelous late-twenties-early-thirties big band, had taught Blackwell, and Blackwell had also had absorbed the rhythmic inspiration of New Orleans parade drummers—"In fact, you can always hear that type of thing in the playing of practically any drummer that's from New Orleans, the parade beats and the street beats, you know."[3] It had been a struggle for Blackwell to play bebop in New Orleans against the tide of popular opinion, yet playing with Ornette at this evolving stage of Ornette's own career proved at times to be the biggest challenge of all. Ellis Marsalis describes a revealing incident when Blackwell and Ornette were rehearsing: "Edward was very adept at playing in the Western form. On playing the 32-bar song, he would usually play a press-roll on the turnaround and start at the top of the song again. And this one time he did it and Ornette stopped and said, 'Why did you end my phrase?' which was to say, 'If I'm playing a phrase and you come to the end of the song, play out the phrase—don't just adhere to the form of the song.' "[4]

In the late 1960s Edward Blackwell said, "But people are so fickle. Like, if you go to California now, everybody's been digging Ornette for *so long*!" The truth was that Ornette and Blackwell seldom got the chance to play for pay and couldn't even find a bassist who would play with them regularly. According to Blackwell, "The only time we could get a bassist was when we had the job. We played for $10 a night, sometimes eight, just to be able to be working."[5] The rejection of Ornette by Los Angeles musicians was massive. He listened to a lot of music, and got to hear Charlie Parker play with a pickup band that included trumpeter Chet Baker and pianist Russ Freeman, about a year before Parker's death; though Ornette was thrown out of the club for not buying drinks, Parker came out and visited with him after the set. Ornette also went around to clubs, at all ends of the sprawling city, to sit in, and he did this many times. The San Fernando Valley is at the opposite end of Los Angeles from Watts, thirty miles away, and he had to hitchhike there and back to sit in with Gerry Mulligan or other jazz musicians. On his return trips, then, cops were sure to stop him and make him put his horn together and play it, just to prove he hadn't stolen it, since they weren't used to seeing black men late at night in white districts. One night he was playing with Dexter Gordon's rhythm section when Gordon showed up at the club late and ordered him to immediately finish the song and get off the stage. A place called the California Club featured Monday night sessions, and one Monday, when the Clifford Brown–Max Roach Quintet was yet a new group, Ornette went to the club to jam. He waited for hours for other musicians to take their turns first. Finally, at 1:45 A.M., after Brown and Roach had left the club, Ornette was permitted to play—at which the pianist, bassist, and drummer left the bandstand.

Why? Was Ornette's music that outrageous? Certainly the white plastic alto saxophone he was playing by that time was considered weird. He'd bought it in Los Angeles in 1954 when he couldn't afford a metal horn; it had cost him the price of a used Selmer. "I didn't like it at first, but I figured it would be better to have a new horn anyway. Now I won't play any other," he later told critic Nat Hentoff. "They're made in England, and I have to send for them. They're only good for a year the way I play them. . . . The notes from a plastic horn are purer. In addition, the keyboard is made flat, like a flute keyboard, whereas a regular keyboard is curved. On a flat keyboard, I can dig in more."[6] In 1981 he said that "when I had the plastic saxophone, it was really nice because you could almost see the shape of the breath of a note. With the metal you can't, the breath just dissolves in the metal. The plastic was like a vacuum." Although Charlie Parker had played a plastic alto sax in his famous Massey Hall concert in Toronto in 1953, musicians still tended to consider it a toy instrument and to not take Ornette seriously because he played it.

The music he played on the plastic alto was cause for rejection, too. Bobby Bradford, who independently of Ornette had moved to Los Angeles at about the same time that Ornette returned there, says, "Bird and Sonny [Rollins] would use the device of playing half a step above the key for one phrase, just to add that little taste of piquancy, but Ornette would go out and stay there—he wouldn't come back after one phrase, and this would test your capacity for dissonance. I was very impressed with the fact that he had the courage and audacity to test Charlie Parker's law, partly because I was at the stage of worshipping Bird. That's when I began to think of him as a genius."[7] Eric Dolphy has stated that Ornette was playing a mature free style as early as 1954: "I heard about him, and when I heard him play, he asked me if I liked his pieces and I said I thought they sounded good. When he said that if someone played a chord, he heard another chord on that one, I knew what he was talking about because I had been thinking of the same thing."[8] Blackwell thought that Ornette still sounded like Parker and was still bound by four-beat measures. He thought his own experiments with time and cadences combined with Ornette's own discoveries to reach "some new grooves," and that since Ornette's sound was changing and he "never used to play the same thing twice,"[9] other musicians concluded that Ornette simply didn't know how to play. Ornette's unique music, then, was making him a well-known, minor local figure, and the Ornette Coleman controversy that was then beginning in Los Angeles is the one that would burst into a national controversy at the end of the decade.

There is a paradox here. The word *jazz*, which originated in the early part of the twentieth century when virtually every kind of lively American popular music was called jazz, had essential denotations of freedom of expression—indeed, stern antijazz bluenoses of the 1920s criticized jazz precisely for this freedom. It was this liberating quality of jazz's rhythms, sounds, and harmonies that attracted audiences during jazz's most popular phases, and it was the prospect of further freedom of expression that initiated every fresh development from Louis Armstrong and Earl Hines to swing to the bop era. Then after each development in jazz became no longer new, but common practice, musicians who had mastered each era's disciplines objected to further discoveries of freedom. For instance, Louis Armstrong, most notably, opposed bebop when it first emerged. The jazz musicians who matured during the bop era evolved styles of life and art that were intolerant of differences, as the careers of rejected artists such as Herbie Nichols and Thelonious Monk show. In other words bop, originally heretic, had become orthodox; since it was precisely Ornette's freedom of expression that was his music's most distinctive quality, his assertion of an essential quality of jazz made him an outcast. Bop ruled in Los Angeles in the mid-1950s, of course; Dexter Gordon, Hampton Hawes, Art Pepper, Carl Perkins, Harold Land, and Red Mitchell were among the leading bop figures there, while an offshoot of bop, West Coast jazz, was commercially the most successful jazz of the day. In general, emotions as strong and personal as Ornette expressed had no place in Los Angeles's jazz orthodoxy.

There was one more factor in Los Angeles musicians' rejection of Ornette Coleman. With his beards and his long hair, which was straightened, then curled—the style was called a "croquignole"—and distinctive homemade clothes, he *looked* different, and moreover he *acted* different.

I remember one night playing in a session where Clifford Brown and lots of guys were trying to play "Donna Lee," and I knew "Donna Lee" [forward and] backwards. So they asked me where I was from—because I have never yet carried myself like I was a musician, I just always have been low-key about being a musician. For some reason musicians always had this phony air about them like they had to have special attention, that they had to have a certain environment. I still don't like that image that people have of musicians—it's a very degrading human image of the way music and musicians have to identify what they do. So I never liked to take my horn out if I went out somewhere, because people treat you as if you're some kind of creature from another planet or something. I'd rather just be normal. When I was in California I don't think lots of people thought I knew as much music as I actually did because I didn't take that air of trying to show them that I *did* know quite a bit of music.

Blackwell described Ornette's personality as "peaceful," adding, "It rubbed off on me a lot because I was very wild in California! . . . There are times when his meekness has infuriated me, but he just doesn't anger very easily."[10]

Perhaps he didn't anger easily—he speaks softly, and I can hardly imagine him raising his voice—but he could hurt. Some Communists found him playing dates at three or five dollars a night and attempted to get him to join their organization: "They made me feel as though they were doing me a great service. . . . I could tell that if they hadn't been Communists they would have been prejudiced."[11] Ornette has also said,

I was born in Texas and I was put in jail for having long hair, and I was called a homosexual, and I was going through so many things, and the only thing I was trying to do was find a way to have my own individual beliefs, freedom. I'd always go somewhere where I thought I'd be accepted, and found out I'd be kicked in the ass. I would always get my cues wrong. I'd go somewhere thinking, because this was music, people were going to let me just be. I was a vegetarian and everything, and I had hair down to my shoulders and a beard, and the cops took me to jail and cut my hair off, and I grew it back and went to California and then in California they told me to strip—I was like a hermit, you know, and Don Cherry said I was walking around with an overcoat on. But I didn't think I was weird, I just thought I was being an individual and not in anyone's way. So what I was really trying to do was be more at peace with my . . . I was more religious. And when I realized no-one treated me better because I was that way, and that I was literally starving and couldn't get arrested, I said, well, I'm failing here as an adult, I'll marry and become a bigger adult. So I cut my hair and I found a woman I married and I said, maybe I can now do it the way it's done—*and it wasn't any better.*[12]

Here is how Ornette's marriage and haircut came about: IIis music had attracted some admirers. One of them was Jayne Cortez, who went to clubs to hear him play. She played the cello herself and was a serious record collector, interested in all kinds of music and knowledgeable about them. She was also a poet—indeed, in the 1970s and 1980s she became a well-known poet via her books, public recordings, and readings—and a distinctive dresser who made her own clothes. When she and Ornette were together, she made his clothes, too. Her friends were among the younger, more adventurous musicians in Los Angeles. Jayne and Ornette Coleman were married in 1954; at first they lived in her parents' house in Watts. "As I remember, it was not a big enough house that they could stay there too long without getting the kind of flak that maybe you'd get from your in-laws," says Bobby Bradford.

Bradford, shortly after moving to Los Angeles, where his mother was living, had run into Ornette on a streetcar—it was the first time they had met since Texas. "That was the main transportation from where we lived in downtown Los Angeles," says Bradford, a reminder that in the 1950s, before General Motors systematically destroyed America's streetcar systems altogether, Los Angeles was still a city where a living creature could breathe without inhaling carcinogens from a perpetual, mile-high cloud of smog.

When he saw me, he remembered me and we talked. He was writing some tunes, he said, and he was trying to organize a band—would I be interested? "Yeah, I'm interested." So I started going down to his place and practising his tunes—the tunes that he did on that first record. One place where we used to work was down there in what they used to call the red-light district in Los Angeles, about a six- or eight-block area where guys drummed and there's transvestites—we sort of looked the other way. We used to play with sometimes two horns and bass and drums and sometimes a piano player. We played some standards and some of his tunes, and some of his tunes were based on "[I Got] Rhythm" or "Honeysuckle Rose." It was Ornette's gig—he hustled the gig.

Fifth Street seemed to be like the key to the whole district, and the nickname for it, in the hip jargon of the day, was The Nickel, and that's where guys would find the prostitutes. "We're working on The Nickel this weekend." . . . Other guys would play down there, too. There was one place where Joe Maini [one of Ornette's early admirers] played, Herb Geller, Teddy Edwards, Walter Benton—all these cats were at that same club. Anyhow, Ornette's band would play around wherever we got gigs. And Ornette rarely got gigs with other people because he was doing his thing by then—he had a reputation across town for playing weird. I was learning to play when I met Ornette—I was a dyed-in-the-wool bopper. . . . My idol in that period was Fats Navarro. I was copying Fats Navarro solos vernotim from the records.

I loved Ornette's music. But if it had been left to me alone to make something with free music, I never would have made up the music. If you didn't play the changes bar-to-bar, forget it, even if you were swinging. There's a difference between playing something mysterious or far-out, and playing something wrong. What we meant by "weird" then was good. It might have been complimentary—weird in your unique way. You know clearly when the guy does not know the changes. Ornette's early songs were real bebop-oriented. He made some changes in the forms, sometimes added extra bars, but those are bop tunes, man.

Bradford was the only one of Ornette's close friends who had a car in 1954; it was a 1941 Chrysler that had a habit of breaking down, particularly when Ornette and Bradford were going to or from someplace where they played. It was Bradford's old car that moved Ornette and Jayne's few belongings out of her parents' house into their own small apartment. In those days Bradford worked as a "stock boy" at a large downtown Los Angeles department store, Bullock's: "When I say 'stock boy,' we were men—it was awfully hard to mistake us for boys. You know, you bring merchandise up to the store. Ornette said he needed a job, so I spoke to the guy I worked for and got him on there at Bullock's as a stock man." And that was when Ornette cut his hair and shaved his beard.

This early Ornette Coleman group—Ornette, Bradford, Blackwell, Floyd Howard, piano, and whatever bassists they could find to work with them—began to fade away when Bradford went into an air force band for four years, at the end of 1954, and then Blackwell decided to move back to New Orleans. One day on Ornette's lunch hour at the department store, "I was walking down the street and I came upon a gallery. On display in this gallery was a painting of a very bourgeois, wealthy-looking white lady sitting there with the most sad and lonely expression; tears on her face, and she had everything that anyone could ever want. I said, 'It's amazing, but I can relate to this painting.' "[13] That day, inspired by the painting, Ornette composed the song "Lonely Woman." At Bullock's he soon moved from stocking merchandise to running an elevator, and this new job gave him the luxury of slipping up to the tenth floor at times when the store wasn't busy, and studying his music-theory books. It was a job that lasted two and a half years—until Bullock's installed self-service elevators. He took low-paying jobs off and on in the fifties in Los Angeles, working as a houseboy, a porter, and baby-sitter.

After his son was born, he joined the Jehovah's Witnesses, and was baptized (in his youth he'd been baptized a Methodist): "One thing that drew me to becoming a Jehovah Witness for a time is that they say you should do nothing you don't want to do forever. Which makes logical sense, but no one's been able to find out what that is."[14] Even the Witnesses had their failings, however. On one occasion, when Ornette returned to Texas for a visit, he telephoned a church to find out when services were held and was told to go to a colored Jehovah's Witness hall instead. "I found out that the church needs God just like the people."[15]

He stayed in touch with his old friends, and in 1956 bought Edward Blackwell a bus ticket to visit him in Los Angeles. This time three other prominent New Orleans musicians—pianist Ellis Marsalis, clarinetist Alvin Batiste, and saxophonist-pianist-composer Harold Battiste—came along. Alvin Batiste played a set with Ornette and Blackwell at the California Club, "across the street"[16] from Ornette's home—but they weren't allowed to play a second set there. Marsalis recalls an experience he and Harold Battiste had on separate occasions while playing with Ornette:

Both of us were playing piano. We were playing somewhere and I started a cycle of 7th chords, just moving 'em up the scale, up the piano chromatically, and Ornette said, 'That's it! That's it! Keep playing that!'. . . I didn't really understand what I was doing, it's just that whatever it was, Ornette related to it. Eventually it kind of disturbed Edward because I had forsaken the rhythmic responsibility of the group in favor of trying to play harmonically what Ornette was hearing and trying to hear myself what was going on.[17]

Harold Battiste stayed in Los Angeles, where he worked in studios and eventually became musical director for a very popular rock act, Sonny and Cher. By the end of summer Blackwell, Marsalis, and Alvin Batiste were back in New Orleans. Meanwhile, thanks to his wife Jayne, Ornette was finding some new musicians to play with in Los Angeles. She knew a jazz-struck Watts teenager, Don Cherry, who had begun playing trumpet in junior high school. Cherry was a student at Fremont High School when he heard the swinging Jefferson High School band in an assembly, and knew he wanted to play in that band. So he got in the habit of cutting classes at Fremont in order to slip over to Jefferson. The teacher there, Sam Brown, played piano himself and led his student band in compositions from the Dizzy Gillespie and Stan Kenton bands' repertoires. Other well-known Los Angeles musicians who played in the Jefferson band included trumpeter Art Farmer, tenor saxman Walter Benton, and pianist Horace Tapscott. After awhile the authorities at Fremont High School began noticing how many classes Cherry was cutting and sent him away to the Jacob Riis detention school, promising that if he stayed out of trouble there, he could go to Jefferson and study with Brown. At Riis he began playing with a teenager from his own neighborhood, Billy Higgins, who had been playing drums since he was five years old.

By the time Higgins was eight, he was already determined that he was going to become a professional musician. "Jazz, at that time, was a major part of the average Black person's way of life. . . . As a community, we were much more aware of jazz than we are now. For example, most of the people on the street then knew who Charlie Parker was, but if you were to ask now, most people wouldn't know. At that time, jazz was dance music—you know, dancing to be-bop!"[18] His first professional gig was with Cherry and pianist George Newman. Then he drummed in a rhythm-and-blues band led by Arthur Wright, in which Cherry played shuffle rhythms on piano. "Later on I played with Teddy Edwards, Ernie Andrews, and Sonny Criss"—pretty sophisticated bop company for a young drummer.

In fact, Cherry and Higgins were themselves becoming known around Los Angeles by virtue of playing bop in a combo named the Jazz Messiahs. Cherry co-led the group with tenor saxophonist James Clay, originally from Dallas, who had moved to Los Angeles in 1955; George Newman was the Messiahs' pianist. They played original tunes by Cherry and Clay during intermissions at The Haig, the club where Gerry Mulligan and his quartet with Chet Baker had become famous a few years earlier, a place frequented by top jazz musicians; they also traveled to San Diego to play. Jayne Cortez Coleman had told young Cherry about her husband, and then one August day in 1956 Cherry and Newman walked into a record store on 101st Street in Watts. Cherry says,

> This record shop was like an institution. It's where everybody would go to get turned onto what was happening in the records, and the man was a musician, so we had all the facilities, valve oil and reeds. . . . Ornette was there to try a reed, and he was playing one of the thickest reeds, which was like a 4½ or 5. He had an overcoat on, it was 90 outside, and he had long hair. Now this was the first person I had seen with long hair, especially a black person—he looked like a black Jesus Christ. . . . And I could hear him—I was a block away, and I heard something like a horse whinnying—it was incredible.[19]

"He thought Ornette was crazy," adds James Clay.[20] Nevertheless, Cherry and Higgins and Newman became friends with Ornette, and one day Newman tried to play Ornette's alto. He didn't have enough breath to play a sound on it; the thick reed and open mouthpiece required too much air. Ornette could play it because through long practice he'd developed neck muscles that helped control his wind; unusual for a saxophonist, his neck swelled as he played.

Clay persuaded Ornette to come to Newman's garage to practice with the Jazz Messiahs. Blackwell came along, too, so until he returned to New Orleans, the band had two drummers. And Ornette brought along his own compositions to the rehearsals. "I could play with him," says Clay. "The music was written wrong, but I could play with Ornette. . . . He'd say, 'You ought to come and go with me' and I'd say, 'No, I can't play that shit. That ain't me, man.' " And one night Ornette came to a club where Clay was playing: "I was getting ready to go out and play some and I asked him to go with me. He muttered, mumbled, didn't want to go. I said, man, let's go! He went out and played, and the next thing I knew he got them *goin'*, Jack! He played and blew their brains out." On another occasion at The Haig, bassist Red Mitchell heard Ornette for the first time when Clay invited Ornette to sit in: "He

said, 'Nah, man.' I said, 'Play, man,' and the cat played 'Embraceable You'. . . . He can play Charlie Parker note for note."[21]

While Clay was merely bemused by Ornette Coleman's songs
and his playing, Cherry and Higgins were discovering themselves
in it. In the few months before Blackwell returned to New Orleans,
he taught drum techniques to Higgins. As for Cherry, there is clear
evidence on Ornette's early records that he was a master of hard
bop phrasing and may have even been on his way to discovering an
original voice, a kind of busy post–Clifford Brown style within the
hard bop idiom. Says Ornette,

> They would come over to my house. I would always be writing
> something, and I'd say,'Oh, try this with me' and 'Try this,' and
> they really started realizing that there was something else to do
> besides the changes. So I couldn't go out and play that music with
> anyone—the only way I could go out and play it was if I could get
> a bass player and a drummer. I used to play lots with Blackwell like
> that, in pickups, because therefore I could just write out what I
> wanted the bass player to play and have the drummer set a certain
> time pattern. By the time I met Charlie and Cherry, I had written,
> oh, God, hundreds of songs.

The rehearsals with Blackwell, then Higgins and Cherry, were
the most important events in Ornette's career up to then, and they
were, of course, the most important events in post-Parker jazz.
They revealed two enormously important facts: First, the freely
mobile harmonic structures were indeed a consistent, viable way of
improvising jazz. Second, other musicians could play that way with
Ornette.

It is at those rehearsals at George Newman's garage and at Cherry's and Ornette's homes, and at the very occasional subsequent
gigs by Ornette Coleman and his young musicians, that the present
era of jazz began. Says Ornette,

> Well, it took me a long time to get them interested in studying with
> me and staying—because when I met Charlie and Billy and Don,
> they were into bebop. . . . But then they got very interested in the
> things that I was trying to write. So when we got together, after
> we'd play the melody—the most interesting part is, what do you
> play after you play the melody? That's where I won them over.
> Because when I started showing them how they could do that—

you see, when you play a melody, you have a set pattern to know just what you can do while the other person is doing certain things. Whereas, in this case, when you play the melody no one knew where to go or what to do to show that he knew where he was going. I had already developed playing like that naturally. And when I started showing them how I'd done that—I'd take a chord. So you play the tonic, you play the third, and then they found out that they were playing the same space. And finally I got them to where they could see how to express themselves without linking up to a definite maze.

It was really a case of "teaching them how to feel more confident in being expressive like that for themselves."

The year 1956 was the year of the best thing to happen to Ornette in California: the birth of his and Jayne's son, Ornette Denardo Coleman. On the negative side, there were still musicians who walked off the bandstand when Ornette came around to sit in. Ornette recalls that Eric Dolphy was among those who were originally cold to his music, and it wasn't until later, in New York, that they became friends. On Wednesday nights, for a time, Ornette and James Clay played rhythm and blues for dancers at a Mexican club named Armond's, though Ornette had long since wearied of that kind of music. Nevertheless, the involvement of his young acolytes in his music was a bright spot. He and Cherry and Clay played an engagement at Club Malamo, and then, in December 1957, came an important event: Cherry hustled an engagement with the Vancouver (British Columbia) Jazz Society at The Cellar, the city's leading jazz club, playing Ornette's songs. The Cherry group for the occasion consisted of himself and Ornette with pianist Don Friedman, bassist Ben Tucker, and a drummer. According to emcee Bob Smith, the group recorded and broadcast at least two sets over radio station CFUN, which was probably the first time Ornette's Free jazz was preserved on tape.

It was at about this time that Red Mitchell, with whom George Newman, Billy Higgins, and James Clay worked and with whom Don Cherry had gigged, spent an evening at Don Payne's house listening to Ornette Coleman play. At the time Payne was the bassist in Ornette's groups, while Mitchell was one of the most in-demand bop bassists in Los Angeles, an improviser of superb technique and refined melodic instincts who recorded often for the Contemporary label. Payne and Newman were strong Ornette Coleman advocates, and Newman had conceived the idea that once

Mitchell, highly respected in the Los Angeles jazz establishment, listened to Ornette at length, he would recommend Ornette for a Contemporary recording date. Mitchell's response that evening was mixed. He wouldn't recommend that Contemporary record Ornette's alto playing, but he liked Ornette's composing and was willing to be a reference if Ornette wanted to sell his songs to Contemporary for use on their recording sessions.

Lester Koenig, the owner of Contemporary Records, had been a friend of Arnold Schoenberg, and a movie producer (he worked on, among other films, two Best Picture Oscar winners) until he was blacklisted for not cooperating with the notorious Hollywood anti-Communist witch-hunts. He had also been recording jazz since 1941, and his Contemporary label had recorded exploratory works by Duane Tatro, Shelly Manne with Jimmy Giuffre, and Sonny Rollins's first pianoless trio. It happened that the beginning of 1958 was a very depressing period for Ornette—apart from the lack of musical opportunity, his marriage was unhappy—so much so that he wired his mother to send him a bus ticket back home to Fort Worth. On the day the bus ticket arrived, Koenig asked Ornette to audition some of his songs.

The result was one of the most written-about incidents of Ornette's life. He and Don Cherry went to the Contemporary studios and introduced themselves to Koenig. "I took him to the piano," said Koenig, "and asked him to play the tunes. Ornette said he couldn't *play* the piano. I asked him, 'How did you hope to play your tunes for me if you can't play piano?' So he took out his plastic alto and began to play."[22] Reportedly it was Koenig's suggestion that Ornette and Cherry play the songs on the horns with which they were most familiar. They did; Koenig bought seven Ornette Coleman songs at twenty-five dollars each. More than that, Koenig liked their playing and proposed that Ornette lead a recording date. As Ornette remembers the encounter, Koenig told him,

"Oh, I'd like to buy some of your compositions," 'cause he wanted Shelly Manne and lots of other professional guys to record them—they'd say they could read the music, but they didn't know what to do with it after they'd read it. The guy [Koenig] said, "Why don't you put a band together?" I said, "Fine with me." So I knew Cherry and Billy and Walter Norris and Don Payne—that was my first record date. I had written lots of songs on the regular bebop changes that most guys played, so I used those songs—all those pieces were written long ago. I didn't record the kind that I call harmolodics now until I recorded "Lonely Woman" on Atlantic.

Something Else! The Music of Ornette Coleman was recorded in three sessions in February and March 1958. George Newman was reportedly struggling with emotional problems, and Norris was his replacement as Ornette's pianist. The songs, which Ornette says were all written between 1950 and 1953, use chord changes—in Nat Hentoff's liner notes Ornette stated, "On this recording, the changes finally decided on for the tunes are a combination of some I suggested and some the musicians suggested. If you feel the lines different one day, you can change the harmony accordingly."[23] Indeed, Norris said, "Each time we played the tunes, we'd change them around a different way. We did everything possible we could do with them."[24] All of the tunes are in standard song forms, though one of three blues, "The Disguise," is a clever thirteen-bar theme in which the turnaround, the final bar of the chorus, also serves as the first bar of the next chorus.

On the recording, then, pianist Norris attends to the chord changes that Ornette and the group selected; in solo, however, Cherry and Ornette can escape the changes to play freely. (Bobby Bradford comments, "I remember Walter Norris saying to me, 'Ornette doesn't seem to know his own tunes.' What he meant was that *he* got all the correct changes, but Ornette's horn didn't fit the changes.") Ornette told Hentoff, "I would prefer it if musicians would play my tunes with different changes as they take a new chorus so that there'd be all the more variety in the performances. . . . Rhythm patterns should be more or less like natural breathing patterns."[25] Hearing Ornette's subsequent recordings, it becomes clear that the piano is an inhibiting factor in *Something Else!* There are passages in "Jayne," "The Sphinx," and three blues solos in which Ornette's alto lines move freely amid the rhythm section's bop.

What the listener hears most distinctly in Ornette's solos here are his sound and his rhythm. "I think you'll find an urgency and dead seriousness in Ornette's music that said things weren't going to be about Jim Crow or a resigned black man or West Coast cool any longer,"[26] Bobby Bradford has said. Ornette sought to play a "human" sound on his alto: "There are some intervals that carry that *human* quality if you play them in the right pitch."[27] It's quite true, as Don Cherry said, that the plastic alto in *Something Else!* has a warmer, drier sound than a metal alto; it may be the plastic in the horn that makes Ornette's bent notes so effective in, for instance, "Invisible" and "The Blessing." The most immediate quality of Ornette's rhythmic character is his force, his eagerness: He seems to virtually eat up the beat, with an eagerness that recalls the drive of Charlie Parker in Parker's 1948 "Crazeology" session. If Ornette's phrasing gives a first impression of spaciousness, like the wide open spaces of Texas, that impression is partly an illusion, for the broken phrases of bebop are reflected in his phrase shapes. In solos such as the fast "Chippie," his phrases often begin in unpredictable places, and his accenting throughout the album is quite irregular; the beat gets turned around often, and sometimes it seems only an accident when accents fall on beats that are traditionally considered "correct." These are features of Charlie Parker's music, too, at its most radical, even if the rhythmic content of Ornette's phrases is typically less detailed than Parker's. While Ornette's soloing captures much of Parker's lyric spirit, the conflicts that arise in his solos are unlike Parker's conflicts—Ornette's lines are less mercurial, though they sometimes hint at emotion as extreme.

Among the best features of *Something Else!* are the way Ornette's sound *moves* in "Invisible," rather in the way Albert Ayler's sound would move five years later in the now-classic *My Name Is Albert Ayler.* There is the fire of his "Chippie" and "Alpha" solos, taken at fast tempos; in the latter you can hear trumpeter Cherry slipping from one point of view to another, playing freely here, a convoluted kind of hard bop there—independently of the young Lee Morgan and Bill Hardman of the period, Cherry seems to have arrived at similar conclusions about phrasing at fast tempos. And then there are the songs that are surely like the ones that had grabbed Red Mitchell's recommendation, including "The Disguise," with its turnaround trick; "Invisible," with distant suggestions of Thelonious Monk; and "When Will the Blues Leave?" with its unique spaces for a drum break in bars seven and eight.

They are certainly good songs, and they helped attract attention to Ornette's music at a time when jazz composers were stretching the boundaries of song form. One, Herbie Nichols, was composing secret masterpieces in those days, and I have heard it suggested that at this evolutionary stage of the Ornette

Coleman groups, the harmonic and emotional ambiguities of Herbie Nichols's songs were a most appropriate parallel to Ornette's writing. Nichols's songs are at least as distinctive as Ornette's, and in elastic length and harmonic movement they stretch song form much more. Their implications for theme-based improvisation were in line with the improvising concepts that Ornette was evolving, too. One of the songs in *Something Else!* became a modest standard: "When Will the Blues Leave?" which Ira Sullivan's quintet, with Donald (Rafael) Garrett on bass and Wilbur Campbell on drums, was soon playing.

About the time when Ornette's quintet was recording *Something Else!* he was making another one of the crucial friendships of his life. Charlie Haden was born in Shenandoah, Iowa, and at the age of two began singing harmony as part of the Haden Family that performed country music together on midwestern radio and television stations. His older brother Jim Haden, who played bass in Nevada show bands, was a major inspiration to Charlie, who, after high school, went to Los Angeles to enroll in a top jazz school, Westlake College of Music. Soon he was playing with alto-sax great Art Pepper, when Hampton Hawes and Sonny Clark were Pepper's pianists; then "Elmo Hope came here with Chet Baker and stayed here awhile, and I got to play with him every day for about six months." Haden abandoned Westlake College to play full-time, and in 1957 he joined pianist Paul Bley's quartet, with Dave Pike, vibes, and drummer Lenny McBrowne at the Hillcrest Club. Once on a night off Haden dropped into The Haig, still a popular Los Angeles jazz spot, and "this guy came up on stage and asked the musicians if he could play, and started to sit in. He played three or four phrases, and it was so brilliant, I couldn't believe—I never heard any sound like that before. Immediately the musicians told him to stop playing, and he packed up his horn, but before I could reach him he'd already left through the back entrance."

Haden told about the incident to McBrowne, who asked in response, "Was he playing a white plastic alto?" Yes, he was. "That was Ornette Coleman." McBrowne invited Ornette to come to the Hillcrest for a Sunday-morning jam session, and introduced him to Haden; after the session Ornette and Haden rode off in Ornette's Studebaker to spend the rest of the day playing music at Ornette's house. "Before I met Ornette," Haden recalls,

I would sometimes feel to play not on the changes of the song, sometimes I would feel to play on the inspiration and the feeling of the song, and create a new chord structure to it in my solo. Whenever I tried to do that, whoever I was playing with would get very upset because they didn't know where I was. And I would have to bring the melody back in, so everybody would know where to come back in. So I had to be careful who I did this with. And the first time I played with Ornette, he was *doing* that! I said, "Man! Finally!"

Ornette and Jayne were separated by this time. One topic they had disputed was his dedication to his original music: "My wife would start in, 'People say you're crazy,' and she sounded as if she agreed."[28] The little circle of musicians whom Ornette had inspired met virtually every day to rehearse at Don Cherry's home, and Haden says he never

really got instructions. Ornette would tell me the chord changes he was hearing when he wrote the song, and then I would usually put a bass line to it. We would talk over the notes I was going to play as far as playing on the composition, and we would come to an agreement on the right notes. On every record that we did I usually heard my own bass line. We discussed the chords to use and I always told him what notes I felt worked in different places, and he usually agreed with me.

The first national recognition Ornette received came in mid-1958. Don Payne had played the test pressing of *Something Else!* for John Tynan, associate editor of *Down Beat*, and Tynan and Nat Hentoff, one of the most prolific and levelheaded jazz critics of the day, voted for Ornette as "Alto Saxophone New Star" in the *Down Beat* Critics Poll. Tynan commented:

Ornette Coleman. Please remember this name. Coleman is a 28-year-old altoist from Fort Worth, Texas who has been living in Los Angeles for the last four years. In my opinion, he is showing more originality on his instrument than *any* of the group of newer instrumentalists on either coast or points between. . . . the president of [Contemporary Records] is to be congratulated for his courage and foresight in recording this vitally important horn man. And if the above reads like a rave, that is no coincidence. . . . It sure is.[29]

Tynan was so enthusiastic, in fact, that he tried to talk the Monterey Jazz Festival into placing Ornette on that year's program, without success. Then, in October, in reviewing *Something Else!* he awarded the album four stars and commented on the music's "wealth of feeling and honesty," while suggesting that Ornette aspired to be as revolutionary as Charlie Parker. Nevertheless, he wrote,

> Coleman is far from being a reincarnation of Parker. About the closest parallel I can make from this 28-year-old Texan's passionate, sometimes almost inarticulate playing is to the piano approach of Thelonious Monk. There is in it the same reaching, striving feeling and also the frustration of not being capable of attaining the heights yearned for so desperately. . . .
>
> On first hearing, this album raises goose bumps. One is puzzled by Coleman's jagged, fragmentary playing, and it is easy to imagine listeners quickly taking sides for or against him. . . .[30]

Welcome praise, but Ornette was still living a life of rehearsing and sitting in. Apart from the recording sessions, the only other playing engagement he had all year was as a sideman. Paul Bley was still at the Hillcrest Club, on Washington Boulevard in a black area of Los Angeles, where he led a quartet six nights a week with Pike, Haden, and eventually Higgins. According to Bley, one day late in the year, after a set in which Don Cherry and Ornette had sat in, the pianist and bassist went into the yard behind the club and, says Bley, "had a confrontation. We said, 'Look, we have been working in this club for a *long* time and most probably could stay here as long as we wanted. If we fire Dave Pike and hire Don and Ornette we won't last the week. We'll be lucky to last the night. What shall we do? And we looked at each other and said, 'Fire Dave Pike!' "[31] Pike went on to considerable success over the years as a pop-jazz vibes performer; meanwhile, Bley recalls that his new quintet lasted "three or four weeks" at the Hillcrest, while Ornette recalls that it lasted about six weeks. Says Haden, "We were there for about two or three months. The audiences were great at first— they started dwindling a little at the end. At first it was a crowd that went there every night to hear Paul Bley's band, then it was replaced by a lot of musicians coming to hear us play." But Bley maintains,

> When you were driving down Washington Boulevard and you looked at the Hillcrest Club you always knew whether the band was

on the bandstand or not. If the street was full of audience in front of the club, the band was playing. . . . And as soon as the band stopped they would all come back in and drink, talk and shout and be happy and be merry. . . . Musically it was incredible. Ornette had a bag of compositions that was so deep that we rehearsed every day of the job. . . . Every single afternoon all day. And every night we played an entire new book from the night before. So I'd say ten or twenty new tunes were added to the band's repertoire daily. That's a rate of growth that was stimulating to say the least.

I spent ¾ of the time tuning Ornette up to see if I could get him to play A440. . . . Unfortunately I didn't have the flexibility that he had when it came to hitting A. . . . Up until the time that those two fellows had sat in with this group, there had been a great deal of thought as to how to break the bondage of chord structures over meter. Ornette was so early that Coltrane was an interim step which coexisted with Ornette, whereas historically it should have preceded Ornette.[32]

The two recordings of the Hillcrest engagement that Bley eventually issued reveal a most extroverted quintet, with solos by Coleman and then Cherry beginning most selections. Bley, who by then had already recorded as a leader and with Charles Mingus, sounds like a somewhat reticent leader, with his piano recorded in the background and his solos sometimes short—perhaps that's understandable, since most of the material is Ornette's, and the alto playing is quite fine. Whereas Ornette's first five studio recordings present comparatively short performances, typically of jazz releases in the late 1950s, the Bley Quintet stretched out and the long alto solos are a revelation. Ornette follows the thirty-two-bar, AABA form of Parker's "Klactoveedsedstene" in his solo with as rich freedom of internal rhythm in his phrases as Parker, but with less detail; certainly the fusion of exultation and fear in Parker's own playing is evident in Ornette's lines and harrowing tone, which peaks at a turnaround and ends with an incongruous quote from "Hawaiian War Chant." Actually, Ornette was in a quoting mood during these performances: "When Will the Blues Leave?" for instance, finds him quoting from "Hey There," "Stranger in Paradise," and at least three other pop songs. These sudden attacks of whimsical mood stand out in contrast to his generally blues-filled lines.

Harmonically, he and Cherry follow their inclinations to juxtapose chord changes on top of the tunes' harmonic structures, an approach particularly important in the alto solos, since most of them include passages wherein Ornette closely develops musical ideas. His freedom of sound, the movement of his pitch and tone quality, and his and Cherry's most harmonically liberated passages, while resulting in musically consistent lines, nevertheless presented an atmosphere of danger, like dancing at the edge of a precipice; to a degree this was also the result of Bley's out-of-tune piano accompaniments, which observed the chord changes. And the sometimes asymmetrical accenting and irregularly falling phrases that Ornette played were prime elements in this danger, while the bop lines that Cherry played on trumpet, with their free gestures, added to the nervous daring. There's further excitement in Ornette's solo in "Free," while his bebop phrasing in the medium-tempo "The Blessing" bespeaks optimism. The thirteen choruses that he creates in- "Ramblin," perhaps more than in any other solo in his career, are an idealized Texas-style improvisation. At the most stimulating of medium-up tempos—what Von Freeman has called "the Chicago tempo"—Ornette creates phrases that suggest he's a missing link between Charlie Christian and Charlie Parker, a more flowing and rhythmically free player than the former, a somewhat less rhythmically and emotionally complex player than the latter. The top notes of Coleman's phrases here are always bent. It's a very tense solo, for all its exultation, and the tension derives from not only his rhythm and the seeming harmonic irresolution of his lines against the altered blues-chord changes, but also from the angular intervals that again and again invade his essentially diatonic phrasing. The beginnings of the frontier myth embodied in the Ornette Coleman Quartet's classic "Ramblin' " of the next year are present in Coleman's big, bold sound and loping phrases, and in the cowboy song variations in Haden's solo, which themselves are a variation on the near-Latin Bo Diddley, or "hambone," bass pattern that underlies the theme. This version of "Ramblin" includes Ornette's lines—are they composed or improvised?—behind Cherry's solo, and it's interesting that for Bley's quintet, "When Will the Blues Leave?" has been provided with a second theme.

Something Else! was not a big seller in record stores, and for Ornette's next album Lester Koenig decided to record Coleman and Cherry with two of Contemporary's busiest and most popular regulars, drummer Shelly Manne and bassist Red Mitchell, in an at-

tempt to stir up more marketplace action. Manne, especially, had
been a leading figure in West Coast jazz, the cool-styled music that
by the mid-1950s had succeeded and exceeded bop in popularity.
The reasons for West Coast jazz's commercial success were complex. Bop had been born in New York City, of an underground
circle of black musicians working in a milieu constrained by racial
segregation. The social circumstances surrounding the birth of
bop—World War II and its ambiguous conclusion, including the
atomic-bomb cataclysm; the conflict in values between an older,
narrower, more idealistic America and a younger generation, many
of whom were aware of the need for drastic changes in society—
were reflected in the collapse of the big band business and the
smaller, more self-consciously radical audience that bebop attracted. The music itself, with its broken phrasing, dislocated
rhythms, frightening ecstasies, fractured ballads, and harrowing
blues, sounded as if it internalized these conflicts: Bop was not
simply the product of a new kind of sensibility, it expressed a new,
more neurotic kind of nervous system. West Coast jazz, on the
other hand, emerged in post-postwar America, the product of white
musicians from the vast, laid-back suburbs of Los Angeles. It fil-
tered bop harmony and rhythm through late–Swing Era melodies,
with a consequent lessening of the music's nervous tension.
Whereas melodic intensity and expression were ideal qualities in
bop, cool, undramatic complexity was the contrasting West Coast
ideal.

The bop milieu had internalized one of the nasty features of
the social tidepool in which it had spawned: intolerance. Bop musicians and audiences tended to ignore the discoveries of such
eastern players as Herbie Nichols, Elmo Hope, and even, for
many years, Thelonious Monk; these artists were simply periph-
eral to the dogmas of taste derived primarily from Charlie Parker
and his successor as a model of taste, Miles Davis. By contrast,
West Coast–styled artists welcomed such exploratory works as
young Richard Twardzik's piano solos, Bob Graettinger's large,
atonal compositions, and Jimmy Giuffre's experiments in free harmonic structure. Shelly Manne was an all-purpose drummer who
had participated in the most radical West Coast experiments as
well as in popular jazz recordings such as those of Shorty Rogers
and André Previn. That the jazz circles in which Coleman and
Manne moved were to a large extent separate and unequal was in

part a result of racial segregation, and of different musical perspectives as well.

Ornette believed that Red Mitchell considered him "out of my skull,"[33] but the bassist's playing in "Lorraine" shows a conscientious attempt to enter Ornette's musical world by accompanying the horns' solos with variations on theme phrases. The song is Ornette's dirge for the late modern pianist Lorraine Geller; his alto solo is a remarkable development of emotion, with dissonant upward leaps adding to the harshness of the sense of loss; helplessness emerges at the beginning of the very fast bridge, which ends with the alto careening unaccompanied over space until it falls, crushed, into a single, bent, defeated note. His final strain is stark, with a dark, despairing phrase repeated four times to conclude. It is one of the most vividly dramatic solos Ornette ever recorded, and its starkness is made more dramatic by the unusual structure, including the fast bridge that ends with the horns dropping tempo, unaccompanied by the rhythm players.

"Lorraine" was the one track preserved from the January 16, 1959, recording session. Over a month later the same quartet recorded the blues "Turnaround" and the fast "Endless." The latter features an insistent, driving alto solo, while the former includes an alto solo beginning with an "If I Loved You" quote that proves apposite as Ornette progresses, as well as unfortunately cute drumming behind Cherry's solo and a long bass solo in which Red Mitchell's phrasing recalls Ornette's own unique sense of space. Nevertheless, Ornette felt that Mitchell's bass playing was, in general, wrong for the group. One of the happier incidents of the previous year had been an occasion when Ornette had been sitting in at a club and Don Payne had talked the Modern Jazz Quartet's bassist and drummer, Percy Heath and Connie Kay, into hearing him. Heath and Kay had enjoyed Ornette's music so much that they'd gone out to get their pianist partner, John Lewis, to hear him that night too, and Lewis immediately became an Ornette Coleman enthusiast.

Between the second and third recording dates for Ornette's second album, he and Cherry drove to San Francisco to persuade Percy Heath to play on their studio session, and sat in with the Modern Jazz Quartet while they were there. Whereas the first two sessions had resulted in a total of three satisfactory tracks, the final session yielded six tracks, suggesting that Heath's presence on bass put the quartet at ease. Ornette's solo in "Tomorrow Is the Question!" suggests that the answer is his kind of rhythmic flexibility, given his rare sensitivity to the effects of displacement and free space (Cherry's similarly fluid sense of space suggests a similar answer). Songs such as "Rejoicing," with the wildly flapping phrases in Ornette's solo, "Compassion," and "Tears Inside" reveal the accuracy of their titles. The last of these is a blues, and in it Ornette's strained sound, bent or splintered notes, and sometimes brutal attack provide an excellent example of the kind of human sound he said he was attempting to achieve on the alto sax. As for "Mind and Time," it includes the bold, headfirst charge of Don Cherry, who by this time was playing his Pakistani pocket trumpet, which looks like a squashed version of a standard trumpet. It also includes an Ornette Coleman solo that breaks wholly away from repeated harmonic patterns: An arching opening run becomes the structural center of the solo as it is turned in multiple different directions, amplified, condensed, and distorted. It is pertinent to the alto-saxophone sound that he achieves in *Tomorrow Is the Question!* that he says he worried at one time that he was playing out of tune by playing the "natural" pitch of his instrument. But he became aware that "My emotions were raising my tone to another level. . . . I could still hear the centre of what I was reading."[34]

After the recording of *Tomorrow Is the Question!* was completed, the friendship of John Lewis was the catalyst for the next major changes in Ornette's life. "I've never heard anything like Ornette Coleman and Don Cherry before," Lewis said. "Ornette is the driving force of the two. They're almost like twins; they play together like I've never heard anybody play together. I can't figure how they start together. It's not like any ensemble that I've ever heard. . . ."[35] Lewis told Nesuhi Ertegun about Ornette; Ertegun and his brother Ahmet operated Atlantic Records, a New York label that had thrived during the 1950s with rhythm-and-blues and early rock-and-roll hit recordings. Nesuhi Ertegun produced Atlantic's jazz album line, which included the Modern Jazz Quartet's recordings, and as a trusted former employee of Contemporary, he was still a good friend of Contemporary's Koenig. The two agreed on Ornette's changing labels, and Koenig later said, "We just couldn't support him in Los Angeles. There was no place for the group to work."[36] In fact, Ornette's two Contemporary LPs were both poor sellers. Though he has received songwriter's royalties from Contemporary's music-publishing subsidiaries for many years, by the early 1980s the albums still had not quite sold enough copies to earn royalty payments.

In the spring, not quite two and a half months after *Tomorrow Is the Question!* was completed, Atlantic's Nesuhi Ertegun went to Los Angeles to record *The Shape of Jazz to Come*. This time the group was Ornette's own quartet with Cherry, Haden, and Higgins—the first recording by this now-classic jazz ensemble. The first piece recorded at this historic session was perhaps its most remarkable work: "Focus on Sanity." It has three separate fanfare themes, and Haden is the first to solo, with an unhurried bluesy line in slow tempo that only hints, by way of a couple of rushed phrases and others that end in precarious dissonances, at the distortions of emotion and reason to come. Suddenly a screeching fanfare intervenes to introduce a madly yelping Coleman solo, a frenzy of terror with lashing trills and insane double-time phrases; there's no continuity here except emotional force—stark and shattering. If the Cherry solo that follows is more of a continuous line, its splintered attacks and brutalized notes bespeak the intrusion of terror, and Higgins's linear solo and the final fanfare finalize the assertion of precarious balance. "Focus on Sanity" is thus a composition, with several tempos and themes, that could only be realized through improvisation—and not the role-playing kinds of improvisation that Charles Mingus often called for from his interpreters. Ornette, instead, used his players' own choices to unite in a whole musical statement. Given its success, it's no wonder that Ornette originally wanted to title this first Atlantic album "Focus on Sanity."

The Ornette Coleman Quartet was remarkably at home in very fast tempos, as selections such as "Chronology" and "Congeniality" demonstrate, the latter with Ornette's loquacious, humorous solo. "Monk and the Nun" and "Just for You" were recorded that day. The latter is a ballad, a love song in which Ornette's alto describes devotion and surrender, and in a central passage, Cherry and Haden create a low-down blues duet. Two Coleman songs from *The Shape of Jazz to Come* quickly went into the repertoires of other jazz musicians: "Peace" and "Lonely Woman," of which the latter is probably the Coleman song most often recorded by other musicians. "Lonely Woman" turns the conventional bop ensemble structure inside out, with its fast tempo set by the drummer, the bass

playing accents rather than meter or velocity, and the two horns
playing the slow, rubato theme over it all. Pity, sorrow, sympathy,
and resignation emerge in succession from the theme, qualities
amplified in Ornette's solo, which is in Higgins's fast tempo and in
identifiable strains, however freely the lengths to which he improvises in the song's two keys. The melody of the slow "Peace," with
its one-note-to-the-bar bass-and-drums bridge, again illustrates Ornette's title, and the conversational mood of his alto solo is an
amplification of the call-response moments in the theme. "Peace"
also has another striking Cherry-Haden duet, the pocket trumpet
almost dissipating altogether over the irregular bass tones in the
bridges.

The final tune at the session was another very fast one, "Eventually," with, for its improvised bridge, a three-note lick that Ornette plays ten times. That lick is the source for his solo, stabbing
up, then down, beginning phrases, or leading to fearful, trapped
phrases that alternate with long screams and saxophone squalls. For
all of the solo's varied thrusts, Ornette's evolution of that three-note
lick makes for compact construction, while his motions contrast
with the optimistic composed portions of the theme.

Musically speaking, *The Shape of Jazz to Come* was a brilliant
achievement, a herald of the era to come in the way that Louis
Armstrong's starring setting with the 1926–1927 Hot Five and
Hot Seven heralded the Swing Era and the first Gillespie-Parker
masterpieces of 1945 announced to the world that bop had arrived.

In August 1959 the School of Jazz was in its third year. It was a
summer school that held its session for three weeks annually at
Music Inn, near Lenox in the Berkshire Hills of western Massachusetts. It was a kind of finishing school for selected young musicians at the onset of their careers, and John Lewis was its director.
True, Ornette Coleman and Don Cherry, with an album in the
stores and two more in the can, were far from unfinished musicians,
but Lewis had an ulterior motive in seeing to it that the pair be
given scholarships to the School of Jazz: The faculty and attending
guests would be leading musicians and writers who could help
Ornette's and Cherry's careers. Nesuhi Ertegun and Atlantic
Records paid for the scholarships and the journey east.

To those who heard Ornette for the first time, the School of Jazz
weeks were a revelation. Gunther Schuller recalls,

In some deep sense he wasn't a student there—he could have taught any of the faculty at Lenox. He burst on the scene completely intact. The only thing I felt I was able to teach him there, I did all the history courses. I remember vividly Ornette Coleman going just out of his mind the first time he heard Jelly Roll Morton's "Black Bottom Stomp"—he thought that was the best thing he'd ever heard in his life. I played a lot of Louis Armstrong, Bessie Smith, God knows what, and a lot of this was a revelation to him about his own heritage.

Ornette had been sort of needling Jimmy Giuffre for days and weeks for being too structured—he wanted Giuffre to break out of himself and play free. I think it was a Sunday afternoon, and they went off into this nice little room and started jamming. Ornette took the lead and Giuffre was sort of listening pensively. Eventually he just came in there and played the wildest, craziest music—I remember him lying with his back on the floor playing his tenor saxophone, just playing altissimo notes and screaming and all this wailing—he was trying to play a kind of Ornette Coleman on tenor.

Back then, Schuller wrote that they "played like two battling wounded animals until a state of utter exhaustion had been reached."[37] But Giuffre, with his unique history of big band and small group adventures (in 1958 he'd led a trio of reeds-trombone-guitar in a folk music–like kind of chamber jazz) was the only other musician at the school whom Ornette could talk into playing freely. Says Giuffre, "The wonderful thing . . . is that it has nothing to do with the ideas or the musical content, it has to do with the statement—and when somebody gets to this point where he can be this free and this sure in his statement, then it's just a matter of his speaking. . . . He has thrown out the bugaboos about being afraid of what he's going to sound like."[38]

At the School of Jazz Ornette edited the tapes for *Tomorrow Is the Question!* rehearsed with other musicians, and performed in a concert with students, among whom bassist Larry Ridley, saxophonists Lenny Popkin and Ian Underwood, trombonist David Baker, and pianist Steve Kuhn were also destined for prominent careers in jazz. Ornette's songs "The Sphinx," "Compassion," and "Giggin' " were among the works played at the final concert. The three weeks he spent as a School of Jazz "student" served John Lewis's purposes admirably, for Ornette's music was now a hot topic in jazz circles. Enthusiasm for it was by no means unanimous; trombonist Bob

Brookmeyer screamed, "Damn it, tune up!" and then left the faculty in protest of the attention paid Ornette. But Guiffre's enthusiasm was typical of Ornette's admirers' responses (indeed, Giuffre's own clarinet music was soon to change direction in direct response to Ornette's liberation), and other listeners were soon to bring important results. For upon returning to New York City, some (most prominently critic Martin Williams, who, with Hentoff, edited the monthly *Jazz Review*) began urging the owner of the Five Spot Cafe, Joe Termini, to offer Ornette his first eastern engagement.

On top of all of John Lewis's other duties, he was musical director of the Monterey Jazz Festival in California, and he saw to it that Ornette was on the 1959 program. There, on the first Saturday in October, he played on an afternoon concert in two compositions. The *Jazz Review*'s Dick Hadlock wrote,"Ernie Wilkins' *The Big Three*, written for Coleman Hawkins, Ben Webster, and Ornette Coleman, was embarrassingly trivial and something of an affront to altoist Coleman, whose talent should not be measured in a Hawkins-Webster-Wilkins context. Coleman, along with trumpeter Don Cherry, was victimized again, this time by John Lewis, in a composition called *Relays*, which seemed to have little to do with Coleman's unique musical philosophy."[39] On the other hand, *Down Beat*'s Gene Lees praised "The Big Three" and singled out Ornette's performance: "Whatever it is he is doing on his plastic alto, his work with Webster and Hawkins was intensely exciting."[40] The next week the Coleman-Cherry-Haden-Higgins quartet returned to the Radio Recorders studio in Hollywood for what turned out to be their final California recording sessions.

The first song they recorded in October was "Una Muy Bonita," with Higgins offering a hat dance on drums and the occasional south-of-the-border phrase in Ornette's solo. "The Face of the Bass" was conceived as a feature for Haden, whose opening solo is pointedly free with tempo. The previous year the Bley Quintet, with Ornette, had played "Crossroads," a brief performance of which is preserved in the *Coleman Classics* LP; it now reappears as "The Circle with the Hole in the Middle," featuring an alto solo notable for its reckless terror: Ornette's sound is strained at times to a shuddering rasp, as his line careens precariously to a held note, before a sense of control is asserted. He is quite the opposite in "Music Always," offering a good humor that Haden quickly catches. As in the sessions for his three previous studio albums, Ornette used songs that he had composed in the past, and even more than in the previous three the program selected for *Change of the Century* showed a variety of mood and material that was special for the time. "Bird Food" has been taken as an attempt at bebop, for instance, "just one of those synthetic Charlie Parker tunes," according to reviewer Hsio Wen Shih.[41] He may have been misled to this conclusion by the song's opening phrase, though the way it is developed is pure Ornette Coleman. "Ramblin' " is still a blues, as it was in Bley's repertoire, though now, without the harmonic restrictions imposed by a piano, the changes are elongated and the performance is much more open-ended harmonically. "Forerunner" and "Change of the Century," both aptly titled, are quite at the "outside" end of the jazz spectrum; the latter, in fact, is played with an independence of component parts that predicts the discoveries made almost five years later by Albert Ayler's first New York groups.

Even in the midst of the most creative period of Ornette Coleman's life, these four performances and "Free" are exceptional, and his own alto-saxophone playing is the most exceptional single aspect. In his "Bird Food" solo, writes critic T. E. Martin, "The construction centres around little teasing accents that are never resolved even in the final passages where he moves to the upper register to complete the dramatic shape while leaving melodic threads adrift."[42] "Forerunner" offers a quite amazing solo conception in which Ornette's unity is achieved through disunity of line and dynamics. It is three solos in one, in fact; the first solo is very tangled and tortured, full of notes, ending suddenly in long, held tones; the second, after a rest, begins with bright material that moves into further painful tangles, and a held tone; the third yet again moves through thickets to a held tone. The long tones are played *piano* in contrast to most of the rest of his solo material, which is quite remarkably varied, from sheets of sound and fierce flurries to little pecking tones. The long tones and long rests provide contrast and an element of formal unity, although admittedly subtle. As for the album's title track, it is a fierce, crying performance at a tempo so fast that Higgins's drums maintain an even, fast counterpoint rather than mark the time. Haden's bass is here bowed, there in contrary rhythm, then there in Ornette's own fast tempo, there again in descending double stops or in isolated tones—

he's motivated, it seems, by impulsive responses to the very sharp angles in Ornette's ferociously aggressive lines. As Martin notes, "The theme is again played with vigorous ferocity far too triumphant to be 'fearing' or 'hating,' rather one might suggest that 'fearsome' is a far more apt description for this torrential performance."[43] As we shall see, this fearsome aggression was a quality to be developed in Ornette's next recording, which lay a summer into the future.

The issues about Ornette Coleman's music that T. E. Martin raised in his three-part 1964 article, titled "The Plastic Muse," are so important that at this juncture it is best to quote from it at length. What critic Hsio Wen Shih described as the "effortless, soaring" theme statement of "Free," notes Martin,

> leads us into the heart of Coleman's most challenging innovations. Careful listening however will penetrate the sharp angularities of the altoist's solo to reveal one of his major methods of improvisation, a process that might be called 'motive evolution'. I can think of no other jazzman who has used this device so meticulously, though Sonny Rollins has sometimes hinted at it; certainly the thematic approach of Rollins and Monk is only a distant relative, and the self-constructing lines of latter-day Benny Carter, a greatly misunderstood soloist, are much closer. It may come as some surprise that a master of 'free form', the 'incoherent emotionalism', has carried improvisational form, consciously or intuitively, deeper into the core of the music than any of his predecessors, indeed to the point where it may imperil the spontaneity of his performance; the *Free* solo for example can almost be described as self-analysing music. Before turning to this however I must explain the term 'motive evolution'. This in Coleman's style involves the modification, transmutation, replication and polymerisation of the melodic germ cell which may be defined in say three notes; the notes themselves are unimportant, so in fact are the strict intervals they imply, thus harmony ceases to exist as a primary concept (the staunch admirers of bop harmony have only Parker to blame for making this step feasible) but the shape of this cell now becomes the essence. In a long solo such as we will encounter later, one of the distant progeny of the original motive will select itself for similar permutation to produce the sequential motive development described by Gunther Schuller in his excellent sleeve-note to "Ornette". In *Free* however there is only one main cell and this is displayed for all to see like the empty hat of a magician who has already drawn forth several rabbits and is about to produce

dozens more. The solo begins with the aforementioned rapid angular phrases but it is soon clarified by a brief slow tempo section which, in the manner of the jazz student elucidating passages on 78's by playing at 33 rpm, allows us to see the germs of his solo. The motive is seen in a simple 'polymerised' form and here sounds like a quote from one of the more sickly tunes of the 'twenties or 'thirties (the name of which eludes me). The line is instantly abstracted by repetition at tempo and its skeleton rapidly developed into 'sheets of sound'; Coleman surpasses even Coltrane by climaxing this sequence with a series of fierce trills. The basic melodic cell also supports the increasingly heated and scourging passages preceding the unaccompanied section which emerges in a long trilling figure and closes the solo.

Cherry begins, unaccompanied, with several sparse notes then immediately adopts the 'sheets' approach. A further sparse region precedes some very boppish lines that move into intense trills. He seems in good lip but submerges his own individuality in Coleman's favour; the rhythm section is quite able to supply continuity without this repetition of material. Once again Haden takes the opportunity of the trumpeter's solo to demonstrate the originality of his accompaniment. Coleman's long snaking lines lead back to a brief out-of-tempo section. He then plays a figure that would seem to be cut from granite so convinced is its melodic strength but the heated passage that precedes the final theme seems a needless self-indulgence merely repeating earlier ideas out of context. Nevertheless it is remarkable how the whole performance approaches a detailed unity despite the demanding tempo (almost 80 bars/minute).[44]

Earlier, Ornette had played excellent solos in "Mind and Time" and "Eventually" that were also closely unified by way of thematic evolution. In describing a later solo, Gunther Schuller pointed out the general formal pattern that Ornette presents: "Little motives are attacked from every conceivable angle, tried sequentially in numerous ways until they yield a motivic springboard for a new and contrasting idea, which will in turn be developed similarly, only to yield to another link in the chain of musical thought, and so on until the entire statement has been made."[45] This is, of course, the very opposite of the formlessness of which Ornette was accused by his detractors. At the same time, the ways he develops these solos illustrate his assertion that his "emphasis is placed on the melodic line rather than on the chord structure of a composition."[46]

The new performance of "Ramblin' " retains the alternating

straight-ahead and Bo Diddley bass patterns (remember the often-imitated guitar rhythm played by Bo Diddley in his 1955 hit "Bo Diddley"), but now they appear in unmeasured choruses. The effect recalls traditional country music or blues singers who form their statements without strict regard for chord-change timetables. "Ramblin'," notes Martin,

> has an outmoving prairie theme over an excellently defined rhythm in which bassist Charlie Haden's repetitive figures fill the expressive gaps. These gaps seem to create the sense of the western emptiness across which men (the horns) move with their mixture of bravado and loneliness, the latter becoming more explicit in the short motive that concludes the first theme statement. The reappearance of this motive is prevented by Coleman's entry after the repeat. This solo is one of his best and most approachable, being played with the contrast of light dancing phrases and gravelly voicings; only the second half shows any superficial signs of emotional disturbance and these are slight. The prairie sound is kept well to the fore and given psychological complexity, hence its life, by the use of short stabbing phrases that fall into a compulsive swing. The whole is straightforward, though individual, and one can see little difficulty in sensing the man's enviable understanding. Trumpeter Donald Cherry also has a fine conservative solo (within the new framework) developing out from the altoist's stabbing phrases. But it is Haden who really climaxes the work by his strict adherence to the prairie concept, rich-toned and very inventive with drone effects and 'guitar' passages. As Hsio Wen Shih says of the bassist (in a review of the LP for *Jazz Review*): "He shows a vivid and dramatic talent in his solo work and his accompaniments are always simple, always fitting, always uncluttered" and compares him with Wilbur Ware in his reaction to the conscientiously multi-noted style of bass-playing that has been dominant since Blanton's revelations. Here I think is the Roach to Ornette's Parker.
>
> The closing ensemble has drummer Billy Higgins overwhelming the bass figures of the theme; a simple but effective formal device. There is at the end a long diminuendo coda based on the loneliness motive which though loose in structure captures both courage and frustration (themes beloved by contemporary art); the result, it is stressed, is not pure optimism or tragedy but myth in the best and most vital sense of the word, the present feeling of the past. It is such a work (Mingus's *Los Mariachis* is another) the basic sentimentality of the 'folksy jazz' of a Brubeck or for that matter Guiffre; Haden's solo does not betray its sources nor bow before them but seems to talk

with them on their own terms, eye to eye, a mixture of satire and respect (quite apart from its sheer rhythmic elan).[47]

The quartet "Ramblin'," it should be noted, is shorter and more concentrated than the Bley Quintet's version of about a year earlier.

The missionary work by the admirers Ornette had won at the School of Jazz brought results of the most valuable kind: His quartet was booked for a two-week engagement at the Five Spot Cafe in New York City, to begin on November 17, 1959. Shortly before that, Contemporary released *Tomorrow Is the Question!* with its liner notes by Nat Hentoff that began, "I'm especially convinced that Ornette Coleman is making a unique and valuable contribution to 'tomorrow's' music because of the startling power of his playing to reach the most basic emotions." Reviewing the album the next year, Martin Williams suggested another way in which Ornette's music was a major innovation in jazz. The major innovations, the ones with the widest results such as Louis Armstrong and Charlie Parker brought about, were based in new perceptions of rhythm, Williams ventured, and recently there had seemed to be two possibilities in which jazz might evolve rhythmically: "There was Coltrane's way, accenting and phrasing his short notes which seemed to want to subdivide Parker's eighth-note rhythms into sixteenths. The other was the very free reorganization of rhythm and meter of Monk, most strikingly used in that *Bags Groove* solo. (It was in Rollins, too, and as Dick Katz once said, something very like it seemed to be in Lester Young's later work.) Rhythmic subdivision seems possible in Ornette's work, but free meters seem more likely. They certainly put fewer inhibitions on melody."[48] In fact, in solos such as "Focus on Sanity," "Free," or "Forerunner," Ornette had already achieved stunning rhythmic freedom, and there would be many more such liberated events to come.

Nine years earlier Ornette had left Forth Worth, seeking the freedom to be himself, and landed in Los Angeles, like it or not. Five years earlier he had left Forth Worth and subsequently found some success in Los Angeles, increasing in small, sometimes minuscule increments: a few musicians to play with, a few listeners (Ornette received 21 votes for best alto saxophonist in the 1958 *Down Beat* Readers Poll—1,425 less than the winner, Paul Desmond), a very few engagements, and, amid much rejection or indifference, some very enthusiastic praise. Despite the influential friends he'd made at the School of Jazz, there was realistically no reason to expect that audiences in New York City would respond differently from Los Angeles audiences. He had no prospects for work after the two-week gig at the Five Spot, but on the other hand he wasn't making much of a living playing his original music—praise and generous press notices did not pay the rent—and two weeks of steady work leading his own quartet was the best offer he'd yet received. It may be, as Barry McRae has suggested, that Ornette would have preferred that Bobby Bradford and Edward Blackwell were still with him in 1959. In any case, Ornette used half of his advance payment for his second Atlantic album, plus money he'd borrowed from the loyal Cherry, Haden, and Higgins, to purchase the group's transportation to New York. On the eve of their departure from Los Angeles, the newsstands displayed an issue of *Down Beat* that included photos of Ornette's last Atlantic recording session and the notice of the group's opening at the Five Spot in New York City.

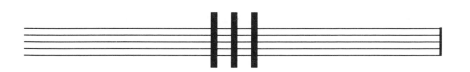

With its large black population and its liberal, elegant café society that grew up after the turn of the twentieth century, New York City, from an early point in jazz's history, has been the art's center of activity. Before World War I, pianists there were transforming folk and popular music into stride piano, and black ensembles, most famously the one led by James Reese Europe, were suffusing ragtime performances with a vitality and originality that took it to the brink of jazz. Amid the outpourings of Tin Pan Alley this prejazz or early jazz was quite avant-garde music; for instance, Europe and his collaborator Ford Dabney composed music for dancers in 5/4 meter, forty-some years in advance of Paul Desmond and Dave Brubeck's modal hit "Take Five." While New Orleans jazz was evolving to its climax in Chicago and Louis Armstrong was predicting the course of jazz's evolution, the most popular kind of jazz, big band jazz, was for the most part living its infancy in New York City (Armstrong and the other two leading former New Orleanians had resettled to New York by the end of the 1920s). Bebop, its successor, hard bop, and its modern alternative, cool jazz, first emerged in New York, too.

Not only was New York plentiful with jazz venues, it was, and is, relatively close to other major northeastern jazz markets, from Boston to Philadelphia and Washington, D.C. Along with the vitality of New York's jazz scene, then, there was the practical matter of saving money on travel expenses to attract musicians into settling there. After the decline of Chicago as a recording center in the 1920s, New York was by far the principal source of jazz recordings; of the six or seven independent record labels that were the leading documentors of jazz, five were New York-based. And since New York was the center of America's publishing industry, it was also the center of jazz journalism.

The Five Spot Cafe was located on The Bowery, the heart of New York City's skid-row district, but by the late 1950s it was not a down-and-out-folks' hangout—rather, it had become a jazz club with the most adventurous of artists among its performers and farsighted critics among its regulars. Before booking Ornette Coleman, the Five Spot's major claim to fame was its six-month engagement of Thelonious Monk's great 1957 quartet with John Coltrane. Charles Mingus, Herbie Nichols, and Cecil Taylor were among others who had graced the Five Spot's stage. With the release of two new Ornette Coleman albums and the recent praise in the jazz press, the Five Spot's owners decided to work his New York debut for its publicity value. On the cold evening of November 17, 1959, before Ornette's first show, the Five Spot held a press preview of the quartet and invited a crowd from New York's jazz establishment. While the Ornette Coleman Quartet played, wrote George Hoefer in an often-reprinted *Down Beat* column,

> some walked in and out before they could finish a drink, some sat mesmerized by the sound, others talked constantly to their neighbors at the table or argued with drink in hand at the bar. It was, for all this, the largest collection of VIP's the jazz world has seen in many a year. . . .
>
> This special preview for the press brought forth mixed-up comments:
>
> "He'll change the entire course of jazz," "He's a fake," "He's a genius," "He swings like HELL," "I'm going home and listen to my Benny Goodman trios and quartets," "He's out, real far out," "I like him, but I don't have any idea of what he is doing."[1]

The reactions, then, were extreme. The Ornette Coleman controversy began with that press party, and quickly generated business for the club, so much so that Ornette's two-week gig was quickly extended to two and a half months. While early opinions were flying freely back and forth, the quartet was quickly added to the program of two November 28 concerts at Town Hall. The performers, besides the quartet, included the bands of Monk, Taylor, Coltrane, the Jazztet, Lee Konitz–Ernestine Anderson, and Count Basie. Critic Whitney Balliett called it "a miraculous and perhaps even historic event" and "a vest-pocket history of most of the radical changes in jazz improvisation during the past couple of decades," devoting nearly half of his review to the "extraordinary" Ornette:

> Although his style suggests that he has forgotten more about Charlie Parker than most people have learned, it is, in essence, unique and indescribable. Coleman's improvisations are apt to be based not on the chords of a melody but on themes that are variations of the melody and that are stated, in a highly oblique manner, in the group's ensembles. Equally important is Coleman's tone. . . . Coleman will state a theme in a disarmingly simple way, interrupt himself furiously, sail into a blistering human-voice run (when these come off . . . it is a shaking experience), return to the theme but from a different angle, career off into another stretch of yodelling, and so on. . . . Cherry, a tall, thin, stick-legged man, who stood attentively beside Coleman during the leader's solos—his posture and attitude were suggestive of a valet holding a towel as he awaits his master's emergence from the bath—is his direct counterpart, . . . while Haden and Higgins realize the rhythmic freedoms preferred in Coleman's work by establishing a restless, continually shifting foundation that is almost completely melodic and ornamental, rather than merely percussive. (Haden, in particular, is remarkable.) . . .[2]

The Jazztet, one of the period's best hard bop groups, was sharing the Five Spot bill with Ornette's group, perhaps to soothe those listeners shaken up by the Coleman Quartet maelstrom. In view of the subsequently successful careers of the Jazztet's principals—Art Farmer, a melodic flugelhornist who phrased uniquely simply; his coleader, Benny Golson, a prolific composer who attempted to wed the disparate arts of Lucky Thompson and John Coltrane on tenor sax; and Curtis Fuller, a clean, very active trombonist—their being relatively ignored by the press at the time is not to be regretted, and in fact the juxtaposition of the two groups served to emphasize the nature of Ornette's advances. The source of hard bop was the late-forties Charlie Parker quintets with Max Roach; hard bop arguably began with Bud Powell's 1949 quintet, which included Fats Navarro, Sonny Rollins, and Roy Haynes. The interplay of soloist and rhythm section, with the latter virtually an equal participant in creating musical line, was a hard bop essential, as in the dense layer of percussion with which Roach surrounded his trumpeter Clifford Brown, or in the Jazz Messengers, in which the rise and fall of performance were determined by the surging drummer Art Blakey and pianist Horace Silver as much as by the horn soloists. The small hard bop combos tried, via dynamics, to project big band power; they often tended to use rhythm-and-blues and gospel-music harmonies, for hard bop was a reassertion of fundamental jazz passions in the face of West Coast cool. And hard bop was the immediate evolutionary ancestor of Free jazz.

But the evolution of hard bop had climaxed several years earlier. There had been already growing a sense that 1959 was a watershed year in jazz. The deaths of four great artists—Sidney Bechet and Baby Dodds, both from the early days of jazz in New Orleans, and beloved swing stars Billie Holiday and Lester Young—heightened a sense of jazz's past receding. With the 1959 recording of Miles Davis's major modal statement, *Kind of Blue*, and a month later, John Coltrane's masterpiece, *Giant Steps*, there was the clear implication that jazz was on the verge of major discoveries—and that Ornette's New York debut was the breakthrough into jazz's future.

Atlantic's title for its first Ornette Coleman album, *The Shape of Jazz to Come*, was intended to be, and to a large extent was, prophetic. It may have been a successful marketing device, too, for this LP's sales quickly outpaced those of the equally new *Tomorrow Is the Question!* But these prophetic titles raised hackles among established New York musicians who had not, in their own opinions, received enough attention. For part of the orthodox bop attitude of the day was the belief that only musicians who had worked as sidemen for established New York-based leaders for a period—paying their dues, the practice was called—deserved success. Not only was Ornette new in New York, the Five Spot engagement was the first time he had kept a band working for any extended period, as was well known.

At the end of January the Five Spot engagement concluded. Ornette and the quartet played another Town Hall concert on

January 30, 1960, then took the band on tour, to ongoing success: For instance, during two weeks at Chicago's top jazz spot, the Sutherland Hotel Lounge, business was good. As it happened, their Chicago appearance coincided with the annual convention of the Nation of Islam, popularly known as the Black Muslims, led by the charismatic Elijah Muhammad. Ornette, no longer a devoted Jehovah's Witness since the separation from Jayne, went to the convention but was not attracted to the religion: "I could hardly play for all the hate around me."[3]

Back in New York City by April 4, the quartet played a concert and then moved back into the Five Spot the next night. In those years New York enjoyed the alleged benefits of its "cabaret card" law, which forbade anyone with a police record of illegal drug possession to perform in nightclubs, thus sparing New Yorkers from the unspeakable horrors of music played by addicts. Billy Higgins's cabaret card was revoked; in April the Five Spot told Ornette to replace him with another drummer. In an extraordinary conjunction of events, the blinded goddess Justice provided Ornette with the necessary new drummer. In New Orleans Edward Blackwell and his wife Frances were arrested for miscegenation and jailed, thus sparing New Orleanians the unmentionable, perhaps even unremarkable presence of an interracial married couple. Fortunately, the Blackwells were released on bail, and skipped; Edward contacted Ornette, who first recommended him to John Coltrane for the new band Coltrane was forming before hiring Blackwell for his own quartet. Blackwell came to New York, played a week with Ornette, and with his first paycheck sent for his wife. There are two interesting sidebars to Blackwell's joining Ornette in 1960. First, Blackwell had turned down Ornette's invitation to play in the *Something Else!* sessions two years earlier, for he was performing regularly not only in rhythm and blues but also with the American Jazz Quintet, with fellow modernists Ellis Marsalis, Alvin Batiste, and Harold Battiste. Second, much later, in 1977, Edward and Frances Blackwell and their family attended a ceremony in the office of the mayor of New Orleans. As the mayor gave the key to the city to Edward, he said, "I hope there's no warrant out for our arrest."

The round of heavy activity continued for Ornette Coleman. In mid-May he played in a concert directed by Gunther Schuller in which he joined Eric Dolphy, the Bill Evans Trio, and the Contemporary String Quartet in seven Schuller compositions. On the Fourth of July weekend the Coleman Quartet played at the Newport rebel festival organized by Charles Mingus and Elaine Lorillard, who had founded and then been frozen out of the famed Newport Jazz Festival. Despite his gig at the rebel festival, Ornette had dickered for a spot on the Newport Jazz Festival until it was finally shut down by the historic Newport riots, which left the rebel festival the only music in town. It was the quartet's only break from the ongoing engagement at the Five Spot, which this time continued to the end of July. By then the group was making $682 for playing a six-night week, and that sum included a $32-a-week raise—hardly the pay one might expect for a group so highly publicized and that continued to draw crowds to the club. The Five Spot attracted a diverse clientele, including artists and writers—it was in this period that Ornette began his art collection with works by audience members such as Larry Rivers and Robert Rauschenberg—and media figures, both the written-about and their Boswells. Dorothy Kilgallen, the leading celebrity-gossip columnist of the day, liked to drop Ornette's name in print, alongside enthusiastic adjectives; when she went on vacation, Ornette's byline appeared over a guest column that filled her space in the *New York Journal-American* (Ornette had a ghostwriter do the job). It became fashionable to sit in with the quartet. Charles Mingus and Leonard Bernstein, then conductor of the New York Philharmonic, both did, on piano; Lionel Hampton and Percy Heath were among other sitters-in. Those who had heard Ornette at the School of Jazz, including, by now, Bob Brookmeyer, were his major supporters among musicians and critics, though the anti–Ornette Coleman side was beginning to be heard from.

Roy Eldridge, the great swing trumpeter, for instance: "I listened to him all kinds of ways. I listened to him high and I listened to him cold sober. I even played with him. I think he's jiving, baby."[4] Miles Davis: "Hell, just listen to what he writes and how he plays. If you're talking psychologically, the man is all screwed up inside."[5] Years later Ornette said, "I'm not mentioning names, but I remember one trumpet player who came up to me and said, 'I don't know what you're doing, but I want to let the people see me playing with you. Why don't you play some blues and let me come up and play.' So I said, 'OK,' and we did some song that he had played with Charlie Parker. Then when they asked him what he thought of my music, he said, 'Oh, the guy's all messed up—you can tell that just by listening to him.' And it wasn't true."[6] Ornette told John Snyder that Max Roach came to hear the quartet at the Five Spot, to find out "what all the fuss was about," and after the set came over and punched Ornette in the mouth. Moreover, at four o'clock the next morning Roach showed up on the street where Ornette lived, screaming, "I know you're up there, motherfucker! Come on down here and I'll kick your ass!"[7]

There were bad jokes. Ornette recalls the bewhiskered old one that maintained a couple went to hear him in a nightclub, and when a waiter dropped a tray of dishes the husband turned to his wife and said, "Listen, dear, Ornette's playing our favorite song!" *Down Beat* columnist George Crater, who claimed to have invented an Ornette Coleman windup doll—"wind it up, and it forgets the chord changes"[8]—raised the question of whether an evening spent listening to Ornette was covered by Blue Cross. *Newsweek* featured Ornette in an article, and the fashion magazine *Harper's Bazaar* maintained that "the intense, cacophonic jazz of alto saxophonist Ornette Coleman has the veteran way-out world all agog."[9] Mingus, who was to have a long love-hate affair with Ornette's music, weighed in with "I'm not saying that everybody's going to have to play like Coleman. But they're going to have to stop copying Bird. . . . It's like organized disorganization, or playing wrong right. . . . And it gets to you emotionally, like a drummer."[10]

Two English critics offered opinions. Stanley Dance, on hearing Ornette's quartet at the Five Spot, wrote, "to none of the blankly stirring patrons did it seem to communicate. They did not applaud at the end of 'numbers,' but when the set was finished they picked up their glasses as though they really needed refreshment. . . . Oh, Ornette will be the next jazz fashion, never fear. Once those numbed patrons realize that, they will understand and applaud."[11] Author Eric Hobsbawm, who wrote jazz journalism under the pseudonym Francis Newton, remarked, "The unforgettable thing about this very dark, soft-handed man playing with a vertical fold over his nose, is the passion with which he blows. I have heard nothing like it in modern jazz since Parker." Newton added, in a telling observation:

> But who has recognized him? The public at the *Five Spot* is overwhelmingly young, white, and intellectual or bohemian. Here are

the jazz fans (white or colored) with the "Draft Stevenson" buttons, lost over their $1.50 beer. If Coleman were to blow in *Small's Paradise* in Harlem, it would clear the place in five minutes. Musicians such as he are, it seems, as cut off from the common listeners among their people as Webern is from the public at the Filey Butin's. They depend on those who are themselves alienated, the internal emigrants of America.[12]

As jazz changes, its audience changes. Newton/Hobsbawm unknowingly was pointing toward a phenomenon that would become an increasing problem in the 1970s: the separation between African-American jazz audiences and the creators, who as in every previous period of jazz history were primarily African-American, of the new jazz.

In July 1960 the Ornette Coleman Quartet, now with Edward Blackwell playing drums, began recording its first New York album. By now Ornette was feeling the pressures of an extremely busy performing schedule, the controversy swirling around him, and tensions within his group as well, which may be why the first of the summer's three sessions included three of the cruelest, harshest solos he ever documented: "Kaleidoscope" and two takes of "Blues Connotation." T. E. Martin, commenting on the qualities of the music and the issues it raised, says the first version of "Blues Connotation," released in the album *This Is Our Music*, is

a slightly eccentric theme in which the notes seem to be constantly displaced from the expected; in his sleeve-note Coleman speaks of the melodic movement by minor thirds. The effect is very forceful and conveys an implacable determination. Coleman improvises very easily giving no sense of lack of control at any time (indeed it will be shown that his solo develops from theme with absolute logic of method) although there are some ideas which may be said to be 'gap-fillers'. This is not uncontrolled passion but a rational statement in a form of which Coleman can now demonstrate a consistent mastery. Its consistency perhaps is a feature worthy of attention by those who feel that the new wave cannot produce solos analogous in its way to those say of Hodges. But more than that study of this performance may help clarify Coleman's attitude to tonality since it seems to be an open form of his more usually dense approach to key centre.

At last it seems important for the jazz audience to have some knowledge of the thorny subject of tonality in its degrees of presence and absence. For the moment may I provide a crude personal glossary:

TONALITY: restriction to a single tonal centre ("key") as fulcrum point.

POLYTONALITY: division of centre between a restricted number of tonalities, usually two or three, as more will give the impression of—

PANTONALITY: where all tonalities are possible, i.e. roughly as defined by George Russell (*Jazz Review* June 1960), not Arnold Schoenberg whose method forms the basis of what became popularly known as—

ATONALITY: where all tonalities are essential.[13]

"Pan-tonal jazz is here," said Russell:

It seems logical to me that jazz would by-pass atonality because jazz is a music that is rooted in folk scales, which again are strongly rooted in tonality. Atonality, as I understand it, is the complete negation of tonal centers, either vertically or horizontally. It would not support, therefore, the utterance of a blues scale because this implies a tonic. But pantonality is a philosophy which the new jazz may easily align itself with. . . . Ornette seems to depend mostly on the over-all tonality of the song as a point of departure for melody. By this I don't mean the key the music might be in. His pieces don't readily infer key. I mean that the melody and the chords of his compositions have an over-all sound which Ornette seems to use as a point of departure. This approach liberates the improviser to sing his own song really, without having to meet the deadlines of any particular chord.[14]

To return to the first "Blues Connotation," Martin adds that Ornette's pantonality can be made to approach tonality or atonality

by simulating the even flow of tonal music (*Ramblin'*) or the vertiginous discontinuities of atonality. The second choice is made here, but in expanded form so that a key centre is retained long enough to be established as point of reference then destroyed by the shifting of the melodic shape to a dissonant key. The effect is something like that felt on a train rushing through the numerous switches of a large railway junction. It is not tonality that is shunned per se but tonal resolution, or "having to meet the deadline of any particular chord"

(Russell ibid.). Coleman reserves the right to change tonality (generally by fourths, minor thirds or more violently by minor seconds) at points which are determined solely by his conception of form, which is course how harmonic development must have been introduced in the first place. Tonality having been almost completely charted ceases to master and is now mastered to become an element used or not as the situation demands.

It is interesting to see how Ed Blackwell who replaces Billy Higgins at the drums has used this example to develop an asymmetric relation of rhythms analogous to the above melodic style. His solo on *Blues Connotation* consists of a brilliant series of short deliberately unresolved figures; rolls are broken midstream, cymbal patterns trail off but somehow these are made to fuse into a new rhythmic logic. Other highlights of the track include Charlie Haden's remarkable choice of stress, particularly behind the introduction to Cherry's solo, and the melodic fertility of Coleman's lines leading to the climax of his solo which is achieved by a series of striking and harmonically disturbing vocalised repetitions.[15]

The alternate "Blues Connotation" was not released until 1975, and then with the title "P.S. Unless One Has." Here the great violence in Ornette's solo, savage as a starving tiger confronted with raw meat, sounds as if it is a direct response to the power and complexity of Blackwell's accompaniments. Much of these descriptions fit "Kaleidoscope," too, except that this performance is even harsher, more violent, and Ornette's solo modulates among unrelated keys so fast that the sense of tonal abstraction is thoroughly pervasive. Wrote Martin, "Coleman is very well able to capture fleeting ambiguities and it is this I think that lends his ferocity a depth lacking in the occasionally empty anger of Mingus or in Coltrane's brilliant self-crucifictions and likens it to traits of the more 'modern' country singers—e.g. Lightnin' Hopkins and Robert Johnson."[16] Sonny Rollins's fierce "B. Swift" and "B. Quick" provide another point of comparison, though the variety of phrase shape in Ornette's "Kaleidoscope" solo makes it a sharper, bloodier work. Remarkably, Cherry's solo sustains the violent mood, as do a rolling Blackwell solo and the great power of Haden's bass. "Here," writes Martin, "the angry, the ugly and the noble rub shoulders, unify, and 'action jazz' reaches one of its most intense moments."[17]

These July 1960 sessions, recorded amid probably the busiest period of Ornette's life, resulted in almost two entire albums—the second, *To Whom Who Keeps a Record*, did not appear until 1975, and then only in Japan—and also provided much of the material for two catchall Coleman compilations that Atlantic issued in the 1970s, *Twins* and *The Art of the Improvisers* (Ornette authorized only the release of *This Is Our Music*). The previous December, as the Ornette Coleman Quartet was entering the extended portion of its first long run at the Five Spot, Lester Koenig wrote a letter to Nesuhi Ertegun that included some tantalizing titles of songs that Ornette had originally proposed to record for Contemporary, including "Circumstances," "The Doctor and the Artist," "My Friend Gabe," "Sound by Yore," and "Vivid Perception." It is quite possible that at least some of these were recorded, with new titles, at the summer Atlantic sessions. In any case, among the documents released were "Joy of a Toy," in which the theme's brevity of phrase and the sharp sound with which Ornette plays it are worlds away from the later "children's songs" of Keith Jarrett and Chick Corea. "The Fifth of Beethoven" is not merely a happy performance; it becomes downright giddy with a passage of alto sax quacking at Blackwell's tuned drums. The song titles in *To Whom Who Keeps a Record* read, in order, "Music Always," "Brings Goodness," "To Us," "All," "P.S. Unless One Has," "Some Other," "Motive for Its Use," and the quality of the performances, remarkably, approaches the standards Ornette set in *This Is Our Music* and the first two Atlantics.

"Embraceable You" is the only pop song to appear on an Ornette Coleman album, and if its performance was intended to entice bop-oriented listeners into his quartet's world, those listeners must have been startled indeed. The grand, sentimental introduction sounds like a parody of a Hollywood love scene, following which Ornette's solo, after two bars, distorts and then abandons the Gershwin theme, and sourness, harshness, and gentleness mingle in his lines. Another ballad recorded that summer, "Some Other," lacks the Gershwin piece's humorous features—"Some Other" is in a much more devoted, even plaintive mood.

On August 2, 1960, two days after the conclusion of the quartet's second long run at the Five Spot, they recorded sixteen tracks, of which thirteen are listed in Ornette's discography under the intriguing title "Untitled Original." A fire in the Atlantic Records vaults in the 1970s reportedly destroyed these along with other tapes; however, in 1992 Atlantic reports the discovery of quartet works previously believed lost. But given the central appearance of a motive from "Beauty Is a Rare Thing" in Ornette's "Poise" and "Folk Tale" solos, it is clear that "Beauty" was the major event on his mind that day, and it is even possible that the thirteen lost tracks are early attempts to play "Beauty." For it was probably a difficult conception to realize, and, more important, it was a prophetic work, a usually unacknowledged precedent to the exploration to come among younger New York and especially Chicago jazz artists in the later 1960s. Though largely improvised, "Beauty" is an orchestral conception, and Ornette says,

> I guess in jazz music, there are two horns and a rhythm section, that's what Charlie Parker and all the guys followed. But what happened with me is that I never was thinking about the format as much as I was thinking about the melodic line not having to be just played with that small structure. So what I was doing was to try and write a melodic line that sounded like it was structured orchestratedly. I was trying to play orchestrated music in a small combo context. . . . I realized that if I changed the harmonic structure or the tempo structure while someone else was doing something, they couldn't stay there. They'd have to change with me. So I'd more or less bring that about myself a lot, knowing where I could take the melody. In other words I could create a showcase of the melody and then show the distance between where I could go and still come directly back to that melody. Instead of trying to show the different inversions of the same thing.

So in the recording of "Beauty Is a Rare Thing," wrote Martin,

> Coleman and Haden are magnificent and the ensembles are amongst the most impressive recorded since the 'twenties'. However one of the most important achievements is the total form which allows the 'theme' to crystallise, dissolve and recrystallise within the fabric of individual statements. So striking is the result that I feel a full description of the work is warranted.
>
> It begins with a few keening alto notes played across bowed bass and drum rolls that move into 'pitched' tom-tom figures as Coleman extends the note values of the melody to prepare the underlying idea of emotional strain. His descents into the lower register and the following high-pitched squeals set an intense mood of sympathy and pathos. A menacing roll from Blackwell introduces Cherry who takes, through a web of cymbals, the same path from pity to disin-

tegration which is assisted by the alto's shrill glissandi and some
groaning bass. There follows a remarkable section in which the
drummer lays down a sparse but beautifully accented figure to set
Cherry's austerely lyrical fragments afloat on a bass ostinato of elas-
ticity and rolling power almost unique in the art of jazz bass-playing
(recalling for this writer the beautiful melodorhythmic phrase used
by Lester Young to lead into his solo on Billie Holiday's *A Sailboat
in the Moonlight*). This has, as so much of Haden's work, a musicality
beyond even the powerful solos and accompaniment of such a virtuoso as Mingus for example. And it forces me to suggest that here
is one of the few great exponents of the new idiom, almost the equal
of the altoist, tremendous in the support he lends to Cherry, who
lacks in himself the maturity and self-confidence to meet the demanding role of free agent, and in the organisational power he effects
throughout all these tracks. To return however, this section which
lasts only for a few bars, continues with Haden's return to sustained
notes for Blackwell to conclude with logical extensions of his introductory passage. The drummer now leads back to the disintegration
motive presented here in a sparse pyramidal form in which the horns
interlock isolated notes to be joined by some remarkable arco bass
similar to Mingus' harbour sounds in *A Foggy Day in San Francisco* (on
the London "Pithecanthropus Erectus" LP) but here shorn of literal
meaning; the effect is similar, an edgy disturbance, terror a hair's
breadth away.

It is Coleman who by an increasing restlessness of line introduces
this section with first the pointillist notes of Cherry then the addition
of Haden, and it is the altoist who resolves it by allowing the restricted tempo to flow out into lines of sixteenth notes. This device
indicates his idea of felt time (see Nat Hentoff), for this multiplica-
tion of notes is not felt as double or quadruple tempo imposed on a
set pulse as it generally is in Parker and Monk and always is in the
other boppers; we instead tend to move with the variable tempo of
the line itself. Haden's accelerandi and 'catching up to tempo' is a
simplified use of this, but only Coleman uses it consistently and his
success is surely indicative of a rhythmic intuition unrivalled in the
new wave and equalled by few other jazzmen. This resolution of
tension also allows his playing to become the dominant solo voice for
the following bars, moving in the low and middle registers, creating
some warm and compassionate melodies that are restrained in the
true sense of damming back, for the tone finally coarsens and after
a brief ascending pointillist duet with Cherry the lines are allowed to
reach their harrowing climax as several coarse high notes in strained
discord with the trumpet. From this catharsis the horns tumble into

concord as the theme reasserts itself to show by its own melodic shape why the climax was felt as a logical end. The closing statement presents the theme rising in its most compassionate form in the final bars. Incidentally Haden's tidal figure is also shown as an integral part of the structure either as cause or effect, when as the horns tumble back to the theme they blend in a melody which has a single recapitulation of the rolling rhythms of that remarkable central section extolled above.

Here the new wave has achieved by "chance" or what-ever-you-will an example of unity (NB—this track plays for nearly seven minutes) almost without peer in previous forms. It maintains a difficult mood and more important, explores the implied complexities with the precision of the original *Mood Indigo* or *Dead Man Blues*, without stumbling into sheer bathos and melodrama or third-stream academicism.[18]

There is not rest for the weary, goes the old saying. In mid-August the quartet began a three-and-a-half-week engagement at the famed Village Vanguard. Ornette now had a booking agent, Milt Shaw's Shaw Artists Corp., one of the leaders in the business—Miles Davis, John Coltrane, and Art Blakey were among Shaw's other clients at the time. So when Ornette once again took the quartet on tour, he received fees of $1,100–$1,250 a week, an improvement on the $850 a week they'd commanded for their tour the previous winter. And now another crisis arose, for Ornette's alter ego, Charlie Haden, dropped out of the quartet. Many years later Haden still had strong feelings about the occasion: "I never really left Ornette. I went to a hospital, then I stopped playing for awhile, and then I rejoined him in 1966." The replacement Haden recommended was his former Los Angeles roommate Scott LaFaro, who had come to New York to work with pianist Bill Evans at about the time Haden had come to New York with Ornette. The tour went from a Philadelphia festival to a San Francisco club to, once again, the Monterey Festival and finally to a club in Los Angeles. At Monterey, reported Kenneth Rexroth, "the whole group showed signs of acute unhappiness,"[19] and they did not even complete the two weeks they were scheduled to play in Los Angeles. Returning to New York, they played opposite the Modern Jazz Quartet, at John Lewis's request, for two weeks at the Village Vanguard before at last taking a vacation.

There was by then absolutely no question that Ornette was a

New Yorker—he took to the city like a duck to water. The audience that he couldn't attract in Los Angeles was certainly present in New York. For instance, at the Five Spot, according to Haden, "I don't remember the club ever being empty; it was almost full every night. And Ornette was always writing new tunes, as he had from the time I first met him. Coltrane used to come hear us every night. He would grab Ornette by the arm as soon as we got off and they would go off into the night talking about music."[20] There were budding friendships with young musicians who were inspired by the advanced ideas of Ornette, Coltrane, and Cecil Taylor, and there may have been an undercurrent of rivalry with Taylor, who, in 1960, was still struggling to present his original music. Taylor long maintained that his very fine, aggressive bassist Buell Neidlinger was Haden's superior, and Neidlinger wrote that Taylor's "Of What," in his Contemporary album *Looking Ahead!* "recorded at Nola's Studios June 9, 1958, is the *original* free piece, preceding its credited invention by Ornette Coleman by several years."[21] Soft-spoken and friendly, Ornette moved easily among New York's circles of artists, writers, and filmmakers, as well as musicians.

On the other hand the extremely busy schedule of performing and recording that Ornette had pursued since arriving in New York was draining him. "I'm not sure but what I lose more than I gain by working every night," he told Nat Hentoff. "I get so tired I don't have the enthusiasm to write or rehearse during the day. I'd much prefer longer sets three or four nights a week, and the rest of the time off."[22] To a *New Yorker* interviewer Ornette said, "What I'd like most now is a vacation, but I've got three musicians depending on me. . . . Sometimes I go to the club and I can't understand what I feel. 'Am I here? How will I make it through tonight?' I say to myself. I'd like to play a couple of nights a week is all. I'd have more to say. I'd get closer to harnessing my feelings, to getting down to the true essence."[23]

The very conditions of the jazz business were antithetical to the creation of fine art—you couldn't imagine classical musicians, for instance, putting up with them. The long hours on most nights of the week; the poor pay; the atmosphere of corruption that pervaded most clubs (including the under-the-table deals with city officials that kept the clubs open); the disrespect for the music from noisy bartenders, cash registers, talkative customers, and employees; all added up to something less than an atmosphere oriented to sensitive musical creation and interpretation. Indeed, the very atmosphere that artists inhaled for long hours each night was objectionable. The Five Spot, for instance, one of the world's leading jazz venues in its day, had its bandstand in front of the rest rooms: "the latrine job, I called that. Urine used to seep in under the piano," said Buell Neidlinger.[24] The rival Newport festival that Ornette played in July was, for one of the first times, a musicians' protest against the jazz business. After the rebel festival, participants such as Charles Mingus, Max Roach, and Jo Jones formed an artists' collective to produce their own concerts and recordings; Ornette was invited, but chose not to join them.

Meanwhile, the musicians Ornette worked with day after day—skilled craftsmen who had so extensively practiced with him and learned the complex harmonic relationships that made his new music possible; artists who had stayed loyal to him through the worst of times and now the new, good times—were, apart from their music, often undependable. Alto saxophonist Jackie McLean and others have argued persuasively that the wide availability of heroin in New York stemmed from the release from a federal prison of New York drugs kingpin Lucky Luciano during World War II, a release brought about by President Franklin Roosevelt in exchange for wartime undercover work; as a result Luciano felt free to organize the city's narcotic distribution and targeted black neighborhoods as markets; one result was the high incidence of narcotics addiction among jazz musicians. There were periods when Ornette was the only member of his quartet who did not use narcotics. During the quartet's second long Five Spot engagement, Jimmy Giuffre's group shared the bill, and Neidlinger, who was Giuffre's bassist in 1960, often was drafted into Ornette's group "because Charlie Haden in those days might not show up until midnight."[25]

Ornette made loans to his addicted sidemen—they sometimes arrived for work without their instruments, which were in the pawnshop—and tried to hustle recording dates so that his players could support their addictions. According to John Snyder, on an out-of-town engagement Ornette noticed that one of his musicians was flying back and forth to New York every day. Ornette asked why. The musician replied, "To cop." "To cop what?" "Heroin"—for himself and Ornette's other two sidemen. Ornette: "I thought we were playing music." The sideman: "We're playing music—

high." If heroin was that good, Ornette wanted to try it himself; he did, once, and was never interested in using it again: "The problem was, you never got anything done, you just sat around feeling good about yourself." The problem within the quartet was not his sidemen's use of heroin per se, but its results, including the need to replace Higgins and Haden. Years later, after an addicted former sideman came to Ornette and Snyder asking for money, Ornette sighed: "He's in such a bad way, but he's got such a good heart."

In fact, though, Ornette was hurt that his musicians continued drugging, so the personal relationships within his group were often strained. At the Monterey Festival Ornette played in Schuller's "Abstraction" and "Conversations" and then with his quartet on Saturday afternoon. The quartet was scheduled to return Sunday evening, but as they warmed up backstage Sunday, Ornette suddenly struck Don Cherry in his pocket trumpet, as he was playing it, tearing his lip. He couldn't play that night as a result, and the set proved to be by the Ornette Coleman Trio. "I don't want to talk about it" was Ornette's only comment after the event.[26]

There was a further source of conflict for Ornette then, and possibly a serious one. Gunther Schuller was a french hornist in symphony orchestras, having by 1960 spent ten years in the Metropolitan Opera Orchestra, and a composer of orchestral and chamber music. He had also played on occasional jazz recordings, including Miles Davis's final 1950 *Birth of the Cool* date. In years to come he would compose an opera, *The Visitation*, based on Franz Kafka's *The Trial* but with the important difference that his hero is a modern African-American. He would also serve as president of the New England Conservatory of Music and write two of the few essential works in the jazz critical literature. Ornette had become friends with Schuller at the School of Jazz; in those days Schuller was composing his early third stream music, works which attempted to unite the disparate rhythmic-harmonic-expressive worlds of jazz and classical music, and in 1960 Ornette played in two concerts of Schuller compositions.

Ornette began taking lessons from Schuller, in reading and notating music. Schuller recalls,

> He'd write things down, and they never made any sense. He'd write B flat when he really was hearing D flat, and it was all screwed up. So he said, "Let me study with you." He came to my apartment

religiously every week for something like eight months—he never was late. All of that ordinary teaching he had gotten as a kid in school, none of that had worked, so I knew I had to think of some new, ingenious ways of breaking through this mental barrier that he had. It never quite happened. There was one incredible moment when I felt I was making good progress and he was beginning to understand—I felt there was like a light going on in his brain.

Suddenly he stared at me and said, "I think I'm feeling sick," and he started to groan. He quickly got up and rushed into the bathroom and vomited for about ten minutes—it was unbelievable. Then afterwards he came back and said, "Gee, I'm sorry, Gunther, I don't know what happened, but I realized something that I never realized before, and it really hurt me." His eyes were full of terror—if a black man can turn white, he turned white. That's not just some casual little experience, that was a mind-blowing, earth-shaking experience for him. He never came back for another lesson.

I'm not a professional psychologist, but I think what happened was, he caught a glimpse of what I was talking about in terms of accurate reading and notation and it was so disturbing because it meant everything he had learned up to then was "wrong." He had the whole transposition thing upside down. Further than that, over a period of years, when I think he was playing in blues bands in Texas, he had for some reason begun to associate certain pitches with certain characters. In other words, certain notes were always upbeats and they could only be upbeats. Certain other notes were always downbeats. I have always said that because he did not learn these things in the traditional way, he became the extraordinarily original improviser that he is, it's his genius. To this day he has people translate, I don't know what the word is, transcribe, transmogrify the things he writes down into some kind of normal notation, and nobody really knows whether those people do it accurately or not.

(In 1961, as editor of a book of transcriptions of nine Ornette Coleman themes, Schuller wrote, "We believe it is precisely because Mr. Coleman was not 'handicapped' by conventional music education that he has been able to make his unique contribution to contemporary music."[27])

At a benefit for comedian Lord Buckley in December, Ornette sat in with Dizzy Gillespie's band. Then came three consecutive days of recording, of which the first two were spent with Gunther Schuller compositions. Schuller had composed "Abstraction" specifically for Ornette and seven strings (including guitar) and drums as an attempt to dramatize by juxtaposition the parallels between Ornette's pan-tonal improvising and serial composition, and also between his "outwardly fragmentary, but inwardly cohesive"[28] line and post-Webern classical form. It's in ABA[1] form, with A as the strings-drums ensemble's development from isolated fragments to intensity; B begins with Ornette's sudden entrance at the peak of ensemble density, and consists of his vivid, unaccompanied, improvised cadenza; A[1] is the exact retrograde of A. The sudden sundering of the ensemble's agitation by the passionate Ornette is dramatic indeed. Schuller's third stream works recurringly contrasts a seemingly constricted, "correct" classical ensemble yearning for expressive freedom with jazz's realization of that freedom, and "Abstraction" is among the best demonstrations. Ornette also played in two of Schuller's "Variants on a Theme of Thelonious Monk (Criss-Cross)"; the first has Ornette's own excellent theme variations as well as strong lines over harmonically ambiguous accompanists, and both the first and final variants feature genuinely stimulating duets, though other players are present, by Ornette and Eric Dolphy. "Abstraction" and "Variants" appeared on *Jazz Abstractions*, an unfortunately ignored album, since much of the playing is fine and Schuller's mixing of distinctive, disparate improvisers is frequently subtle and stimulating.

Possibly the heat generated that day by Coleman and bass clarinetist Dolphy together was a warm-up for *Free Jazz* on Ornette's third day of recording. It was the same day that Dolphy had recorded for the first time with Booker Little in Dolphy's own group. For *Free Jazz* Dolphy again chose to play bass clarinet, and Ornette's other collaborators on the recording's "double quartet" were his latest quartet partners, Cherry, LaFaro, and Blackwell; his former bassist and drummer, Haden and Higgins; and Dolphy's roommate, young trumpeter Freddie Hubbard, who had arrived in New York to stay at about the same time that Ornette had first opened at the Five Spot. Not only did Dolphy and Hubbard make minor sensations themselves at the turn of the 1960s but Dolphy was Ornette's rival in the sense that conservative journalists held him to be a model of respectable jazz exploration, as opposed to Ornette's "wrong" exploration. And it's true that Dolphy played his woodwinds—alto sax, flute, bass clarinet—using chord changes or modes, which is all the conservatives really required, but with a sense of harmony and a free associa-

tion of solo form that often came much closer to atonality than
Ornette.

Free Jazz is a series of collective improvisations separated by
composed themes, at first fanfares, with each horn in turn taking
the lead and the others improvising ongoing responses at will, ending in bass, then drum, duets. For most of the work's forty minutes
the basses play an up-down, hugga-bugga shuffle rhythm. Insofar
as *Free Jazz* is successful, much of that success results from Dolphy's responses to other "soloists" lines. Ornette's own "solo" is not
among his major works, but halfway through *Free Jazz* comes Don
Cherry's "solo," in which Ornette's objective of responsive ensemble improvisation actually succeeds—the trumpet phrases are liberated from the shuffle rhythm's dominance, Cherry responds to
Ornette's interjections, and this "solo" section ends with Cherry
playing obligato to an alto-bass clarinet game of phrase catch. The
idea of *Free Jazz*, certainly imperfectly realized here, had emerged
on record with Lennie Tristano's "Intuition" and "Digression" as
early as 1949, as his sextet improvised, without themes or fixed
harmonic structures, on and against each other's lines. Compared to
the radical Free jazz that Ornette Coleman and Cecil Taylor were
conceiving in the early 1960s, the interweaving of pianist Tristano
and saxophonists Lee Konitz and Warne Marsh sounds to modern
ears almost like bop.

January found the Ornette Coleman Quartet back at the Village
Vanguard for two weeks, and then into the recording studio for the
Ornette! session. Changes in Ornette's music were now quite evident, the most obvious being the abandonment of lingering links to
material based on standard chord changes ("Embraceable You" had
been the last) and the replacement of Charlie Haden's close empathy by Scott LaFaro's virtuoso accompaniments. Upon coming to
New York in 1959, LaFaro joined the Bill Evans Trio at something
near the pianist's peak. Apart from his work with Ornette, much of
LaFaro's reputation rests on his gradually claiming the role of central voice in the Evans Trio. LaFaro was a strong player, possibly
even as forceful as Haden, but his technical facility and his harmonic choices often made his lines appear merely ornamental,
whereas Haden's had been integral. Thus much of this particular
quartet's music leaves the effect of brilliant rhythmic interplay between Ornette and Blackwell, joined by brilliant and decorative
bass. About LaFaro's personality, Ornette once said, "He felt su-

perior not only to Negroes but to whites as well,"[29] while Haden remembers, "I'd come home and Scotty would be on the bed, upset, saying, 'I'll never be good enough.' He was a perfectionist, though. I'd tell him how great he was, but he wouldn't be satisfied."[30] These seemingly disparate attitudes about himself, far from being mutually exclusive, seem to be opposite sides of the same coin.

The most integrated work at the session was the fastest, "The Alchemy of Scott LaFaro," with quite fiery playing by Ornette and his bassist. "T and T" is an excellent, West African–inspired drum solo—Blackwell by then was already an experienced student of international percussion cultures—while the other three works originally released in *Ornette!* are all in a similar tempo and feature, for a change, extended soloing. The most remarkable performance, "W.R.U.," is slightly faster than the others, at a medium-fast pace that's an ideal stimulus to Ornette's eight-minute solo, which from a thrilling beginning moves through a world of vibrant melody, constantly challenged by Blackwell's ingenious rhythms; LaFaro's bass solo, with "twisting sitar-like glissandos and doublestops,"[31] is excellent, though largely unrelated in mood to the rest of the performance. "C and D" includes a similarly fine bowed-bass solo, this one suggestive of a classical music sensibility, while "R.P.D.D." is almost entirely a strong Ornette solo. The last of these alto solos, while it is in his motive-evolution style like the others in the album, proposes a problem for critic T. E. Martin:

> The structure is much looser, more obvious (hence possibly the greater understanding shown by critics) and less rewarding. To me the tonal centres, or modal pedal-points often become painfully obvious and despite the many melodic attractions and unflagging invention we might well wonder on this evidence what all the fuss of "free jazz" was about. After a very promising beginning the dramatic space rapidly weakens and a playfulness which on one hand reveals his assurance undermines the unity that he can achieve.
>
> This failure is interesting and certainly understandable but unlike my colleagues I sincerely hope that this is not indicative of the main line of Ornette's future development, for it will represent a dangerous retreat from the boldness of his achievements in *Free, Beauty is a rare thing, Kaleidoscope* and more hopefully *W.R.U.* from these same sessions.[32]

This kind of stylization would become increasingly evident in Ornette's soloing in the years to come.

There's no way of knowing whether additional experience in the quartet would have furthered the integration of Scott LaFaro's music, or how his and Ornette's forceful musical personalities might have gone on to affect one another, for the group did not perform again that winter, and soon LaFaro was working with Evans again. Six months after _Ornette!_ LaFaro died tragically in an automobile accident. Meanwhile, Ornette replaced him with Jimmy Garrison, and this Ornette Coleman Quartet recorded _Ornette on Tenor_ in March. It was the first time Ornette had recorded jazz on tenor saxophone—the first time he'd recorded anything at all on tenor, in fact—since that lost 1950 rhythm-and-blues date; he'd seldom played it in the intervening years, and he would not record on tenor again for another sixteen years. But he'd never lost his affection for the instrument. In the album's liner notes he said,

> The tenor is a rhythm instrument, and the best statements Negroes have made, of what their soul is, have been on tenor saxophone. Now you think about it and you'll see I'm right. The tenor's got that thing, that honk, you can get to people with it. Sometimes you can be playing that tenor and I'm telling you, the people want to jump across the rail. Especially that D flat blues. You can really reach their souls with that D flat blues. . . .[33]

The album is more than an attempt to recapture the happiest times of Ornette's early musical years. The tenor saxophone adds visceral power and richness of sound to his playing here; his cry and his vigor in "Enfant" and "Eos" are marvelous. Again motive evolution organizes his soloing, to the point of motive tyranny in "Ecars," while "Enfant" is a unified work by virtue of Cherry's solo expanding on the same central motive that Ornette uses in his solo. "Mapa" is an attempt at a _tour de force_ of collective improvisation, at unity of development despite contrary rhythmic thrusts, with one or more players in tempos or meters unrelated to the music's principal velocity throughout. "Cross Breeding" is an excellent Ornette showpiece, with his tenor expressing enormous rhythmic liberation in tempo and over stop-time and suspended sections as contrasting lines, often of great complexity, again and again meet a recurring resolution motive, a grand performance that once again is stimulated by Edward Blackwell's interplay.

The second *Ornette on Tenor* session, recorded on March 27, 1961, was not only the end of Ornette's association with Atlantic Records, at least as far as documents that have been released, but it was also the last appearance by Blackwell and Cherry in the classic Ornette Coleman Quartet. The recordings of Cherry with Coleman over slightly more than three years document the progress to maturity of a remarkable trumpeter. To have achieved what must have been a high degree of mastery in one discipline, hard bop, in the later 1950s, and then to apply his gifts to an utterly fresh, indeed, unprecedented one, Ornette's music, required rare boldness of spirit. The listener can hear alternating tentativeness and confidence as the vestiges of hard bop vanish over time from Cherry's discourse. While his subsequent use of Ornette's own phrasing as a model for his own lines indicates dependence on the leader's vision, it also indicates a sense of the importance of his own improvising as an element of a unified ensemble viewpoint. By Don Cherry's Atlantic recordings there is surely no mistaking him for any other trumpeter in jazz—the melodic contours, the rhythm, the sense of space were unique—and in time the occasional fragmentary passages in some earlier solos were replaced by a compelling sense of the tension of sound and space. His 1961 solos in *Ornette!* and *Ornette on Tenor* show a most rewarding mastery of developing whole statements out of complex material, while his duel with Ornette in "The Alchemy of Scott LaFaro" shows that he is quite willing, at last, to challenge the leader at his own strengths. By the time Don Cherry left the Ornette Coleman Quartet, he was a major jazz artist in his own right.

From the near-constant activity of most of 1960, in 1961 Ornette had come to hardly perform at all. This would be reason enough for a sideman to seek full-time employment elsewhere, and for Cherry there was another reason, perhaps not felt or only dimly felt: Now in his musical maturity, his most personal growth might very well occur in other settings. His 1962 work with Sonny Rollins strongly suggests that, for if next to Ornette, Cherry appeared to be another aspect of his master's vision, next to Rollins, Cherry, wholly confident and masterful, made an excellent contrast. It was a period when Rollins had been stimulated by Ornette's music to explore freely structured improvisation himself, though—perhaps surprisingly, considering Rollins's great discoveries in improvised form in the late 1950s—without a corresponding development of form. The resulting live album, *Our Man in Jazz* (RCA), tends to sound brittle, disconnected, during the long tenor solos that are its primary content; for a change, the highly dramatic inclinations of Rollins's art sound quite unfocused. Cherry, lyrical from top to bottom, is wonderfully poised; even given the comparative delicacy of his sound amid the otherwise extroverted Rollins group, the flow of Cherry's melodies and his purposefulness gives the music an island of confidence. He was to play a somewhat similar role in the New York Contemporary Five the next year. The Five was a more fulfilling group, for its musicians were all experienced in Free jazz territory. The unique, acidulous lyricism of alto saxophonist John Tchicai in those days was something never to be repeated in jazz, while tenorman Archie Shepp was at the early height of his improvising and composing powers. Even among this exciting company, Don Cherry's trumpet melodies were the NYC Five's greatest merit.

And just as Charlie Haden had been the perfect bassist for the realization of Ornette Coleman's art, Edward Blackwell had been the perfect drummer. This was probably true as early as 1956, reported Ellis Marsalis, for the things Ornette and Blackwell did "accentuated a certain kind of rhythmic importance and rhythmic emphasis that was in Ornette's music," making their teaming "sufficient" without any other rhythm-section players.[34] As a child Blackwell had listened to his sister practice tap dancing and had tried to imitate her taps with improvised drumsticks. In New Orleans he also followed funeral and festival parades, "just follow behind the band clapping and dancing, what they would call the second line, and we would just follow the band all the way to their destination. . . ."; as a young drummer he "had this fantasy in my head of people dancing to the rhythm."[35]

Paul Barbarin, who once had played with King Oliver, Luis Russell, and Louis Armstrong, had tutored Blackwell, had even let him sit in on occasion; also in New Orleans Blackwell had played rhythm and blues and been one of the city's first modern jazzmen. Why was he such a provocative drummer for Ornette's music? Part of the reason may be the New Orleans–bred concept of drumming as an ensemble art—"for the benefit of the band," as the city's greatest drummer, Baby Dodds, once said. Most important, surely, was personal empathy—Ornette's playing inspired Blackwell's rhythmic impulses and vice versa. After leaving Ornette in 1961, Blackwell found employment with the Montgomery Brothers group, which included guitar favorite Wes Montgomery, and in Eric Dolphy's short-lived Five Spot quintet, one of the high points of Dolphy's pathetically short life.

There was an obvious replacement available for Don Cherry in Ornette Coleman's quartet—Bobby Bradford, at last. A few months earlier Ornette had tried to recruit Bradford to play in *Free Jazz* instead of Hubbard, had even sent Bradford money and plane tickets; Bradford had returned them. As a Dallas teenager, Bradford had played in his city's top band, led by local institution Buster Smith, a multi-instrumentalist whose alto work in the 1930s had been one of Charlie Parker's first inspirations. Besides Ornette, Eric Dolphy and Wardell Gray were among the other notables with whom Bradford had played in Los Angeles. After his four air force years, Bradford had attended the University of Texas for two years before joining Ornette in the spring of 1961; by then he was no longer modeling his improvising on Fats Navarro.

Ornette rehearsed with a fine hard bop drummer, Pete La Roca—he'd abandoned his given name, Pete Sims, when he'd worked in Latin bands—and considered using Charlie Parker's onetime drummer, Roy Haynes, but Blackwell's replacement proved to be Ornette's old friend from Fort Worth high school days and the Jam Jivers, Charles Moffett. Moffett had had a highly successful career teaching high school music in Rosenberg, Texas, near Houston, and then in Fort Worth; the bands he had led won state contests, and he had played Ornette's early recordings for his music-appreciation classes; in that period Moffett still played drums, too, including in Trudy Coleman's band and, like Blackwell, with Little Richard. Indeed, during a brief visit home in 1960 Ornette had visited Moffett's class, met Moffett's students, and promised Moffett a job if Moffett would move to New York. "No way would I leave the kids," Moffett said. "I thought I really had the best band I'd ever had, that year." But when the band was awarded only a second-place rating in the state contest, Moffett became disgusted with the music-education bureaucracy; "I thought I better play and do it myself." Arriving in New York, then, he played club dates with former schoolmate King Curtis, then still riding his R&B fame (when Ornette had come to New York in 1959, Curtis had met him in a Rolls-Royce), and rehearsed with Ornette. "After rehearsing a week or two weeks with him, he said, 'Well, fellows, we're opening up at the Five Spot,' " Moffett recalls. "I said, 'Me, too?' He said, 'Yeah, what do you think you've been rehearsing for?' "

The new quartet of Ornette, Bradford, Garrison, and Moffett played the Five Spot from July 17 to August 19 and again from September 11 to October 15. In the meantime, apparently, Ornette had put together a new double quartet of his regular quartet plus, probably, Cherry, Blackwell, Steve Lacy (soprano sax), and Art Davis (bass) to record for Atlantic during the summer; no tapes exist, and there is no record of the session or sessions in Atlantic's files. Then in October, after the Five Spot run ended, Ornette was scheduled to perform an "unrehearsed concert" in Cincinnati with his double quartet, by Encore Productions. Ornette had a personal manager, now, Mildred Fields, formerly of the Monte Kay agency (she also managed George Russell). Ornette and Fields arrived in Cincinnati the day before the concert to promote it, and by late the next day the rest of the musicians arrived, too. While the double quartet was rehearsing for the "unrehearsed" event, Fields went to the concert promoters to ask for the $1,000 advance that the musicians were to receive. No, Encore Productions told her, we already advanced you $900 to fly the band to Cincinnati, and the musicians drove their cars instead. "Nonsense," responded Fields. "Who ever heard of travel money with restrictions on it." She called the musicians off the stage; it was later discovered that Encore had collected less than $500 in advance sales. To make matters worse, Encore had put up posters in Cincinnati that read "ORNETTE COLEMAN—FREE JAZZ CONCERT," which attracted a crowd that expected to be admitted into the concert without paying, and turned angry when confronted with the demand to buy tickets. The Cincinnati affair was a fiasco that could have turned violent, for that was the crowd's mood.

Ornette then went on alone to California. In San Francisco he crossed the bay to Berkeley, where he sat in with The Group, house quartet at the Tsubo Club (The Group's bassist Barre Phillips called the event "real scary"). In Los Angeles tenor saxophonist Gene Ammons canceled his opening at the Flamingo Club at the last minute; Ornette, his old supporter James Clay, and Dexter Gordon, beginning his career anew after his long incarceration, were Ammons's replacements. Back in New York, Ornette had to make another change in his quartet. Jimmy Garrison had played some of the best music of his career in *Ornette on Tenor*, yet playing in Ornette's quartet always made him uncomfortable:

With Ornette I learned how to resolve notes instead of chords. Ornette writes phrases the way he feels them; if it comes out 3½ bars, then that's it. His playing sometimes leaves you hanging the same way, leaves you wanting more, leaves you thinking, 'Is there anything else to come?' But it just means it's the end of the phrase and he's moved on. . . . He said, 'Well, James, just play, and listen, of course, and if there's anything you want to know, just ask.' . . . You can only go so far in his music without *knowing* about it, and one night I just exploded.[36]

One night in front of a packed house at the Five Spot, Garrison stopped the band and, according to Ornette, said, "Stop this goddam music, ain't a fucking thing happening, what do you Negroes think you're doing? You going crazy, I mean it's nothing, you know, nothing's happening, what are you doing? I mean let me have it, I know what's happening."[37] Reflecting on the incident later, Ornette could respect the intensity of Garrison's musical beliefs, and in October when Garrison left him to join John Coltrane, he did so with Ornette's blessing.

A bassist who had sat in at the Five Spot, David Izenzon, took Garrison's place. Izenzon was another man with a strong sense of conviction; he had not even begun to study the bass until adulthood, and with a background in classical music, had not played jazz before playing informally with Ornette. By the time Izenzon became part of Ornette's quartet, though, Ornette was taking fewer and fewer engagements. He'd seen Dave Brubeck receive twice as much money as himself to play before smaller crowds than his own quartet attracted, and all around him was more evidence of others' financial success, including that of John Coltrane, with Garrison in his band. Ornette decided to triple his price, which may have brought it more in line with his music's value but which did not make him a more successful commodity, and which reportedly horrified his agent. There was very little work for him in 1962, then. When the Newport Jazz Festival offered him fifteen hundred dollars to play at an afternoon show, Ornette's response, according to Bradford, was "That's all right for me—now what about the rest of the band?"[38]

He led his group in a concert for the American Institute of Architects' First Conference on Aesthetic Responsibility in April, in New York. With Izenzon and Moffett he played a week at the Jazz Gallery in June. Bradford was by then only playing irregularly with Ornette, and spending more time in Dallas. According to Charles Moffett, both Bradford and Izenzon "challenged" Ornette to work more: "They went out and got engagements and Ornette said, well, it's not enough money. They said, how much money do you want, and Ornette named his price and they went back. Then, here they come back with the contract for the price that Ornette said! Ornette still said, I'm not gonna take it. So that's when Bobby left to go back to Texas. . . ."[39] Fortunately Moffett was substitute teaching in New York schools and Izenzon was playing classical music in orchestras and chamber ensembles, so they did not have to depend on Ornette for an income, unlike the original Coleman Quartet. At the end of the year, Ornette rented New York's Town Hall with his own money to present a concert of his new music, played by his regular trio, a trio of rhythm-and-blues players to join his own trio for one selection, and a string quartet; he paid all the musicians himself, and he and Moffett and Izenzon put up posters advertising the event. The nightclub business that sustained jazz and the New Orleans whorehouses of legend where Jelly Roll Morton had played were "built on the same two things: whiskey and fucking,"[40] whereas with the Town Hall concert, Ornette said, "I believe that the music is best heard in this kind of presentation."[41]

The Town Hall concert was a major event. Izenzon's solo bass piece "Taurus" was composed by himself; of the other works on the concert, all were composed by Ornette and eight were trio pieces. "Blues Misused," the rhythm-and-blues piece for alto, guitar, piano, two basses, and drums, was reviewed by *Down Beat*'s Bill Coss as "a sometimes historical, sometimes satirical, sometimes plain funny piece that exhibited the best and worst of rhythm and blues." It is one of the seven Town Hall works that was never issued on record; could it have been an ancestor of Prime Time's music? "Dedication to Poets and Writers" was composed for string quartet; Ornette has said, "I had been trying to write classical music since 1950." In 1984 he told a curious story: NBC-TV news anchors Chet Huntley and David Brinkley "came to the Five Spot and asked me, 'Can you read?' And I said, 'Only the newspaper,' because even when I told people I could do things like read music, it never helped me. So after that, write-ups always picked up on that quote. . . . I realized that my image was sort of 'corn-pone musician,' this illiterate guy who just plays, so I started writing classical music."[42] Shades of the Original Dixieland Jazz Band, one of whose members had claimed more than four decades earlier, "I don't know how many pianists we tried before we found one who couldn't read music."[43] "Dedication to Poets and Writers" begins as a dance, though the minor qualities of the initiating five-note cell motive are soon emphasized; much of the work is the adventures of that motive, evolving in a way reminiscent of his soloing; with fast and slow sections, harmonic and contrapuntal turmoil abet the work's development, resolving in the end, after agitated dissonance, with an unanticipated consonant, hymnlike chord, a touch of pure Ornette humor.

The three trio works issued on record along with the "Dedication" show drastic changes in Ornette's music, for Izenzon and Moffett were quite unlike any bassists and drummers who had recorded previously with him. Very often these two did not support the alto improvisations with a regular pulse, and Moffett, whose technical accomplishments made him a master of several styles, often changed the character of his accompaniments. At times he sounds like an experimenter, detached from the high purposefulness (which even bordered on the brutal) of the alto and bass lines. "The Ark" is a long, discursive piece, with the players seemingly independent of each other at the beginning, moving in fast, slow, and medium tempos, and Izenzon often contradicting the others by playing half-time or windstorms of bowed sound; a sustained drumroll kicks Ornette into an unaccompanied passage and, finally, the trio finds the swinging medium–up tempo that Ornette may well have loved best. By contrast "Doughnut" is more closely knit, even if Ornette avoids his usual motive-evolution methods; his optimistic playing and the creative flow of his ideas are truly beautiful to hear, while the central bass solo, which ends in a bass-drums chase, is just as brilliant. "Sadness," which might more accurately been titled "Despair," is essentially Ornette Coleman blues phrases slowed down into long, beautiful tones over the piercing, microtonal sounds of the bowed bass.

The recording is the first document of Izenzon's work in an Ornette Coleman context, and makes clear that he is a major advance in the jazz bass. He bowed as often as he plucked notes, often improvised in microtones, contradicted his partners' tempos, and in general stimulated Ornette by way of counterpoint and contrast as often as with direct support. True, he swung in the swinging trio passages; at other times he created a second melodic line to underline Ornette's own lines. Izenzon's music was a development of the most extreme adventures in Charlie Haden's work with Ornette; from Charles Mingus and Wilbur Ware to Haden, LaFaro, and Garrison, modern bassists had ventured in the direction of the kind of independence that Izenzon projected (even LaFaro's successes with the Bill Evans Trio had come about from the pianist's deference). Izenzon and Coleman, however, did not defer to each other, but projected boldly; their objective was a new kind of ensemble music, and as a result of Izenzon's ensemble orientation he played without the self-dramatizing qualities of virtuosos like Mingus and LaFaro. He was a soft player, and remained devoted to the sound of his unamplified bass through the years when other jazz bassists were making electric amplification a standard procedure.

The concert broke even financially. After that, from Ornette, came silence. The haggling with club owners and record companies over money, the demands of leading a band, the atmosphere of jazz clubs, the negative aspects of the jazz life in general, have discouraged many other musicians down through the decades, and some very fine ones have abandoned music entirely for other careers. As a matter of fact, Ornette's silence after the end of 1962 came when jazz in general had entered a long period of economic decline, after its peak in 1960. While the vitality of rock and roll as a popular music had declined somewhat at the beginning of the decade, rhythm and blues was once again developing as a separate marketing entity and attracting large young audiences. While jazz clubs were disappearing one by one around the country, folk music, including bluegrass and prebluegrass country music and preelectric blues, was becoming popular; folk music clubs and a college concert circuit for folk performers was growing, fortunately, since some of the best country blues artists were still at the height of their powers; moreover, though the great era of electric city blues was largely over, artists such as Muddy Waters and John Lee Hooker had begun to discover young, educated, largely white audiences for their musics. A few years earlier much of the audience for these musics would have been drawn to jazz—witness the popularity of Brubeck, Miles Davis, and the Modern Jazz Quartet among fifties college youth—but as jazz was moving into greater rhythmic and harmonic complexity, these simpler, newly fashionable musics were drawing away potential audiences. The one truly popular artist in the new jazz was John Coltrane—his quartet and Miles Davis's quintet were the period's leading jazz commodities.

Coltrane communicated what Cecil Taylor called "the hysteria of the times," and this may well have been one reason why he was such a sixties favorite. American society was severely divided. While Ornette was retiring from the jazz wars an American president, John Kennedy, was assassinated, and a watershed event in American history soon followed: The enactment of the Civil Rights Act. The struggle of African-Americans for equality of opportunity did not end there or with the 1965 Voting Rights Act—indeed, the prolonged nature of the struggle and popular dissatisfaction with the slowness of progress led to riots in segregated inner cities. The expansion of the orgy of slaughter and lies in Vietnam was another source of division. White reaction against the progress of justice and prowar attitudes were popular. The modern jazz audience, though, in general tended to be progressive in its attitudes and among it, especially among those who'd become attracted to the new jazz, there was a sense that a great moral and spiritual revolution was occurring in America, and a wonderful transformation of values, both in society and in personal lives, was waiting at the end of the struggle.

IV

There was another reason why Ornette chose to drop out of the jazz wars in 1963–1964 and at other times in later years. "I think that's because of a certain kind of fear of offending just to get ahead. It's a fear that just tears me up. It must have something to do with being black, or it's something instinctively in me that I can't explain. *There's always the tragedy of your not being totally understood* because someone suspects some other motive outside of you expressing yourself" (emphasis added).[1] It's a tragedy that's been in the human chromosomes since the time of Adam and Eve, and one that Ornette had had to confront again and again from the time he first played that Conn alto saxophone in his youth. That fear of being misunderstood has again and again been immediate to Ornette, and may have even had literal consequences—Ornette had been suffering from ulcers caused, he believed, by "horrible things" written about him and his music.[2]

During those two years of near-complete silence, Ornette seriously considered alternative courses of action. For example, he began making plans to open his own jazz club, a place where the performance of music would be primary. It might or might not sell liquor, for "whiskey and fucking" were not factors in his plans;

what was important was that it would be a place to play and to listen, and the musicians would be paid according to the take at the door. He even acquired a property for his club and contracted for alterations—and only then discovered what the landlord hadn't bothered to tell him: that the location of his big new jazz room was in a residential area where New York's zoning laws prohibited a nightclub. (There was another instance of Ornette's ill fortune in business in this period when he attempted to launch a music publishing company without success.)

His old schoolmate from Fort Worth, Prince Lasha, was one of the jazz musicians who had found a degree of success in the wake of Ornette's own fame. Lasha had left Fort Worth at about the same time that Ornette had first gone on the road; he had gravitated to New York, then to California, and in 1962 recorded his first album, *The Cry*, for Contemporary. For his second Contemporary album, Lasha announced that he would be joined by his California partner Sonny Simmons, Ornette—three saxophonists, in other words— and a string quartet. "I've already got clearance on Ornette," he told John Tynan.[3] Later in 1963 Ornette hired a new personal manager, lawyer Bernard Stollman, and announced plans to issue an album of the Town Hall concert on Fugue, a new record label; Stollman also became Lasha's manager, and *Down Beat* noted that Ornette was "reportedly" preparing a composition for Lasha.[4] There was rather less than meets the eye to these reports. Lasha and Simmons had joined with Sonny Rollins's group to play in a benefit concert at the Village Gate that spring; Charles Moffett had played in that group, and he and Lasha and Simmons also recorded with Eric Dolphy in the spring sessions that were a major breakthrough in Dolphy's evolving art. They did not, however, record with Ornette; for that matter the Fugue label, if it ever existed anywhere except on paper, never released an album of Ornette's Town Hall concert. The major event in Ornette Coleman's career in 1963 was the premiere performance of his composition "City Minds and Country Hearts" by pianist David Tudor and cellist Charlotte Moorman, in New York.

Ornette was hardly a hermit during his 1963–1964 sabbatical from bandleading. One night he and Cecil Taylor played informally together at the home of Byron Allen, one of the first Ornette-inspired altoists. On another occasion he and tenor saxophonist Albert Ayler, whose work was nearly an evolutionary step equal to

Ornette's own discoveries, and, on C-melody sax, Charles Tyler jammed together, and for nearly three decades the tape recording that captured their playing has been a jazz legend to rival the ones told about the Buddy Bolden cylinder and Freddie Keppard's 1916 rejected master. It was in this period that Ornette was studying the trumpet, violin, and guitar, and in fact, during the classic John Coltrane Quartet's January 1964 engagement at the Half Note in New York he sat in with the band on trumpet. Of course, as in all other periods of Ornette's adult life, he was busy composing, too. Along with "City Minds and Country Hearts," his song "War Orphans," which Charlie Haden recorded in his 1969 *Liberation Music Orchestra*, dates from this period; Ornette also composed music for the soundtrack of a short Robert Frank film, *O.K. End Here*, in which Sue Graham, later to become Mrs. Charles Mingus, played the lead role.

Ornette and Jayne were divorced in 1964. They had been together during some of Ornette's most difficult years in Los Angeles, but had separated even before his first Contemporary recording. According to Barry McRae, economics, finally, was the cause of the breakup of their marriage, as it has been in so many other divorces; Jayne felt that "very little compromise" was required for Ornette to be performing regularly;[5] for that matter, Spellman reports that in 1963–1964 Ornette was indeed willing to lower his price tag on occasion, even to prices lower than he'd previously been offered, but the timing in each of these occasions had been wrong and he'd received no offers.

It may have been in this period when Ornette attempted the unusual experiment that he describes in the film *Ornette: Made in America*. Back during his teenage years, when simultaneously he was learning to play the saxophone and sexual maturity was beginning to blossom, he noticed that he was attracting girls; Ornette dismissed the facts that he was handsome, smart, friendly, and polite, and concluded that the fact that he played music was the source of the attraction. A few years later, as a touring musician, he said, "I always found I could pick up a girl because I was playing music," and of course being attracted to the music is not the same as being attracted to the man. Finally there came a time when Ornette decided he wanted to eliminate sexual feeling. He explained this to a doctor, who must have been astonished when Ornette asked the doctor to castrate him; the doctor recommended that Ornette undergo circumcision—"symbolic castration"—instead, and Ornette agreed. After the operation Ornette "still did not feel any changes." He insisted, "I'd rather be a man than a male."[6]

The Town Hall 1962 concert recording that was first announced as a release on the Fugue label also attracted Impulse Records, the ABC-Paramount subsidiary that was scoring much success with its John Coltrane series. It was Blue Note, the most respected of jazz recording companies, that at last made serious plans to issue the concert on two LPs, BN 4210 and 4211, including Izenson's solo bass performance "Taurus" but omitting one trio selection and the rhythm-and-blues piece. But legal entanglements arose; the agreements with Blue Note were renegotiated and BN 4211, which had reached the test-pressing stage, was turned over to Bernard Stollman; it appeared in record stores, minus "Taurus," as one of the first releases on Stollman's own record label, ESP-Disk, late in 1965.

Meanwhile, the evidence had been mounting that Ornette Coleman's music had indeed been stimulating a revolution in jazz. His success had drawn attention to Cecil Taylor, who had been stretching standard jazz tonality to its limits, and sometimes beyond, since the middle 1950s. One of Taylor's former sidemen, Steve Lacy, the only post-Dixieland soprano saxophonist of the period, had rehearsed often with Don Cherry soon after Cherry's arrival in New York, and Cherry also rehearsed for the Taylor-Buell Neidlinger 1961 Candid date, though he did not play on it. The Ornette Coleman Quartet, with John Coltrane replacing Ornette, recorded an album of Ornette's songs in 1960; the Modern Jazz Quartet had added a John Lewis arrangement of "Lonely Woman" to its repertoire, and probably the first great tribute to Ornette came from Art Pepper, in his shatteringly intense blues solo on "Tears Inside." There were the 1962 Sonny Rollins Quartet with Cherry and Higgins, the New York Contemporary Five, and "Peace" by Bill Dixon and Archie Shepp, all, again, strongly influenced by Ornette's music.

A few musicians of earlier generations had begun wholeheartedly to follow Ornette's lead into tonal freedom, including his 1958 employer Paul Bley and, perhaps most boldly, Jimmy Giuffre, who, with Bley and bassist Steve Swallow, ventured into freely moving tempo and meter, while his clarinet playing, on which he now concentrated, arrived at a new expressiveness and angularity of line. By 1964 modal musicians, particularly ones centered around the groups of George Russell, Jackie McLean, Andrew Hill, and Eric Dolphy, were stretching the language of conventional jazz toward its far limits. Charles Mingus had led a 1960 quartet that attempted to convey the same excitement as Ornette's quartet, and Mingus's altoist-flutist-bass clarinetist Dolphy was at last, in 1963–1964, writing music and forming groups that provided appropriate contexts for his most personal and daring ideas; his pathetic story—he died in 1964, of complications of diabetes—is one of the great unfinished careers in jazz.

By that time, of course, John Coltrane had long been creating his brilliant conflicts of harmonic tyranny and harmonic freedom, and in Chicago tenor saxist Joe Daley's trio and the young Experimental Band, led by pianist Muhal Richard Abrams, had begun their adventures. Moreover, Ornette's inspiration was international: Czechoslovakia's first jazz festival included Karel Krautgartner's Radio Prague band, which played "jazz a la Ornette Coleman and George Russell";[7] there were Coleman-derived bands in the USSR; the British quintet of gifted altoist Joe Harriott had produced a series of important "outside" recordings; while at the Antibes jazz festival in France, Chris McGregor's Blue Notes with altoist Dudu Pukwana—it was their debut outside their home country, South Africa—sounded to reviewer Alan Bates "not unlike" Ornette's Los Angeles recordings.[8]

In October 1964 Ornette attended a six-day series of concerts produced by Bill Dixon in a New York club, a series billed as The October Revolution in Jazz. One band after another took the plunge into "outside" jazz, and reviewer Martin Williams wrote, "The music needs the return of Ornette Coleman to active playing, I know. Hundreds of young players are learning from his records. . . ."[9] The popular success of Dixon's series led him to recruit other liberated musicians, including Carla and Paul Bley (then married), pianist Burton Greene, trumpeter Mike Mantler, keyboard whiz Sun Ra, trombonist Roswell Rudd, and Archie Shepp, Cecil Taylor, and John Tchicai, to form the concert-producing Jazz Composers Guild; Ornette was invited to join, too, but declined. Meanwhile, there was one very important invitation that Ornette did accept: the one to bring his trio, with Izenzon and Moffett, to the Village Vanguard. On January 8, 1965, his long silence ended—the trio played a week there, laid off for a week, and then returned for another two weeks.

Ornette's return was a major event in jazz. *Time* and *Newsweek* covered it, and *Down Beat*'s Dan Morgenstern reported, "Coleman never sounded better. . . ." Along with the alto Ornette played trumpet and violin at the Vanguard; it was his first public appearance on the violin, which he played left-handed, and Morgenstern commented,

> Coleman attacks (there is no better word) the violin with intense concentration. . . . His bowing technique is unorthodox—a rapid, circular arm motion that almost enables him to touch all four strings simultaneously.
>
> Coleman rarely plays one string at a time. He produces a cascade of sounds—sometimes surprisingly pleasing to the ear, sometimes almost abrasive, but never with the scratchy uncertainty of incompetent violinists. He seems to have tuned the instrument in his own manner, but it is, so to speak, in tune with itself.
>
> Coleman may not know the rules, but he knows the point of the game. . . . Coleman, after all, did not develop his unique and beautiful music in order to "revolutionize" jazz; he did it because he had to, because this was the way he heard and felt it.[10]

Then for the rest of the winter, silence again. With his recent divorce, his discouragement over the jazz scene, and the unlikely prospect of being paid what he felt were appropriate fees for his performances, Ornette was ready to make a major change in his life, and removing himself to Europe seemed increasingly to be that change. The urge to leave may be why he originally hesitated when Conrad Rooks, a young filmmaker, asked him to act in and create the soundtrack music for his new movie *Chappaqua*. But Rooks offered Ornette a bundle of money to do the job, reportedly in the five-figure range, and Ornette agreed. Before the *Chappaqua* sessions in June, Ornette went to Los Angeles and spent three days with pianist Jack Wilson planning a duet album on which he would only play trumpet and violin, an album that never materialized. Back in New York for *Chappaqua*, Ornette, Izenzon, and Moffett were joined by tenor saxophonist Pharoah Sanders, conductor-arranger Joseph Tekula, and an eleven-piece orchestra; the recording sessions took three days, and when Rooks heard the music Ornette had created, he decided against using it in his movie after all. The music was too beautiful, Rooks allegedly said, it would have distracted the audiences from the film itself; instead, Rooks commissioned sitarist Ravi Shankar to provide *Chappaqua*'s soundtrack music. The movie was not released until 1969, to bad reviews, and quickly sank without a trace; the only other well-known work of Conrad Rooks was his critically acclaimed film of Herman Hesse's novel *Siddhartha*, in the 1970s. Indeed, the major reason the seldom-seen *Chappaqua* is at all remembered is that rejected Ornette Coleman soundtrack, which was released in an edited version on the French and Japanese CBS labels, without Ornette's authorization, and titled *Chappaqua Suite*. Much the greatest part of the *Suite* is Ornette soloing, accompanied by Izenzon and Moffett; Sanders solos fairly briefly, and there are occasional passages of orchestral background to provide color for the vigorous Ornette.

He went to London in August and immediately set about finding someone to present him in concert. His unannounced appearance surprised the local modern jazz community, who immediately responded warmly to him. Photographer John Hopkins shared his apartment with Ornette, and headed by Mike Horovitz, New Departures, a group that presented experimental arts performances and published a literary magazine, *New Departures*, joined forces with jazz critic Victor Schonfield to present a concert at Fairfield Hall, in the suburb of Croydon, south of London. Immediately the British Ministry of Labour raised obstacles. It maintained a quota system that classified Ornette Coleman as a "jazz musician," which meant that he could not perform in England unless certain nominated British musicians were engaged to play in the United States—of course, those engagements did not occur. This quota system did not apply to classical musicians or to Asian improvising musicians, whom the British musicians union and the Labour Ministry classified as "concert artists." Ornette could be reclassified as a "concert artist" by composing a piece of classical music. With just two weeks to prepare for the concert, he set to work writing a woodwind quintet, even working on it while at social gatherings. He managed to complete the piece, *Forms and Sounds*, in time, it was approved, and he brought Izenzon and Moffett across the Atlantic to play with him. There was time for just one rehearsal of *Forms and Sounds* by the classical musicians of the Virtuoso Ensemble. It was the first time an African-American musician, playing his own music, received the "concert artist" classification, and Ornette financed the concert himself. At the last moment the British musicians union threw up additional obstacles, forcing a change in the musicians who accompanied poets Horovitz and Pete Brown in the opening set; after the concert the union blacklisted both New Departures and Schonfield.

The Croydon concert took place on August 29, 1965. It included new versions of "Sadness" and "Dough Nut," the latter as a hard-blowing closer for the concert. "Happy Fool" presents the trio initially in a fast, innocent mood; Ornette adds a three-note tag to the theme, and that tag becomes the motive of a solo that proves not at all happy and childlike, but rather an investigation of the loneliness of childhood: His lines in general turn downward, even those that begin with the forced cheer of a fast rise. The tenderness of his "Ballad" theme is met with dissonance from Izenzon and fiery drumming from Moffett. The bowed-bass solo is a long line with long note values, so melancholy that it fades into near inaudibility, suggesting a Lisztian sensibility informed by Bartokian harmony. The melancholy affects Ornette's second solo, overcoming the tenderness, and the tension of the return of throbbing drums completes the transformation: This is a painful ballad.

Three new pieces in Ornette's trio repertoire are perhaps most remarkable. "Clergyman's Dream," with its two-tempo theme, is a thoroughly exultant affair and Ornette's long opening solo is quite brilliant, with strong, aggressive accompaniment. Izenzon's solo completely breaks from the original tempo and meter, with many notes and tempo changes; Moffett's clever solo is then broken up by fast bowed bass lines, and when Ornette returns the trio becomes three independent voices, altering momentum at will. "Silence" begins loud and fast, until a huge split alto-sax tone leads to sudden silence; passages of fiery phrases alternate with rubato silences, then, though at times faint, momentary bass and percussion enter the silences (once, a soft instance of bass is struck dead by a drum shot); the silences are the theme of the work, with interludes of happy or passionate or ferocious playing. And "Falling Stars" is a piece that features Ornette's trumpet and violin—an energetic performance with plenty of spaces for good-humored bass and catchy percussion, including one of Moffett's most Art Blakeyish solos.

After the Croydon concert, Ornette went on to Paris, where he spent September. His trio played at the Lugano (Switzerland) Jazz Festival, winning a fifteen-minute standing ovation, and this may also have been the month in which Ornette was commissioned to create another film soundtrack. The Living Theater had made a terrific impact in the American theater a few years earlier. Formed by directors Julian Beck and Judith Malina in the early 1950s, it had offered New Yorkers works by leading contemporary authors (including for instance, a long run of William Carlos Williams's *Many Loves*) and revived neglected older works (its production is the reason Alfred Jarry's *Ubu Roi* is no longer neglected); the Living Theater may have been best known for its sensational production of Jack Gelber's *The Connection*, which included onstage jazz by Freddie Redd's quite fine quartet (replaced briefly by Cecil Taylor's quartet in 1960). By the midsixties the Living Theater, however, was in exile in Europe; while in Belgium in 1965 it had made a film—*Who's Crazy?*—without dialogue, which was intended to include a musical background. Ornette may not have been the Living Theater's first choice to provide that music, but his excellence and proximity and willingness made him a natural choice for the job.

The two LPs of the music for *Who's Crazy?* are valuable on their own merits, apart from the music's film function. It is trio music, with Ornette now giving as much attention to his trumpet and violin as to his alto saxophone; indeed, some alto passages lack the intensity that had hitherto been characteristic of his work, and he is preoccupied with sequences and variations of simple motives. The material includes "Sadness," "European Echoes," a Keystone Kops theme titled "Fuzz," the truly dancing "Dans la Neige," a melancholy "Wedding Day"; "The Mis-Used Blues" is almost the same title as the long-lost rhythm-and-blues piece Ornette had played at the 1962 Town Hall concert—can it be the same work? The song's title is appropriate to the music in any case, for here, over Izenzon's blues lines, Ornette improvises the kind of bright melodies that disguise inner darkness.

Who's Crazy? in particular brings a new element in Ornette Coleman's music into relief via its many trumpet and violin improvisations. Whereas his solos on his early albums, especially the 1959–1960 masterpieces, had been developments of inherent emotion, he had in the mid-1960s been more inclined to invent what might be called slices of life—solos whose structures depended largely on his ingenuity in inventing motivic variations and sequences, solos that might be short or long at will, rather than the result of necessity. This became frequently true of his 1965 alto and trumpet work; on the latter horn, because it, too, is played with human breath, his phrase lengths are equivalent to the irregular lengths of his saxophone phrases, which may lead the listener to infer that he's attempting to approach the saxophone similarly. Yet the persistent imprecision of his pitches indicates otherwise, and his violin playing confirms it: Ornette Coleman with these two instruments is transforming himself.

The parallel is Albert Ayler, who originally had played bop tenor saxophone but by 1964, had moved grandly, extravagantly, outside bop's conventions: First, he abandoned standard chord changes, and after that, standard ideas of tuning altogether. Not only were his pitches imprecise, then, but he dwelt largely in split tones (multiphonics) and in the high, screaming overtones and low honks of his horn's extreme ranges. His solos were squalls of sound at the fastest possible tempos, with bass and drums playing independent, rather than accompanying, lines. His 1965 group, with trumpeter Don Ayler and altoist Charles Tyler, alternated these squalling solos with themes that sounded like barely disguised nineteenth-century pop material. Altogether, what Ayler managed to do was to bypass the entire sixty-odd-year-old traditions of jazz altogether to go back to prejazz material and primitive concepts of sound and musical line. True, his performances were structured—his longer solos involved thematic variations, or more accurately, distortions, and climactic developments, for instance—but in general Ayler's aim seemed to be to reinvent jazz in most of its aspects from his own vitals. His influence was considerable, and persists to the present. All of Ayler's innovations, of course, came in the wake of Ornette Coleman's own innovations, while the bassists who accompanied Ayler appeared quite indebted to Ornette's bassists, especially to Izenzon and his bowing and plucking techniques, freedom of tempo, juxtapositions, and microtones.

Ornette's violin music in particular was at least as radical as Ayler's music in bypassing not only the jazz tradition, but Western musical traditions altogether. He had no teachers or guides to show him how to play trumpet and violin and purposely avoided learning standard techniques, for his objective was to create as spontaneously as possible—"without memory," as he has often been quoted as saying. "I'm very sympathetic to non-tempered instruments," he told critic J. B. Figi. "They seem to be able to arouse an emotion that isn't in Western music. I mean, I think that European music is very beautiful, but the people that's playing it don't always get a chance to express it that way because they have spent most of their energy perfecting the unisons of playing together by saying 'You're a little flat' or 'a little sharp.' . . . A tempered note is like eating with a fork, where that if you don't have a fork the food isn't going to taste any different."[11]

Another critic, Max Harrison, points to the advantages of Ornette's teaching himself a new instrument:

> Anybody who has attempted really free improvisation, especially as a member of a group, will know how readily one falls back on stock responses, above all on the muscular habits acquired through years spent with an instrument. Speaking of a crucial stage in his development, Marcel Duchamp said, "I didn't get free of that prison of tradition, but I tried to, consciously. I unlearned to draw. The point was to forget *with my hand*."[12]

Of course, with an instrument so unlike the alto saxophone Ornette did not have to unlearn technique. Comparing Ornette's music on the two instruments, Harrison wrote that in his violin improvisations

> he sounds less civilised, more complex, the showers of notes, matted in dense, frantic textures, seem to well up with little conscious supervision. Because the player intervenes at key points to shape the solo only in a very general way, this music, like certain compositions by two other great American musicians, Charles Ives and John Cage, appears to mirror life's flux rather than to subject it to a personal and therefore arbitrary order. . . . Certainly Coleman's violin playing may represent an indeterminacy as drastic as Cage's.[13]

The *Who's Crazy?* soundtrack recordings include many instrument changes and tempo shifts, much movement of textures and balances; the textures of Ornette and Izenzon playing stringed instruments together is especially attractive.

The touring picked up in October. The trio probably played in Barcelona that month and definitely, on October 29, in Amsterdam (the other group on the concert was the New York Art Quartet, with Tchicai and Rudd); at the Berlin Jazz Festival the next night (this event had been advertised as Ornette's European debut); and in Copenhagen the next; there were additional appearances before they played at the Paris Jazz Festival in November. They made a television documentary, which was released two decades later as a video, *David, Moffett and Ornette*. And they created a sensation virtually everywhere they went.

They played for two weeks at the Golden Circle nightclub in Stockholm, and on their last two nights there Blue Note recorded them. Certainly Ornette's alto sax improvising is brilliant on these sessions, including his oom-pah-pah waltz variations in "European Echoes" and his fast, optimistic variations on "Dee Dee" (with its superbly simple theme) and "Faces and Places" (with its recurring rolling theme motive in his solo). "Dawn" and especially "Morning Song" are sweet ballads, indeed, among his best ballads. Amid many tempo changes by the group in "The Riddle," Izenzon offers a witty bowed solo. "Snowflakes and Sunshine" alternates many brief improvisations by trumpet and violin over mostly fast tempos, usually separated by brief interludes of solo drums or bass; each of Ornette's sections is relatively static in development, and wildly energetic.

The Paris musicians union proved not far behind its British counterpart in concocting obstacles to touring foreign musicians. Since 1933, French law had stipulated that no more than 10 percent of any musical group that played in a French club could be non-French musicians; it was an archaic law that French club owners repeatedly broke, of course. But in 1965 the Paris union local sent letters to twenty-five club-owners asking them to observe the law, and late in the year Ornette's Parisian engagement at Jazz Land came to an early end as a result. The club maintained that the union rule was the reason for cutting the trio's stay short, although the union had in fact agreed to extending his contract. The problem was that the letter of approval from the union arrived too late for Jazz Land to publicize Ornette's extension; too few customers showed up, so the club simply could not afford the Ornette Coleman Trio any longer.

Nevertheless, Ornette would enjoy further performances in Paris over the winter. The final stage of the European sojourn took him back to England, where it began, with a four-week run in April and May at Ronnie Scott's nightclub in London, a short tour of England, and a final concert at, once again, Fairfield Hall in Croydon. The nine months in Europe, for all the hassles, won enthusiastic audience response for Ornette, and he was now, it seems, dealing better with his trio as a commodity in the fluctuations of jazz commerce.

Blue Note, which had not been able to issue the Town Hall concert or record the Ornette Coleman–Jack Wilson duo, had been more than eager to issue his music; the two Golden Circle albums appeared in stores less than four months after that famed Stockholm engagement. These and the ESP-Disk of the Town Hall concert gave American listeners documents, at last, of how Ornette's music had changed since his Atlantic recordings. When the Ornette Coleman Trio returned to their native land at the end of May 1966, they found themselves a prized commodity. There were concerts and club engagements in New York and California, and then, during their late-August–early-September stay at the Village Vanguard in New York, they had a new drummer sitting in: Ornette Denardo Coleman, who was spending his vacation with his father.

Four years earlier, when Denardo reached his sixth birthday, Ornette, in New York, called him in Los Angeles to find out what he wanted for his present. The boy's first suggestion was a toy gun; when his father countered by proposing to buy a drum kit, Denardo said, "Dad, you can forget about the gun, send the drums air mail express!"[14] By the time Ornette had left for Europe, he and Denardo had played together; Denardo had taken lessons and read music well, and Ornette had promised to record with him one day. The day came on September 9, 1966, four days before Denardo was to return to elementary school. Izenzon would have been the obvious choice of bassist, but he had not wanted to play without Charles Moffett, and meanwhile a touch of good fortune arrived for Ornette: Charlie Haden was available. After losing his New York cabaret card in 1961, Haden, on probation and barred from playing in clubs, played concerts and in coffeehouses, then broke probation by going back to Los Angeles, where he worked with Buddy DeFranco and Charlie Barnet, among others, "trying to stay clean by drinking." He won the "New Star" award in that year's *Down Beat* critics poll, while his personal life got worse: He returned to New York for awhile, living like "a walking dead person, doing nothing constructive, not playing any more";[15] he rested with his family in Missouri, took the cure for alcohol abuse in the federal hospital in Fort Worth (Hampton Hawes was there, and the two played every day), and relapsed again. In 1966, after living in Synanon houses in

California (where he played with altoist John Handy and pianist Denny Zeitlin), Synanon asked him to help set up a New York house, which is when Ornette asked him to make the *Empty Foxhole* session. "The music was completely fresh and brand new," Haden said. "Denardo is going to startle every drummer who hears him."[16]

Startle he did. "Unadulterated shit," said Shelly Manne. Cannonball Adderley praised the "logic" of Ornette's playing but called the contributions of Haden and Denardo "interruptions."[17] Freddie Hubbard thought Denardo sounded "like a little kid fooling around."[18] Pete Welding wrote that Denardo "works well with this music," even if his playing is "nothing earth-shattering . . . quite open and responsive to his father's playing. . . . He draws a quite broad range of colors from his drum kit." Welding put his finger on an essential aspect of Denardo's contribution: "What I particularly like about his participation is the sense of space in his music." Wrote Ornette, "I felt the joy playing with someone who hasn't had to care if the music business or musicians or critics would help or destroy his desire to express himself honestly. But the fact that he got paid and is helping to sell the record . . . hasn't meant anything to him. . . . I am very sad to have to sell my son's talent without his knowing the life this type of existing might make of him, as a man to be."[19] Ornette's regret was somewhat misplaced: after all, he did not *have* to hire Denardo.

It was nevertheless an appropriate choice considering the changes that were occurring in Ornette's own playing. As opposed to the precision and, often, the complexity of Charles Moffett's drumming, as well as to the patterns he sometimes slipped into, Denardo's drumming was loose, erratic. This was a time when Elvin Jones's own free relations with the beat in the John Coltrane Quartet had led to drummers such as Andrew Cyrille, Sunny Murray, and Milford Graves eliminating timekeeping altogether, and in fact ten-year-old Denardo's freedom of movement, his imitations of his father's rhythmic patterns, his commentary, are indeed elements of freshness. The music's pulse depended on Haden alone, then—in fact, "Sound Gravitation" might have benefited from Izenzon's wild flights of humor, for both Haden and Ornette bow their fiddles throughout it, making dark, foreboding textures. "Sound Gravitation" was the first time Ornette devoted an entire track to his violin, and the album includes two tracks devoted to his trumpet, "Freeway Express" and "The Empty Foxhole." That title track is brief and perfect: Over Haden's reiterated three notes and Denardo's erratic, wounded-soldier beat, Ornette plays the frail theme on his fragile-sounding trumpet, resulting in a lost, wounded mood. To accompany the song, Ornette wrote, "bury not the soul/in a hole,/ whose life has yet/to exist."[20] Ornette is in characteristic good form on the two faster alto-sax pieces, but the theme of the ballad "Faithful" includes a drooping sequence and his alto solo, then, is overripe with falling sequences that leave a cloying feeling—compare this work to his parody of sentimentality in the 1959 "Just for You."

Returning to work with his regular trio, Ornette, with Izenzon and Moffett, worked three days that fall at Slug's, New York's new-music bastion. In a concert featuring both of their groups Ornette and Coltrane produced themselves at the Village Theater on the day after Christmas. Busy again in 1967, Ornette made a major change in his group by adding a permanent fourth player, Haden. The presence of two bassists proposed a different kind of balance for his music: Haden was one of the great straight-ahead bassists; Izenzon brought to the instrument an element of counterpoint, contrast, and probably greater freedom of motion. Moreover, the momentum that Haden would have provided the group would have been valuable, since it was often drumless. While in Europe the previous year, Moffett had occasionally played a set of orchestra bells; back in the United States Ornette bought a set of vibes for him, and moreover he was also occasionally returning to his first love, the trumpet: "The trio had developed tremendously, and it had opened up all kinds of freedom for me," Moffett says. It was at some point during this period, probably in 1967, that Coleman, Izenzon, and Moffett, without Haden, recorded the soundtrack for a short animated cartoon "about international injustice,"[21] which was titled "Population Explosion."

At the same Village Theater concert in March at which Haden had rejoined Ornette's group, and at which Ornette had played musette on "Buddha's Blues," the Philadelphia Woodwind Quintet performed *Forms and Sounds*, the work he had composed for the 1965 Croydon, England, concert, this time with his trumpet interludes added. That concert, by the way, included the woodwind quintet's performance of *Titles* by classical composer Talib Rasul Hakim, a friend of Ornette and brother of the important jazz percussionist-composer Joe Chambers. Classical composition was certainly on Ornette's mind in this period, in any case. The next month came the announcement that Ornette Coleman was receiving a fellowship from the Guggenheim Foundation (at the same time jazz historian Marshall Stearns also received a Guggenheim to conduct research). In past years Teo Macero and William O. Smith had both received Guggenheims, but for classical composition—in jazz, Macero had produced albums and been part of Charles Mingus's circle of composer-players; Smith had recorded jazz clarinet for Contemporary and played with Dave Brubeck—so the award to Ornette was the first Guggenheim granted for jazz composition. There's a fine point about these categories, for what Ornette planned to compose was music for a symphony orchestra with jazz soloist, which fell in the in-between world that Schuller and John Lewis called third stream music; these fine points about how to categorize his music, and the imposition of categories upon the music's reality, had bugged Ornette throughout his career and continue to bug him today.

A week after the Village Theater concert in March, Ornette recorded an album on which he played only trumpet, to the exclusion of his other instruments—and for only the second time, it was a date in which he was a sideman. The album was *New and Old Gospel* by hard-bop altoist Jackie McLean, who five years earlier had been among the established musicians whose own music had opened up in response to Ornette's ideas; at the time, he wrote, "The new breed has inspired me all over again. The search is on. Let freedom ring."[22] Since then he had recorded with modal settings as often as with chord changes. "I felt it was inevitable I should record with Ornette Coleman some time,"[23] he said, and the presence of Ornette, Billy Higgins, and the aggressive bassist Scotty Holt, who had recently played with Roscoe Mitchell and Muhal Richard Abrams, raised the possibility that McLean was poised to take a leap into free tonality. Pianist Lamont Johnson, however, worked resolutely within modes, however, and determined that *New and Old Gospel* would be modally based.

Blue Note was unique among jazz recording companies in the extent to which it prepared its recording sessions, and even by these standards McLean prepared for this date with much care. One side of the LP is two Ornette Coleman songs. McLean was the most passionate, intense saxophonist of his generation, and in "Old Gospel" his solo is dotted with split-tone screams of joy. Johnson's rolling accompaniments make sure that the track fits the gospel-soul-jazz subcategory, and over him Ornette's trumpet darts freely. In the collective improvisation section, Ornette is the lead voice, and McLean plays loose, riffing support. As McLean plays the melody of the ballad "Strange As It Seems," Ornette plays a muted, outside obligato. The alto solo is on chord changes, while the long-toned trumpet solo is a distant melodic line. The other side of the album is McLean's *Lifeline* suite, "an attempt to parallel in one piece of music a complete life experience, from birth to death," said the composer.[24] Especially in the "Offspring" section the contrast between the two horns is effective: McLean hits his notes hard, his phrasing is comparatively unstructured, his notes are decisively sharp or flat; Ornette's tones are imprecise, however, lending additional free motion to his fluttering line that extends a motive from the theme riff into a unified solo. The suite's conclusion has fabulous, long, bent alto tones, and then Ornette and McLean bend pitches together as the work fades into the unknown.

The album in general was a success, and should point out for all time the intrinsic merits of Ornette's trumpeting. In his hands the horn is wholly an instrument of melody, and delicate melody at that; his imprecision of pitch is on purpose, and heightens the delicacy. It was a time when other trumpeters, too, such as Lester Bowie, Donald Ayler, and Leo Smith were exploring the construction of melodic lines from similar material, and Bowie's work in particular points up the blues sources of these expressive ideas. Of what use would the facile technique of, for instance, Freddie Hubbard or Donald Byrd be in music like *New and Old Gospel*? The musical purposes of Ornette's trumpet playing were quite different from theirs, different even from Don Cherry's trumpeting, and despite the features of Ornette's alto sax phrasing that lingered in his trumpet work, the airy quality of his playing made it seem at times like the freest of his instruments.

The first result of Ornette's Guggenheim grant appeared in May, with the first performance of a symphonic work by him. John Carter had been teaching elementary school in Los Angeles, and Ornette had stayed in touch with him over the years; it was Carter who conducted the premier of Ornette's *Inventions of Symphonic Poems* at the UCLA Jazz Festival. It's unfortunate that no recordings of the work are available; it was performed by an orchestra joined by Ornette on alto saxophone, and the question arises, was it a direct ancestor of *Skies of America*? In 1964, when Bobby Brad-

Ornette Coleman during his time at the School of Jazz in Lenox, Massachusetts, c. 1959 PHOTOGRAPH BY BOB CATO, VAL WILMER COLLECTION

From left: Charlie Haden, Ornette Coleman, Edward Blackwell, David Izenzon, and Yoko Ono, rehearsing *Emotion Modulation* for Ornette's 1968 concert at the Royal Albert Hall, London   VAL WILMER COLLECTION

Ornette Coleman and Anthony Braxton at Ornette's Prince Street home
in New York City, Artists House, 1971 PHOTOGRAPH BY VAL WILMER

Ornette Coleman Quartet, New York City, 1971: (*left to right*) Edward
Blackwell, Dewey Redman, Ornette Coleman, Charlie Haden

Ornette Coleman, alto saxophone, David Measham, conductor, and the
London Symphony Orchestra recording *Skies of America*, 1972

The trumpeter, alto saxophonist, and violinist of the Ornette Coleman Sextet at the 1973 Ann Arbor Blues and Jazz Festival, held at Otis Spann Memorial Field, Ann Arbor, Michigan PHOTOGRAPH BY HERB NOLAN

Edward Blackwell and Ornette Coleman at the Happy Medium, Chicago, 1974 **PHOTOGRAPH BY HERB NOLAN**

Ornette Coleman and Prime Time at the Jazz Festival, August 1984
PHOTOGRAPH BY LAUREN DEUTSCH

Ornette Coleman at the 1982 University of Illinois, Chicago Jazz Festival
PHOTOGRAPH BY LAUREN DEUTSCH

ford had moved from Texas to Los Angeles, Ornette had suggested to Carter that he would find Bradford a stimulating artist to play music with; Carter and Bradford met, and by 1967 were beginning to find other musicians with whom to form a group. The music they played was strongly suggestive of Ornette's own early quartets, but the ensemble used original material, mostly composed by Carter.

Ornette performed in another concert of music from *Inventions of Symphonic Poems* in San Francisco in early June; his quartet was with him on this California tour for concert and club engagements. Back in New York, there was most unhappy news in July: John Coltrane, whose saxophones had been silenced by illness since spring, died of a liver disease. He had been a friend of Ornette's since the original Coleman quartet's early days in New York:

> Actually, after I had done *This Is Our Music* or something, I wrote lots of music, and I wrote some for John and Miles Davis, and Gerry Mulligan and Cannonball and lots of people. John called me and said he wanted to find out just how I went about playing music and writing without having a chordal structure that connected resolutions. So I said, "Okay"—about six months, almost a year, he studied with me. And then one day I received a letter from him in Chicago saying he had found it, and there was a check in the envelope with it. . . . He was really very sincere about growing.

It was surely appropriate that the Ornette Coleman and Albert Ayler groups, as Coltrane had wished, played at his funeral. Coleman's innovations had introduced Coltrane to the possibilities of free playing that he was to explore throughout the 1960s, while Ayler's innovations in sound and structure were the next major tenor-saxophone development.

On August 1 the quartet of Ornette, Haden, Izenzon, and Moffett began a six-week engagement at the Village Gate in New York. With both Ornette and Moffett playing multiple instruments, it was ripe with unique possibilities for sound combinations (two trumpets and two basses, or three string players and vibes). "On the third or fourth night, then, we looked around, and Ed Blackwell was setting up his drums—David and I didn't even know he was coming," recalls Moffett. "Now this was without any rehearsal at all. I took that as, well, I've *really* got some more freedom now, so we still have a drummer when I move off on vibes and trumpet. After one or two nights like that, the next thing I knew, I was fired. Maybe, I don't know, I played myself out of a job [by doubling on vibes and trumpet]."

In fact, after the six years of steady partnership with Izenzon and Moffett, Ornette was going through a period of changing the makeup of his group fairly often. During that same Village Gate engagement, Billy Higgins replaced Blackwell, who went to work with Randy Weston, the Ellington-like pianist with whom he'd worked off and on since 1965; with Higgins, Ornette traveled west and then to Japan that fall. In midwinter Blackwell replaced Higgins for a tour of Europe. In the spring, when Izenzon at last departed the band, Ornette recorded two Blue Note albums with Coltrane's longtime bass-drums team of Jimmy Garrison and Elvin Jones and added a second horn, tenor saxophonist Dewey Redman, who then became a regular in Ornette's groups. For the summer Ornette's quartet was himself, Haden, Redman, and Denardo in East and West Coast clubs and concerts. And with Izenzon departed, the freely moving, impulsive accompaniments of the mid-sixties to a large extent were replaced by the steady pulse of Ornette's first New York groups.

Four of these events in 1968 were more than special, and two of the special events came on the trip to Europe. It took them to Italy, Holland, and England, and an unauthorized recording from the quartet's Rome concert, *The Unprecedented Music of Ornette Coleman*, reveals what a creatively exciting group it was. There's a long new version of "Lonely Woman" to rival the 1959 classic; theme paraphrases arise in Ornette's blues lines, once after particularly dramatic low honks and a split tone. The recording quality is poor, and it sounds as if Izenzon, the softer of the two bassists, sometimes drowns out Haden. Nevertheless the massed density of the basses joined to Blackwell's enormously uplifting drums results in terrific swing, which in itself is inspirational enough to elongate Ornette's alto solo. There is a stunning moment in the final theme statement when the defeated A in the ninth bar is raised an octave, suddenly interjecting a note of exultation into the tragic theme. Ornette's dancing alto phrases in the swinging, up-tempo "Monsieur le Prince" are not in the least disturbed by Izenzon's very long, harmonically acidulous bowed tones, not even when Izenzon attempts to distract with broadly dissonant low notes. At last Izenzon enters the others' world, playing double-stopped riffs and lines based on Ornette's own.

Ornette plays trumpet in "Forgotten Children," one of his loveliest dirge themes, built on tragic cadences. A brief bass duet rises to complexity, after which, Ornette, muted and in fast tempo, plays one of his very finest trumpet solos, constructed, moreover, in the classic building-climax-anticlimax form that is ordinarily irrelevant to his art. Blackwell's drumming, so excellent throughout this concert, is in particularly close interplay here, and when Ornette pauses for a few bars in his second solo Blackwell unleashes a stunning break. "Buddah Blues" once again swings in a medium-up "Chicago" tempo, beginning with very earthy, folklike introductory passages from the basses, and their swing is now of primary interest. Ornette plays a double-reed instrument— a shenai? a musette?—in "Buddah's Blues," and his exotic sound, often in very long phrases, is complemented by one of the players interjecting piping lines on a flutelike instrument. This quartet was surely the most remarkable that Coleman had led since his classic 1959–1960 works. The effect of the electrifying Blackwell and the two complementary bassists on Ornette's playing is wonderfully stimulating—more's the pity that this quartet is not better documented.

In England the 1965 problem with the musicians union and the Labour Ministry happened all over again: Ornette could only play his concert, at London's Albert Hall, if he was classified a "concert artist" instead of jazz artist. His history of classical composition— the 1961 "Dedication," the 1965 *Forms and Sounds*, the 1967 *Inventions of Symphonic Poems*, his Guggenheim—were all irrelevant to the British authorities, and worse, this time he had even less time to prepare a piece of classical music. The work he composed was titled *Emotion Modulation*, written for himself (trumpet and violin), bassists Haden and Izenzon, drummer Blackwell, and singer Yoko Ono; it was several unbroken movements long, with themes upon which the players improvised. The only portion of *Emotion Modulation* that was issued on a record is from a rehearsal; Ono, with experience as an interpreter of John Cage's music and as composer of two operas, is the featured performer in the section titled "Aos," improvising the cries and moans of a woman in the throes of sexual ecstasy. *Emotion Modulation* was half of the concert; the rest included "Buddah's Blues," "Lonely Woman," and a selection for string trio plus drums. McRae, commenting on Ornette's performance, stated, "In

order to get a work permit, he had spent many hours convincing the
authorities that he was not a jazz musician. In the Albert Hall, he
spent little more than two proving that he was one of the greatest."[25]

The Blue Note quartet recorded in April and May; of the first
LP to be issued from the sessions, *New York Is Now!* critic Max
Harrison wrote, "The richness and vitality of Coleman's inspiration
is staggering."[26] Elvin Jones, in more than five years in Coltrane
groups, had developed his already complex drumming in response
to John Coltrane's tenor sax. Since Coltrane continually accented
downbeats hard and Garrison also carried pulse, Jones was freed
from the strictest adherence to keeping time. So he liked to maintain two or three simultaneous rhythms, with his drum set's heavy
resonance, in accompaniment, while still responding quickly to
Coltrane's lines, a thoroughly virtuoso art. As for Garrison, the
reunion with Ornette was not altogether happy, for an element of
freshness had disappeared from the bassist's music since the two
had played together in 1961.

The extraordinarily strange sound in "The Garden of Souls," a
low, rasping scream, is Redman's tenor sax as he hums through it
while he plays; his phrasing and at times his tone recall the young
Ornette. Again and again in Redman's playing there are passages
with a loping quality that suggest a long, tall Texan, and in "Broadway Blues" his long, bent tones resonate with a blues feel that is a
lingua franca from Chicago to Texas. Throughout these sessions
Garrison drops, doubles, halves time on impulse, pauses to strum,
and in general provides bass lines with no apparent connection to
the soloists' lines; his choice of tones, too, is distracting rather than
supportive; he seems by now to severely misunderstand how Ornette's music goes. Jones, however, plays very well, constructing
lines as dense and complex as he had played with Coltrane, and
seems to want to enter into and support Ornette's music. Like a
polar bear in a tropical rain forest, though, he sounds unnatural in
Ornette's ecology. The drums are fine and intense during wearing
permutations of a three-note motive that open and close Ornette's
"Airborne" solo and are irrelevant during Ornette's superbly intense central passages—Jones at his best and Ornette at his best are
not a unity on these LPs. The high point of these sessions is Ornette's alto solo in "Broadway Blues"; elsewhere (note especially
"The Garden of Souls"), illuminated alto playing exists side by side

with much motive repetition and sequencing, and, indeed, by now sequencing is his favorite way to initiate changes of key, of tonality. Is all the repetition and sequencing a conservative response to Jones's complexity? In any case, Jones's music, so appropriate for a modal music in which structure was governed by the accumulation of weight and mass, is at odds with Ornette's more directly linear music here. There is much fine alto saxophone playing in these LPs, and "We Now Interrupt for a Commercial" is a wild, frantic, violin-driven collective improvisation, while Ornette, on trumpet in "Love Call," attempts to organize a solo via motivic/thematic means.

The fourth member of the quartet, tenorman Dewey Redman, had been a high school friend of Ornette's in Forth Worth, had heard Ornette at jam sessions in those days, and had been another of the young musicians on the scene who had been encouraged by Red Connors. Originally a clarinetist, Redman began playing alto and tenor at Prairie View A&M College, and received a master's degree in education—not music—at North Texas State University. He played in Austin on weekends, sometimes with Ornette's cousin James Jordan, while teaching in a nearby town, and moved to San Francisco in 1961: "Kids from all over America were coming, 'cause it was a little liberal. It was the center of things—not New York, not Chicago, or L.A." There Pharoah Sanders, bassist-multi-instrumentalist Donald Raphael Garrett, and drummers Eddie Moore and Smiley Winters were among his musical mates. He co-led a big band with altoist Monty Waters and lived with Waters and the Montgomery Brothers in a lighthouse near Berkeley; he recorded his first album, *Look for the Black Star*, in San Francisco in 1966. He'd heard Ornette on the Coleman groups' visits there and played with the quartet there in 1967.

After Redman moved to New York in late 1967, he began visiting Ornette; one day "I brought my horn over and we just ran down some tunes, and the next thing I knew, I was playing with his band, I had a gig, with Denardo and David Izenzon." Of course, being the other saxophonist in Ornette Coleman's quartet was the ultimate challenge in modern jazz: "Some nights he'd be just on fire, you know? He'd be playing his ass off, and he always took the first solo, and when he got through playing sometimes there'd be nothing left to play, 'cause he'd played everything, the bebop, the avant-garde, whatever. And I said, what the hell am I gonna do, I play the saxophone, too."[27] What first startled listeners about Redman's tenor playing was his technique of singing through the horn in order to release overtones, resulting in harsh, growly multiphonics chords. There was also his sensitive adaptation of Ornette's own manner of playing, with emphasis on melodic qualities rather more than on the organizational features—repetition, variation, sequencing—that often preoccupied Ornette's own late 1960s improvising. For about six years, then, Redman participated in Ornette's groups.

He was, along with Haden and Denardo, in the Coleman quartet that played at the Fillmore West, San Francisco's famed rock-music temple of the sixties—this was a year before the first of Miles Davis's Fillmore gigs—and then in the August 11, 1968, Berkeley concert in which Ornette conducted the premiere of his latest extended work, *Sun Suite of San Francisco*. The *Sun Suite* was in seven movements without breaks between movements; Ornette had composed it for a thirty-five-piece orchestra, his quartet, and trumpet soloist Bobby Bradford. The important modern filmmaker Shirley Clarke, who had achieved an important success with her film of the Living Theater's *The Connection*, wanted to make a film documentary about Ornette, and filmed the entire concert. Snatches of *Sun Suite* eventually appeared in Clarke's 1986 *Ornette: Made in America*. The entire concert was recorded, but Ornette told David Wild that he'd placed the tapes in the ABC-Paramount/Impulse Records vaults, and the record company had managed to misplace them. However, thirty-two minutes of the concert, from the quartet's portion, was preserved in the *Ornette at 12* album. Compared to the fine recent Blue Note studio sound, this recording sounds strange— the saxes, especially Redman's tenor, sound rather light. Denardo's free drumming now often draws Haden into free, arhythmic bass bowing reminiscent of Izenzon, which means that the steadily improving twelve-year-old percussionist takes responsibility for the music's momentum, which is usually fast. Along with characteristically inventive alto solos of the period, Ornette plays much lyrical trumpet in "Rainbows"; in "Bells and Chimes" he and Haden offer multiple-stopped violin-bass lines that create dense textures indeed, while Redman, though underbalanced in the recording, at times adds split tones that further thicken the ensemble sound. Once again, the listener wishes for further examples of the Coleman Quartet expanding on these sonic ideas.

The year 1968 also saw the release of the revised *Forms and*

Sounds, with Ornette's trumpet interludes, as played by him and the Philadelphia Woodwind Quintet at that 1967 Village Theater concert. In the liner notes Ornette wrote that he composed for the wind quintet

> so as to allow them to create a new piece every time the composition was performed. My term for this is "improvise reading," where an instrument has the possibility of changing the piece by a change in register. For example, the flute and bassoon can both play a C in the treble clef and be three octaves apart—in other words, when the piece has a performance the instruments can change the register of their passages, causing the music to sound different and thus changing the form each time it is played.[28]

But, Max Harrison wrote,

> even with quite different teams of musicians on the two recordings [the Croydon, England, and New York performances], this does not happen. . . . Whatever indeterminate procedures are written into the *Sounds and Forms* score do not work, and he does not appear to have grasped that the demands and consequences peculiar to this kind of activity do not parallel those implicit in a jazz solo's indeterminacy. . . . Even more than the string pieces, this music drifts on steadily, departing from nowhere and arriving nowhere: when there is no change of emphasis there is no scope for expression.[29]

Two string quartets by Ornette, *Saints and Soldiers* and the brief *Space Flight*, make up the album's second side; the players are the Chamber Symphony of Philadelphia Quartet. The former work had its inspiration in his December 1965 visit to Rome, when he observed the remains of saints and soldiers in urns in churches: "How incredible that persons of such opposite beliefs—each in his own way attempting to influence our world—could end up in exactly the same place—a jar."

Because of its brevity (under four minutes), fast momentum, and structured, growing turbulence, *Space Fight* is quite the most vivid of the album's three works. Otherwise the most remarkable features of the LP are the trumpet interludes that Ornette composed to insert between the many varilength fast and slow sections of *Forms and Sounds*. Although the interludes are written, they could not be played by any other trumpeter with *this* sound, *this* attack, *this* rubato, *this* sense of pitch. In a way that's unfortunate, for many of his solo passages include wonderfully melodic phrases, too; moreover, as *Forms and Sounds* progresses, the trumpet interludes become increasingly dramatic. For instance, after the woodwind quintet plays a troubled, tense section, Ornette plays long tones concluded by a sudden, Leo Smith–like, isolated staccato note; then, after a slow, dark quintet section, we hear low trumpet tones; at the end come the work's brightest passages as the trumpet briefly joins the woodwind quintet.

And then, months of little performing. In the midst of a cold January, Ornette's sister Truvenza came to New York to visit him at his home on Prince Street, with the "wind right off that East River, and I nearly froze. A lot of people claimed to be Ornette Coleman's sister or Ornette Coleman's wife. I had a hard time getting into Ornette's apartment—I told the super I was Ornette's sister, and he said, 'Well, too many people have told me that.' It happened the electrician said, 'Well, I just got to let you in and wait till Ornette comes to see if you really are his sister.' " A few years earlier Ornette had told A. B. Spellman, "You don't know how many times I've come off the bandstand and had girls come up to me and hand me a note with their address on it,"[30] and it seems his attractiveness to ladies continued with time. It was, however, not a very satisfying part of his life: "But you know when it comes to women, that's my failing. . . . I don't ever have any women to really go to bat for me. I can tell a woman about a bad thing someone has done to me, and she will try to convince me that it's my fault."[31]

It was soon thereafter that Trudy Coleman began singing in New York—"I wasn't known, but wherever I'd play I'd draw a crowd, because I was Ornette's sister"—and she and Don Cherry and Dewey Redman rehearsed for her John Hammond recording at Ornette's loft. In March 1969 came a major event—a concert by Ornette's quintet (Redman, Haden, Denardo, and now Don Cherry added) that resulted in *Crisis*, a particularly provocative album. It occurred at New York University, and perhaps the preceding several months' layoff lent an edge of intensity to the music, for the aggressiveness of the playing, especially by the fiery Haden and Ornette himself; the wealth of creativity, especially by Ornette; and the dark drive of the performances made for most immediate music. That's particularly true of the encore piece

"Trouble in the East" (mistitled "Space Jungle" on the LP), with its exciting collective improvisation, and "Song for Che" in this finest performance of the loveliest of all Haden songs. It had first taken shape as a bass solo for his *Liberation Music Orchestra* (upon which both Redman and Cherry played), and here the urgency of the Coleman quintet's theme statement, the turbulent song of Ornette's alto sax, and Haden's thundering solo make this a major Coleman-group performance. Among the features of the long "Comme Il Faut" are Cherry's poised, glistening trumpet solo and very blue tenor melodies from Redman. A second collective improvisation, "Space Jungle" (mistitled "Trouble in the East" on the LP), opens with Cherry's flute, to which Redman's clarinet and then Ornette's violin are added. The long, dissonant, descending theme of "Broken Shadows" is repeated as the horns play obligatos over it; the melody features aching, hollow drops of augmented thirds, reflected in the horns' harmonies; thus the work is drenched in despair until the final theme statement, in which now-triad harmonies bring a final grace and resolution, somewhat reminiscent of the conclusion of "Beauty Is a Rare Thing."

There were few other performances for Ornette in 1969; another period of general withdrawal from the marketplace had set in. There was a rather brief trip to Europe late in the summer, including concerts in Belgium and France. The one in Paris was historically important because it was there that Ornette Coleman (with Redman, Haden, and Blackwell) first appeared on a bill with the Art Ensemble of Chicago and Anthony Braxton's quartet, two liberated groups from Chicago that had resettled in Paris that summer. Ornette was bitter about the music business. While in Paris he met Arthur Taylor, one of the most-often recorded of modern-jazz drummers, who was interviewing fellow musicians for a series of Sunday-supplement newspaper articles that later became a book, *Notes and Tones*. To Taylor, Ornette played a tape of a composition and said,

> I have come to love writing music. This is a piece of music I wrote for the Black Composers' Society in America. They are all black composers, but they're classical. . . . I don't feel healthy about the performing world anymore at all. I think it's an egotistical world; it's about clothes and money, not about music. I'd like to get out of it, but I don't have the financial situation to do so. I have come to enjoy

writing music because you don't have that performing image. . . . I don't want to be a puppet and be told what to do and what not to do. . . . When I can find some people who are in a position to accept me as a human being on my own terms, then we can work together.[32]

He spoke of his struggles as a commodity in the music business:

I have had black people and white people against me. The white people created something that didn't exist in my life. The black people were the ones that were already established. They thought I was going to be a threat to them, so they were against me. To this very day I'm in the same position I was in ten years ago. The only thing that's healthier is that I can make more choices. . . . They're running that same philosophy about how people don't understand my music, but I know what the real problem is. It's the people who want to design and control the music consumption the way that they want to dictate it. . . . They say: Black people don't buy your records! . . . Maybe the reason black people don't buy my records is that they don't make it possible for black people to get them. They make it possible for black people to get the blues, so they can be depressed all the time.[33]

After Edward Blackwell, Ornette's favorite drummer was Denardo:

I can't get him to practice or anything. He can read drum music, but he's rebelling. Like, I don't want to be a musician because my father is. . . . Every time I wanted him to play for me, I had to damn near beg him.[34]

Which led Ornette back to his struggles in the marketplace:

I tell you, man, the music world is a cold world. Very cold! The way Denardo is playing now on the record, *Ornette at 12*, would be a novelty for any other race of people. Someone would have gotten in and said, We can make lots of money with this father and son, the whole trip. Instead they put it down. . . . It's still a big problem for any heterosexual person in the music world. Most people who control the music business become bisexual, homosexual or whatever because their nature is so tense from all the wrong they're doing. . . . I have never in my life seen anyone explain how and what I'm doing in music. But everybody knows that it's something that hasn't happened before, and that it's not important enough to back. . . . They have created a society where any unknown white person can put something on the market and become successful. I don't see why a black person can't do that.[35]

The first decade of the revolution in jazz had happened in an essentially progressive period in American history. The beginning of the end of sixties optimism followed the assassination of Reverend Martin Luther King in 1968, followed by the election of Richard Nixon as president. It was an omen of times to come that he invited to his inauguration officials of both the Teamsters Union and the Blackstone Rangers, representing the old and new eras of organized crime—the growing popularity of drugs, from narcotics to psychedelics, was gangsterdom's greatest marketing success since Prohibition, and the Rangers (later renamed El Rukns) were an especially vicious Chicago drug gang. A vengeful mood came to darken American life, yet the social advances of the sixties were as irretrievable as Ornette Coleman's brilliant recordings, and the ongoing evolution of the new jazz would demonstrate that this victory of sensibility was also permanent.

V

At most times of Ornette's adult life, he has traveled light. Accumulating a great many material goods was never one of his ambitions, and whether he was rich or poor visitors have had pretty much the same descriptions of the circumstances amid which he has lived, wherever he's been. Charlie Haden comments on the first time he met Ornette:

> I walked into his room and he had music everywhere. It was on the floors, the chairs—even on the bath. You could hardly move in case you stepped on it. He'd just pick up a piece and say, "Hey, play this."[1]

And Bobby Bradford in 1976:

> Sure, Ornette's got just reams of tapes on us. But of course he's kind of a packrat, you know what I mean? He has his video tape machine, and saxophones that he's broken hanging in big bags from the walls, Uher tape recorders that he's broken and tried to fix himself, but that's just the kind of cat he is. You know what kind of mess tapes make when they are unwound, well he'll have them shoved under beds or stacked up in the corner.[2]

But Ornette wearied of living in old, rented New York apartments, and in the late 1960s he bought himself a home.

It was at 131 Prince Street in Manhattan's newly fashionable SoHo area, south of Greenwich Village and west of the Lower East Side. Real estate developers had been converting old industrial buildings, of which 131 Prince Street was one, into artists' lofts; at first Ornette lived upstairs, and then, also at the end of the decade, he also acquired the first-floor storefront. He named the room Artists House, with the objective of encouraging all kinds of music and dance performances there. By and large the audiences that came to Artists House were not asked to make donations, though often they left gifts. In contrast to nightclub and concert settings, the feeling and setting of Artists House was informal—Ornette's place was an alternative to the way in which arts were usually presented—certainly an alternative to the way the music business was typically operated—and in keeping with the do-it-yourself attitude that Ornette had demonstrated when producing concerts at Town Hall in 1962; Croydon, England, in 1965; and, with John Coltrane, at the Village Theater in 1966. Indeed, Artists House must have been something like an ideal situation. Besides Ornette's groups, other artists performed there, including saxophonist Julius Hemphill, a distant relative of Ornette's by marriage, who offered one of his early mixed-media events (he continues to do so in the 1990s). At least two albums were recorded at Artists House, Ornette's own *Friends and Neighbors* and a Chet Baker-Lee Konitz session for which Ornette is credited as producer.

At times musicians lived with Ornette at Artists House, including Truvenza Coleman and, upon their return to America in 1970, saxophonist Anthony Braxton and violinist Leroy Jenkins. They too had had firsthand experience at self-production as members of Chicago's Association for the Advancement of Creative Musicians (AACM). Though still relatively unknown in 1969, they'd found considerable acceptance and musical employment in Europe as the Creative Construction Company, joined by trumpeter Leo Smith and drummer Steve McCall. It had been one of the first free-improvisation groups in Europe as well as in America. Kunle Mwanga, who sold AACM records along with imported African art and sculpture in his store, Liberty House, wanted to introduce New York audiences to the new Chicago jazz; Jenkins assumed leadership responsibilities, getting bassist Richard Davis and pian-

ist Muhal Richard Abrams to join with the quartet and rehearsing
the ensemble at Artists House. The concert was at the Washington
Square Methodist Church—the Peace Church—and Ornette arranged for an engineer to record the event. But Ornette's financial
affairs were in flux, and a year later he offered Mwanga the concert
tapes if Mwanga would pay the engineer; Mwanga eventually sold
the tapes to Muse Records for their excellent *Creative Construction
Company* LPs.

The blooming success of the AACM musicians by that time—
still more musical than financial—dramatized how drastically the
jazz scene had changed in a decade as a result of Ornette's innovations. While isolated, sometimes irregular activity was occurring
elsewhere in America outside of New York, the Chicagoans' music
in particular had been pushing in directions away from the energy
music that had come in the wake of Ayler, Taylor, and Shepp. The
Chicagoans could be lyrical as well as intense, and featured a more
immediate sense of both composed and improvised form. While
they knew Ornette's music mostly from recordings rather than
immediate contact, his influence was evident in their improvising
(to this day saxmen Fred Anderson and Roscoe Mitchell recurringly reveal links to early Ornette) and composing (Braxton's
songs). Moreover, some Chicagoans, most remarkably Joseph Jar-
man, had composed extended works for large ensembles for which
the only precedents were the compositional adventures of Ornette
and his third-stream-music friends.

Free-jazz activity was growing in Europe, too—for instance,
there was no problem finding adept European musicians to join
Don Cherry in his Eternal Rhythm Orchestra at the 1968 Berlin
Jazz Festival. The Blue Notes, South African exiles since 1964,
added British musicians and grew into a big band—Chris McGregor's Brotherhood of Breath—playing works that linked jazz and
South African popular and folk music; drummer John Stevens and
his freely improvising friends were another important center of
British activity. John Tchicai, home in Denmark after his pioneer-
ing years with New York groups, stimulated activity in Scandina-
via. In Holland the Instant Composers Pool included, most notably,
pianist Misha Mengelberg, drummer Han Bennink (these two had
played on Dolphy's last recording in 1964), and saxophonist Willem
Breuker. There were pianist Giorgio Gaslini in Italy, versatile saxman Michel Portal and composer-trombonist Vinko Globokar in

France, pianist Alexander von Schlippenbach, trombonist Albert Manglesdorff, and sax virtuoso Peter Brötzmann in Germany, all with associated musicians.

Among the more conservative explorers in America were those musicians who had chosen to explore modes rather than Free jazz. Miles Davis by 1965 had evolved a quintet music that he and his players admitted was highly indebted to Ornette's discoveries. By the seventies Davis and a largely new set of associates had worked out their fusion music, which would largely exhaust itself during that decade but which, again, would have been inconceivable without the doors Ornette had opened.

From 1969 to 1973, when Ornette did perform he was usually joined by Redman, Haden, and Blackwell, with Denardo assuming the quartet's drum chair on occasion. But Ornette did not perform very often. Blackwell is the drummer in the 1970 *Friends and Neighbors: Ornette Live at Prince Street*, recorded at Artists House; this is, according to the Jim Gicking discography (included in Ornette's LPs for the Artists House label), among the releases that Ornette did not authorize, though the liner credits read "Produced by Ornette Coleman and Bob Thiele." An audience is on hand and in fact sings on the first take of the title tune; three of the five tracks are brief by the usual standards of Ornette's recordings. Once again the interplay of Ornette and Blackwell is quite a happy highlight, for in "Long Time No See" the drummer plays the notes of the alto improvisation and the two lead and anticipate each other in dancing phrases. The other long alto solo is in "Tomorrow," with much typical sequencing in key changes that move a whole step up or down; here the up-tempo drumming and Haden's unbroken tones sound distant from Ornette's own playing, though a central section of intense alto lines played with a biting sound draws his mates into close accompaniment. Blackwell also offers a closely structured drum solo here. He plays marching band–style snares in two versions of the title tune, which feature very blues-ripe tenor by Redman over Ornette's wall-of-sound violin.

Flying Dutchman issued this album; the label apparently went in for fairly informal productions, for in May Ornette joined in an amateur chorus that sang "We Shall Overcome" and "Give Peace a Chance" for the *Louis Armstrong and His Friends* album. Armstrong was no longer playing trumpet by then, only singing, and while Ornette's participation was more symbolic than integral, this *was* the only occasion when two of jazz's three greatest artists appeared on the same record.

Among the Ornette Coleman Quartet's few engagements that year was a week at the Village Gate opposite Alice Coltrane's group; at one point she joined the quartet to play harp on one of Ornette's compositions. The next spring she recorded her *Universal Consciousness*, in which her organ and harp playing were joined by four violinists and a rhythm section that included tamboura and two percussionists. Ornette is credited with transcribing Ms. Coltrane's string arrangements, and his participation in the project apparently went no further. Years earlier Ornette and John Coltrane had discussed recording an album together, but the project never got beyond the talking stage; perhaps later projects, such as the ones with Alice Coltrane, Jimmy Garrison, and Elvin Jones, were a way of making up for the missed opportunity.

Despite the fact that Ornette's discoveries had inspired the major line of jazz evolution for over a decade, 1971 was the first year that he appeared at the Newport Jazz Festival. In a watermelon-red suit, according to Barry McRae, Ornette played trumpet and violin in "Skylight" and in a saxophone duet with Redman, "Broken Shadows." The Coleman Quartet was the climactic act of Newport's Saturday-afternoon show. In 1960, when Ornette had played Charles Mingus's rebel festival in Newport, riots had shut down the main festival. Eleven years later history repeated itself: On the hot Saturday evening following Ornette's performance, as stoned youths flogged drugs openly around the festival grounds, a mob of young rioters tore down the fences, stormed the stage, and trashed the area. After eighteen years, it was the end of the Newport Jazz Festival in Newport, Rhode Island.

And now a major record company beckoned Ornette. Columbia signed him to a contract, and he prepared for his first sessions there by enlarging his group. He brought Cherry and Bradford back to play with him during three early-September nights at Slug's Saloon and then, with Billy Higgins also returned to the fold, the band recorded a group of mostly new compositions. Ornette's cousin James Jordan was now a New York resident, and he became the producer of Ornette's Columbia albums; of the two albums that resulted from the 1971 sessions, *Science Fiction* was released soon after it was recorded, while *Broken Shadows* was not issued until 1982. Actually Ornette led five somewhat different groups—two septets, two quartets, and a quintet—for the three days of recording. It is particularly interesting to hear Bradford responding to Ornette's music as he may well have responded a decade earlier as a member of Ornette's quartet. In general his trumpet work on these sessions lacks the nervous, tense quality of Cherry's; his sound is warmer, the contours of bop phrasing enter his lines in "Law Years," and in "The Jungle Is a Skyscraper" his solos have a naturally flowing quality that Cherry lacks even in such a fine improvisation as "Civilization Day," which is largely variations on a single motive, in both simple and very complex phrases. Ornette's own playing is most inspired in the three quartet pieces with Cherry and Higgins; in "Civilization Day" his own rhythmic variety and ingenuity extend Cherry's already inspired ideas. All of Cherry's playing is a development of Ornette's improvising concepts, while in the septet pieces "Happy House" and "Broken Shadows," Bradford also incorporates Ornette-like phrasing.

"Broken Shadows" is a slightly faster version of the slow dirge, with, as in *Crisis*, solos over the long theme. One other piece by this septet, "Science Fiction," is a poet reading into an echo chamber, joined randomly by a crying baby, while in the background the band plays a violent collective improvisation; it's a long, static performance. A slightly different septet, without Cherry and Bradford, includes an interesting singer, Asha Puthli, who suggests both a Sheila Jordan with an extended upper range and the little-girl quality of pop singer Dolly Parton; most of her singing, however, is obscured by the unison band lines. From Bombay, and also a film actress, Puthli's background was in pop and Indian classical music. (A year after these sessions Ornette's quartet, plus pianist Cedar Walton, guitarist Jim Hall, and a woodwind quintet, recorded a Coleman blues and a Coleman ballad, both featuring Texas singer Webster Armstrong; these minor works were included in *Broken Shadows*.)

Festival producer George Wein was aware that the crowds at Newport had responded enthusiastically to Ornette, and in the fall, on his annual Newport tour, Wein brought the Coleman Quartet to Europe. Ornette flew to Europe ahead of the rest of his band; he had completed the composition of his symphonic work *Skies of America*, and now he spoke to several conductors, searching for one to record it. Haden missed the beginning of the tour, in mid-

October, to stay in New York while his wife gave birth to triplet daughters; Barre Phillips was his replacement. It was a very busy tour, with stops in at least thirteen countries in little more than a month. After a four-day rest, the last concert of the tour was in the resort city of Cascais, Portugal on November 20. This was in the period when Portugal, ruled by a dictatorship, was still attempting to maintain a hold on what was left of its colonial empire. Said Haden, "The guys who were recruited in Portugal to go fight the black liberation armies in Africa refused to fight, like the guys [Americans] who go to Canada here [rather than fight in the Vietnam War]. If they refused to fight, they weren't put in jail—they were put on the front lines to be killed." The quartet had played Haden's "Song for Che" at each concert on the tour. At the stadium in Cascais, with Ornette's blessing, Haden dedicated the song to "the black liberation movements in Mozambique, Angola, and Guinea-Bissau."[3] At least twenty thousand people attended the concert, including many students who opposed their government's policies, "and the cheering continued through most of the song. It was incredible."[4]

The quartet played one more song after that, and at the conclusion of their set Haden, Redman, and Blackwell gave the raised-fist salute. Meanwhile, fights had broken out in the audience, and backstage, Haden was warned not to stay alone that night. In the dressing room, says Haden, when someone asked Ornette why he had let Haden make the dedication, Ornette replied ironically, "Oh, hey, Charlie, would you go back up on the stage and take back all the stuff you said?"

What Haden had done was, to say the least, not politically correct. The next day's concert, the last of the festival, was to have included performers such as Phil Woods and the Giants of Jazz, including Thelonious Monk and Dizzy Gillespie, but the police canceled the event. Haden had left the hotel just before the police arrived to nab him, but he said, "I was arrested at the airport and taken to the Lisbon prison. They kept me alone in a room for several hours, and then took me to another room and interrogated me. What organization was I in? Who was I speaking for?"[5] They made Haden sign a statement in Portuguese; they showed him photos and brochures of their African colonies and told him "about all the good things they were doing for black people there. Suddenly their expressions changed from cold to polite. A man had come into the room to tell me that someone from the U.S. Embassy was there to pick me up."[6]

Haden stayed at the American cultural attaché's house that night and flew to London the next day. But he couldn't find Ornette, Redman, and Blackwell there, so he continued on home to New York. In London the Coleman Quartet, with probably Jeff Clyne substituting on bass, was recording the soundtrack to *Run*, a Stefan Sharp film. It was in this period, probably after the recording sessions in London were completed, that Ornette flew to Nigeria. There, at a village festival in the northern part of the nation, he met a group of Hausa musicians playing percussion instruments and a one-stringed gourd fiddle. Ornette joined them and played his alto saxophone. He also had his movie camera along, and documented some of the visit on film (an excerpt of the visit appears in *Ornette: Made in America*). The stimulating effects of the music on Ornette were much like he would feel in his famed visit to Joujouka, Morocco in 1973.

But between 1971 and 1973 came *Skies of America:*

> I grew up in Texas, in the South, where there was lots of discrimination, lots of problems for minorities. Sometimes the sun is shining and beautiful on one side of the street, and across the street, just maybe three feet apart, there'd be big balls of hail and thunderstorms, and that reminded me of something that happened with people. In America you see them all enjoying themselves and next moment they're all fighting. They're the same way as the elements. When I titled that piece, it was to let me see if I could describe the beauty, and not have it be racial or any territory. In other words, the sky has no territory; only the land has territory. I was trying to describe something that has no territory.[7]

Ornette has also spoken of another inspiration for *Skies of America:* a starry night he had once spent in the open on a Crow Indian reservation in Montana.

> I participated in their sacred rites, and it made me think about the many different elements existing in America, in relation to its causes, purpose and destiny. For some reason, I got that feeling from the sky. I feel that everything that has ever happened in America, from way before the Europeans arrived, is still intact as far as the sky is concerned.[8]

Skies of America was composed as a symphony. It annoyed Ornette that he'd been told that his scores used wrong notation: "At
the British Museum, I saw the original manuscripts from
Beethoven, Mozart and all those guys, and it looked like chicken
scratches."[9] It's possible that portions of *Skies* had been composed as
early as 1963, for Ornette has said that he once hired "lots of
first-chair guys" from "different symphonies in New York" to rehearse it with him,

> and I was having trouble with several of the musicians who were
> classically trained—they couldn't play certain passages. I decided to
> get the trumpet and violin to see if I could play the thing that I was
> hearing myself, and that's what really got me started with those
> instruments, because I didn't want someone to say that I was just
> trying to get them in a position to make them feel inadequate. When
> I came up to a certain problem, I played the part to show them it
> could be done.[10]

The conductor whom Ornette found to record *Skies of America*
was David Measham and the orchestra was the London Symphony.
The Ornette Coleman Quartet was also to have performed the
symphony in concert with the orchestra, but once again the British
musicians union struck its customary blow against Ornette's music
and the concert had to be canceled. At the recording session only
Ornette played with the orchestra, improvising over his composed
sections. Later he said,

> I'm so pissed-off with Columbia. I was put in the situation where
> they're supposed to be humanitarians, aware of everything that's
> going on. But I didn't get the same interest in my music as Boulez
> did recording someone else's music. I didn't even get all of it on the
> record, only 40 minutes. The budget that Boulez could get for re-
> cording a Bartok piece—the rehearsal money—would have allowed
> me to finish my whole piece. I could've done my record exactly as I
> wanted to do it, and if it didn't sell, I still would have the privilege
> of knowing they were *with* me.[11]

(Indeed, Columbia's behavior in its 1970s dealings with Ornette was often shameful. Once he went to Columbia president
Clive Davis to complain about what he considered the insuf-
ficient promotion his recordings were getting. Davis replied that

Columbia had not signed Ornette for his anticipated success as a commodity but rather for the prestige of having his name on its artist roster. It also kept certain widely renowned pop performers and classical artists under contract whether or not the sales of their recordings justified the very high fees they were paid.)

Following two rehearsals, *Skies of America* was recorded at the London EMI studios in April. James Jordan and a CBS classical music producer, Paul Myers, were the producers. But then CBS insisted that the album be released by its jazz division, not its classical music division, and that the LP be banded into separate "songs," each with its own title, allegedly to encourage radio airplay—"but basically," Ornette later said, "they were trying to keep it from having the image of a symphony. I realize now that it was another social-racial problem. . . . I've always thought of myself as a composer who also performs music. I'm classified as a jazz saxophonist. It eliminates people from trying to find out if I've done anything else."[12]

And to J. B. Figi he said,

I really wrote the music because I have the ability to write the music. I wasn't trying to change my class or category or become blacker or whiter. I was just doing something that I could do. And yet, I haven't had any, really, white people that's in the field try and relate to me on a musical level. It's like they were trying to discourage me that there's something that I shouldn't think about.

[*Skies of America* is] the way I play. I just wrote it out for a larger orchestra, that's all. It's like writing a letter, you know. I don't sit down and try and *figure out* something. I just heard something in my head and took the pen and wrote it out. But that was because I've been playing for twenty years and after doing that for twenty years, I should be able to do it. . . .

I would like to have a large orchestra for about five years, where I could teach them to play a large composition without always having to reach and get the music, you know. Like when you go to the Philharmonic and they pull out Bartok or Beethoven. I mean, does it look more elegant to put out music? It doesn't sound any better. They have been playing those pieces for 5 or 6 thousand performances. I'm sure they must know the parts by now.

It costs $750,000 to have a large orchestra. And I'd need it for five years. So that needs 3-½ million dollars. I need 5 million dollars. I'd put it all into an orchestra.[13]

In the liner notes to *Skies of America*, Ornette wrote, "The voicing of the orchestra is written in very high parts because I wanted the sound of the orchestra to create a very clear earth and sky sound as much as the feeling of night, stars and daylight." Indeed, the weight of the orchestra is in the treble clef, leaving a sense of hovering over the landscape. Much of the first half is in long, dissonant tones suggesting night, including an orchestration of "All of My Life," which Asha Puthli had sung with Ornette's jazz group in *Science Fiction*, although there is also an early lively section titled "The Good Life"—Ornette had recorded it in the quintet with Bradford as "School Work," later issued in *Broken Shadows*, and subsequent versions by his electric bands would be titled "Theme from a Symphony" and "Dancing in Your Head." Part I of *Skies of America* concludes with the sudden appearance of Ornette's alto singing over a repeated string figure and percussion writing that appears to be an attempt to create a simplified kind of Edward Blackwell–like setting; Ornette's closing, unaccompanied solo lines, ending on a questioning high note, are especially glorious.

In general the more active music is in the second half of *Skies*, where Ornette's alto is especially prominent. There's his agitated improvising over long, separated chords in "Foreigner in a Free Land," his lovely, sad melodies over solemn tones in "Love Life," and three orchestral tracks that offer much of the vitality of his small groups: "Jam Session," with alto solo, medium-tempo percussion backbeats, and several orchestra sections in various simultaneous tempos; "Sunday in America," without alto but with separate melody lines entering one by one over slow string tones; and best of all "The Men Who Live in the White House," which also includes very alive, unaccompanied alto. Throughout *Skies of America*, and especially evident in the tracks featuring long, dissonant tones, distant tympani maintain faint, brooding throbs—a kind of detached commentary. All of the twenty-one separate tracks into which Columbia divided the composition are short (some are under a minute in length), and some of the breaks between them indeed appear arbitrary—for instance, "Birthdays and Funerals," "Dreams," and "Sounds of Sculpture" sound like a single line of development. As to the absence, dictated by the British musicians union, of the rest of Ornette's quartet, it is especially notable in sections with open spaces that fairly cry for Edward Blackwell's drum commentary, as in "The Soul Within Woman" and "The

Artist in America." The Wild-Cuscuna discography notes the similarities between "Holiday for Heroes" and Ornette's earlier quartet piece "Forgotten Songs," and between Skies' "The Soul Within Woman" and his quartet's "Street Woman." John Rockwell wrote of Skies' alternating "driving polytonal passages" with "slower, grander statements that recall the chordal calm of the American folk symphonists. There are, certainly, moments of naïveté and clumsiness in the conception, arrangement and execution of this fresco. But the overall impact is Ivesian in scope and in spirit, too. Very few first efforts are so powerful as this."[14]

How much had Ornette edited from Skies of America to fit the LP's forty-one and a half minutes? On the Fourth of July, 1972, less than two months after the recording sessions, the composition received its first public performance, which lasted nearly fifty-four minutes, at the Newport Jazz Festival—now moved permanently to New York City—in a concert at Philharmonic Hall. The performers were the American Symphony Orchestra, conducted by Leon Thompson, and at last the Ornette Coleman Quartet. Now the composition was divided into not two but four parts, with at least three new sections added and three others repeated; some sections that had been played by the orchestra alone on the LP now found the orchestra joined, variously, by Ornette, Redman, Blackwell, or the quartet. Down Beat reviewer Jim Szantor wrote of the concerto grosso structure of Skies and commented that "if Coleman's harmonic modulation theory was being practiced (it allows the orchestra to choose any octave of a given note), it did not work at this performance. . . . Too many players were opting for lower notes because the occasional clarinet/ flute passages were a welcome relief from the lower voicings heard most of the time."[15]

It's in Ornette's liner notes to Skies of America that he first publicly refers to the harmolodic theory:

> "Skies of America" is a collection of compositions and the orchestration for a symphony orchestra based on a theory book called The Harmolodic Theory which uses melody, harmony, and the instrumentation of movement of forms. . . . The writing is applied to harmolodic modulation meaning to modulate in range without changing keys.[16]

That theory book has not yet appeared; John Snyder has, and perhaps others have, tried to edit Ornette's manuscript without success. Ornette contributed an essay on his use of harmolodics to *Down Beat*, in which he said, "The way to listen to harmolodic playing as soloist or to listen to the collective harmolodic whole is to follow the idea of melody and listen to the many different ways the idea can affect the melody."[17] And in an essay on harmolodics in the book *Free Spirits: The Insurgent Imagination*, Ornette wrote that he "realized harmolodics can be used in almost any kind of expression. You can think harmolodically, you can write fiction and poetry in harmolodic. Harmolodics allows a person to use a multiplicity of elements to express more than one direction. The greatest freedom in harmolodics is human instinct."[18]

Neither essay is definitive. Perhaps a crucial summary was provided by Ornette when he spoke of the harmolodic "theory method" as "using the melody, the harmony and the rhythm all equal. . . ."[19] Two of Ornette's most experienced colleagues have helped clarify the concept of harmolodics. According to Don Cherry, it is

> a profound system based on developing your ear along with your technical proficiency on your instrument. . . . We have to know the chord structure perfectly, all the possible intervals, and *then* play around it. . . . If I play a C and have it in my mind as the tonic, that's what it will become. If I want it to be a minor third or a major seventh that had a tendency to resolve upward, then the quality of the note will change.[20]

In a lecture Cherry said, "In the harmolodic concept, you're reaching to the point to make every note sound like a tonic. . . ."[21] And Charlie Haden described playing with Ornette's groups in this way: "Technically speaking, it was a constant modulation in the improvising that was taken from the direction of the composition, and from the direction inside the musician, and from listening to each other. . . ."[22]

Is *harmolodics*, then, a name for the way Ornette's first groups in California in the 1950s learned to play together? According to Ornette,

> I had always called it that, but I never started using it as much as I did say in the last five years . . . probably because I was always interested in trying to get to the place where I could be secure and

successful in what I was doing, and I didn't want to appear as if I was trying to be an intellect or something, just to have a chance to play music. When I came to New York in '59, I could have said the same thing, but I didn't say anything—I just let everyone take me apart the way they heard me. And after I started being dissected in so many parts, it seemed like I started making this plan to put the pieces together so someone could understand what chord they were talking about. . . . Like I heard them playing changes, and I left changes, and they'd say, "Oh, he doesn't know that [set of chord changes]. . . ." Because a person saw you play a certain line and they see you get away from it, they assume that's all the further you could go with that.

It's important that Ornette says "harmolodics has not only the variety to expand, it also allows you to be an individual. I mean, a person doesn't have to play like myself in order to know he's playing harmolodic. He can play like himself." He once jotted down the following for interviewer Art Lange:

C	E	G	B	—	Cma7
E$\flat$	G$\flat$	B$\flat$	D$\flat$	—	Emi7
D	F	A$\flat$	A$\sharp$	—	Dmi$\flat$5

He told him, "Play this over and over, and you'll know everything you need to know about harmolodics." And when Ornette dictated the same twelve notes to interviewer Rick Senger, he emphasized that none of the notes is repeated:

In harmolodics, most people think that you just take a horn and play anything off the top of your head and don't have to play any changes. Well, Western music wasn't designed to be played that way because no *one* instrument is designed to play all the music. But most Western instruments *can* play a unison melody. When I realized that unison melody also has its own rules whether you follow the map or not, I realized that harmolodics could be as rewarding as any other form of musical expression.[23]

And Ornette insists that harmolodics is "not supposed to be a secret; it's supposed to be something that anyone should be able to do."[24]

This brings up the question of *unison*, a term that Ornette uses often. Ornette does not usually use "unison" to mean musicians playing the same notes simultaneously, but rather in some of the word's other senses. As the *Oxford English Dictionary* defines it, "A union or combination of concordant sounds; a united and unanimous declaration or utterance . . . Sounding at once or together . . . United and consenting, as the pronouncement of a number of persons; expressing complete agreement; unanimous, concordant, consonant, harmonious."[25] The objective of the concentrated study and practice together of the harmolodic system is to get musicians to play—to feel and think—in this kind of unison. Or as the great bassist Wilbur Ware used to say, "Let's play this music *together*."[26]

Joujouka is an isolated village in the foothills of the Rif Mountains of northern Morocco, a village far from other towns, paved roads, or electricity, and with no running water. In Joujouka live a family of musicians who reportedly trace their ancestry back to Persia, approximately a millennium ago. Since the thirteenth century this family provided, exclusively, the court musicians to the sultans of Morocco—the sultans themselves had not the authority to remove these musicians from their office, or to supplement them. During the 1950s painter Brian Gysin operated a nightclub in Tangier, across the Strait of Gibraltar from Spain, through which passed a unique stream of people including diplomats, aristocrats, and Gysin's fellow expatriates such as writer William Burroughs and writer-composer Paul Bowles; the house musicians in the club were the Master Musicians of Joujouka. Years later, Gysin took Rolling Stones guitarist Brian Jones to Joujouka to record the Master Musicians, and then American music critic Robert Palmer, who wrote an article in *Rolling Stone* magazine about the experience. It was Palmer who played his tapes of Joujouka music for Ornette Coleman, and Ornette's response was immediate: He wanted to journey there and record an album of the Master Musicians himself.

Ornette did not perform often in the second half of 1972; the most notable event, perhaps, was his appearance, for the second year in a row, at the Berlin Jazz Festival, this time alone on alto sax and piano in a concert titled "The Art of the Solo." In January 1973, then, he and Palmer, James Jordan, and a few others traveled to Joujouka, arriving at the beginning of the annual Bou Jeloud festival, which attracted tribesmen and families from surrounding areas to Joujouka to participate in the Master Musicians' rituals. Though a Muslim festival, its origins probably go back to the ancient rites of the Lupercalia, a Roman festival honoring Faunus (Pan in Greek mythology), the god of shepherds and flocks. Arriving there, Ornette found thirty musicians playing *raitas*—a raita is a local, oboelike instrument—and drums. "The youngest guy there was in his 20's and the rest were in their 60's and 70's and they had more energy than any young person I've ever seen play music. They could play music for hours. And the thing that was so incredible is that they were playing instruments that wasn't in Western notes, wasn't no tempered scales, and yet they were playing in unison."[27] "Musicians are magicians in Morocco," wrote William S. Burroughs.[28] On the first night Ornette, sleeping like the other visitors on the dirt floor of a mud hut, took his pouch full of the money with which he intended to pay the musicians and laid it under his pillow. The next morning the pouch was gone. The panic-stricken visitors hunted high and low for it, without success. At last they unlocked the only door of the hut to find the pouch, with money intact, on the doorstep, and two musicians-magicians watching and smirking nearby. Clearly Joujouka was a magical place.

Ornette had composed some themes to play with the Master Musicians. After the first night of playing with them, he composed more, and when he began recording he and Bob Palmer, on clarinet, matched his themes with the ritual music. He continued to record through the several nights of the festival, "with tribesmen screaming in trance all around us," said Palmer. "Once in a while somebody would start frothing at the mouth and dash screaming past the horn mikes: we got this amazing Doppler effect on the tapes."[29] "Bou Jeloud in his black goatskins is dancing in a little square lit by bonfires snatching up switches to whip the women who run screaming before him," wrote William S. Burroughs. "If he touches a woman with his switch she will become pregnant before the year is out."[30] "All the villagers, dressed in best white, swirl in great circles and coils around one wildman in skins," wrote Gysin. "He is wild. He is mad. Sowing panic. Lashing at anyone; striking real terror into the crowd. Women scatter like white marabout birds all aflutter. . . ."[31] As for the music itself, Ornette said,

Well, I've heard lots of music and it just sounds like music. But I've had two experiences of knowing that it sounded like music, but the air smelled so differently, and the activity of the people around them, it changed them. . . . I know in Morocco I had this experience, and I had it in Nigeria. And I had it with Chinese music—any music that doesn't cause you to use your language to identify the name of it will start affecting you in a much more imaginative way. The music that tells you when it's going to go a certain way—it's like everything, it's like hip background stuff. . . . In Texas when I used to have to play for a country evangelist, healing people, doing things. . . . We'd get there and the piano would be in G, H—there'd be no such thing as a key. . . . Those same things would happen. So I had that experience myself, when I was playing for evangelists or in church, that particular thing we're talking about—I think that's more in church music. What I mean by church music, music that is totally created for an emotional experience.

After several days of the festival's intensity, Ornette was taken to a cave that had apparently been a religious shrine in the long-ago past. The music that Ornette had already recorded at the festival had been a meeting of cultures: ancient Berber and America's modern jazz. Now Ornette composed "Music from the Cave" for himself on trumpet, drummers, a string section, including the village violinist and players of the gimbris (three-stringed guitarlike instruments, reported Palmer), and wooden flutes. The theme that Ornette composed, said Palmer, "was a perfect bridge from his idiom to theirs. . . . All the musicians on 'Music from the Cave' were playing in one world, and I think that world was equally new to all of us."[32]

To Ornette, the meaning of the music at Joujouka went far beyond its obvious excitement:

The thing that really fascinated me is the atmosphere of how people get along. I didn't see anyone getting uptight about not relating to somebody. That was really beautiful to see that a person could maintain his own identity without trying to get you to like him and yet get along with you. . . .

It's a human music. It's about life conditions, not about losing your woman and, you know, baby will you please come back, and you know, I can't live without you in the bed. It's not that. It's a much deeper music.

There is a music that has the quality to preserve life.

The musicians there I'd heard had cured a white fellow of cancer with their music. I believe it. Because if you ever hear the music, man, you can understand it. . . . The thing that was very beautiful about Joujouka and at the same time very sad was that all the musicians have to survive is their music. I mean, they don't have *anything* else but that. . . . The oldest musician up there was 110, and I asked him, you know, how was the music when he was a youngster and then how was it different than that it is now. He said he doesn't think about anything like that. He said that if he had a young woman he could live another fifteen years.[33]

Back home in New York Ornette, with Jordan and Palmer, selected two LPs' worth of their Joujouka recordings for release as a Columbia double album, and the tapes were stored in Columbia's vaults. But later that year came the notorious "Bad Day at Black Rock," Columbia's New York offices, when the bean counters who by then ran the company cut off most of its jazz roster, including Ornette; he reportedly did not recover the tapes until sometime in the next decade.

Among the events in Ornette's career in 1973 were lectures at Queensborough Community College in Bayside, N.Y., and teaching at a ten-day Creative Music Studio seminar held in New York—the Studio, headed by vibist Karl Berger, was the new jazz's leading institution of higher learning in the 1970s—and in September an appearance at the Ann Arbor (Michigan) Blues and Jazz Festival with Redman, Haden, Higgins—not Blackwell—singer Webster Armstrong, and Solomon Olonari playing traditional African talking drums. Late in the year came the announcement that Ornette had been awarded another Guggenheim fellowship for composition.

Meanwhile, Edward Blackwell, who had been Ornette's first choice as drummer since 1967, was ill. First he thought his pains were ordinary back problems, but a chiropractor discovered it was considerably more serious than that. Indeed, soon thereafter Blackwell lost the use of both of his kidneys. He'd moved in with Ornette at Artists House for a time, but now he required constant dialysis-machine treatment. In hopes of raising money for a kidney-transplant operation for him, the jazz community rallied around. Billy Higgins and Roger Blank, Sun Ra's drummer, organized benefit concerts at Artists House at the end of December; the performers included Blackwell's two employers, Ornette and pianist Randy Weston, and saxophonists such as Sam Rivers, Charles Brackeen,

Jimmy Heath, Clifford Jordan, Rahsaan Roland Kirk, and Frank Lowe. In mid-December Bobby Bradford, beginning his first tour of England, was featured at an Edward Blackwell benefit in London; early in 1974 there were benefit concerts in New Orleans, Baton Rouge, and two colleges in Ohio; *Coda* magazine began a campaign to raise money for Blackwell, while *Down Beat* printed bulletins soliciting contributions.

Kidneys had actually been offered for a transplant operation for Blackwell, but no one was permitted to provide an organ for transplant unless he or she possessed a Uniform Anatomical Gift card at the time of the donation. Also, most physicians refused to perform kidney transplants in any case, fearing malpractice or negligence lawsuits. The money that jazz fans donated helped pay for treatments, but fell far short of the huge sums required for a transplant.

Problems were mounting for Ornette with Artists House. He had been offering concerts irregularly there for several years. He and others had used it for a rehearsal studio, and fellow musicians liked to meet there. But it was an old industrial building with floors of three-quarter-inch wood and no sound insulation. In fact, the floors of the building had not even been divided into apartments. Ornette and his friends had played music there at almost all hours of the day or night, which meant that their music would resonate through the homes of the others who lived at 131 Prince Street, whether they were awake, asleep, praying, crying, or attempting to listen to their phonographs; the music at Artists House may have been great music, in fact it probably was, but it was an intrusion. Ornette had moved into the building in the early days of the conversion of old SoHo buildings into artists' lofts, "before," says John Snyder, "the law was actually settled on how it was going to be done. He had bought two floors in the building, and it was not really set up legally correct. So he got into a lot of disputes with his neighbors over the noise. He said he owned his spaces, he could do what he wanted, which was not entirely the case." After Ornette was evicted from the bottom floor of Artists House, lawyer Snyder said, "then it became my job to prevent his eviction from the other floor. He considered that his harassment was a racist problem, and it was a very confusing story." Ornette also referred to it as a "homosexual problem"; the neighbors, in turn, began to think of Ornette as vindictive.

What Ornette had originally expected would be a small community of artists living and creating together had turned into warfare. Ornette told McRae that "one of their wives told me that they were going to pick a way to get me out because they didn't want any minorities there. . . ."[34] Court battles followed. It was a most discouraging conclusion to something that had begun most promisingly, with the highest of motives, but Ornette, disgusted with the fighting, finally abandoned Artists House in the mid-1970s.

VI

Edward Blackwell could no longer play regularly with Ornette. Charlie Haden and Dewey Redman had begun playing with pianist Keith Jarrett's quartet; this former Miles Davis sideman was another jazz artist who had been liberated by Ornette's discoveries, and since he was striking forth on his own while Ornette was playing only irregularly, the Jarrett Quartet became Redman's and Haden's main source of employment. So the group that Ornette took with him to Europe in the spring of 1974 included drummer Billy Higgins; bassist Sirone (Norris Jones), who with violinist Leroy Jenkins and drummer Jerome Cooper had played in the important Free trio the Revolutionary Ensemble; and a midwestern guitarist who was beginning to make a name for himself in New York, James "Blood" Ulmer. Like Ornette, Ulmer first made his living in music playing blues and rhythm and blues before graduating to modern jazz and playing for four years with the well-traveled, Ohio-based organist Hank Marr. In 1971 Ulmer was, he says, the first guitarist to join Art Blakey's Jazz Messengers, a job that lasted four months; he also began playing Free jazz with Rashied Ali, who'd drummed in John Coltrane's final groups.

For a time Ulmer lived at Artists House while he studied the harmolodic theory with Ornette: "The harmolodic theory helped bring out things in me rather than completely change my artistic direction"—remember Ornette's insistence that harmolodics allows the player to expand while yet remaining an individual. ". . . What Ornette did show me in music was a special kind of freedom that allowed me to experience and project what I felt. . . . I had to learn instant modulation and orchestration, which are now important parts of my conception."[1] It had been nearly sixteen years since Ornette had worked with an instrument that provided a harmonic backdrop for his soloing; the pianos of Walter Norris and Paul Bley had been either irrelevant to his shifting tonalities or else constraining. Ulmer, however, had a "great big ear," and instant modulation and orchestration became his unprecedented role with Ornette:

> He never had a guitar before me. I was orchestrating his improvised parts as he played them. Instead of setting up sounds for him to play, I would play where he went to. It's different from following the patterns of chord changes. In Ornette's music, the change comes after the phrase. It allows the soloist to make whatever phrase he really wants. . . . I got a chance to solo—I think the guitar worked more with his music than with anyone else.

The music was moving into new territory, now, with Ulmer. With Ornette's irregular performing schedule, however, his rhythm section was in flux: Haden followed Sirone as bassist, and David Williams was Ornette's bassist for a European tour in the summer of 1974; for part of one of the last Artists House events Blackwell took over Higgins's drum chair. In June 1975, at the Jazz Showcase in Chicago, the quartet was Ornette, Ulmer, David Izenzon playing bass, and Denardo, drums: "After Ornette decided he liked the guitar," says Ulmer, "we tried quite a few drummers, and he would ask my suggestions about who we should play with. I thought playing with Denardo would be great. I think he always really wanted Denardo to be the drummer." The sound of this quartet was certainly startling; I recall less a sense of unity than of four distinctive individuals exploring adjoining territories, and was surprised at how softly the highly creative Izenzon played.

According to Ornette, he was now beginning to realize

> that the guitar had a very wide overtone, so maybe one guitar might sound like ten violins as far as range of strength. You know, like in

a symphony orchestra two trumpets are equivalent to twenty-four violins. So when I found that out I decided, well, I'm going to see if I can orchestrate this music that I'm playing and see if it can have a larger sound—and it surely did. So about 1975 I started orchestrating the same music that I was playing, that I've always written, for the kind of instrumentation I was using.

Electric amplification had to be a factor here, both in enhancing the guitar overtones and in "range of strength," for Ulmer was definitely a forward player. And Ornette was experimenting with his group's instrumentation, occasionally adding percussionist Barbara Huey to make it a quintet.

Ornette was now seeking a new music, quite different from his three previous lines of development—his Free jazz combos, his violin improvising, and his classical or third-stream composing. Although playing in rhythm-and-blues bands had been restricting in his youth and playing the Free jazz that he'd discovered was creatively enormously rewarding, he missed the visceral contact with audiences that he'd felt while playing for dancers in his youth. The Joujouka experience, according to Palmer, showed Ornette that it was possible to play creatively while making that immediate audience connection, and he came to believe that he could similarly move audiences in the Western world by playing music based on rock rhythms and electric guitars.

For all Ulmer's harmonic sophistication, he'd begun in rhythm and blues, and blues ideas remained a large element of his improvising. Now, Ornette began seeking musicians from comparable backgrounds to play with. A guitarist with Miles Davis told Ornette about a teenage bassist from Philadelphia, Rudy McDaniel, who later changed his name to Jamaaladeen Tacuma, and Ornette invited him to come to New York and rehearse. Charles Ellerbee, a guitarist in disco bands, began playing with Ornette. Ronald Shannon Jackson, an older drummer from Texas, had played with Charles Tyler, Albert Ayler, and Betty Carter, among others, before meeting Ornette and moving into his loft. Ornette taught these players, showing them harmonic relations—"it's incredible, he's like a wizard because he'll show you so many ways to combine chords," said Tacuma—and encouraging them to express their own ideas:

> We'd often be in a frame of mind where we would try to play in a
> certain way to please him, but on the breaks we'd be playing other

things we knew, and he'd say, 'Why don't you guys play like that when we play?' . . . Basically what we do is compositional improvising in which each person acts like a soloist. We work from a melody in a tonal point, and anything that you play has to be equal to the melody or better. If you play anything less than the melody, you have to go to the doghouse (laugh). The rhythmic pattern, the melodic structure of it, anything you improvise has to be stronger than the original melody.[2]

After a month of rehearsing constantly with his new group of young musicians, some as young as Cherry and Higgins when Ornette had first met them in the 1950s, Ornette "really polished up the band,"[3] according to Tacuma, after which they went to France for yet two more weeks of rehearsing. That short visit, it turned out, stretched into four months of rehearsing. A singer named Claude Nougaro was at the time enjoying considerable popularity in France, and Ornette was asked to play a saxophone solo on an album Nougaro was recording. Not only did Ornette ask for what was, at the time, an outlandish amount of money—ten thousand dollars—to play, but the record company paid it! (The solo is in Nougaro's song "Gloria," and John Snyder calls it "like a rocket taking off . . . fantastic, really incredible, worth every cent of the money.")

With the fresh money Ornette took his quintet into a recording studio to make the *Dancing in Your Head* and *Body Meta* albums at the end of 1975; his players were McDaniel, Ellerbee, Jackson, and guitarist Bern Nix, but Denardo and Ulmer were not part of this group. One of the selections recorded that day was "European Echoes," which Ornette, Izenzon, and Moffett had recorded ten years earlier in Stockholm, and a comparison shows how his alto-sax playing had changed to fit his new group's music. Much of the trio version is gentle satire on the theme's oom-pah-pah waltz rhythms by bassist and drummer, who at times slip subtly into four-beat meter. Ornette's phrases are more even in the 1975 quintet version of "European Echoes," and more evenly spaced; while his players exaggerate the three-beat meter, Ornette now consistently plays waltz phrases that emphasize the downbeats, thus eliminating the element of humor; the guitars' consistent playing against the meter soon leads Ornette and the others to play in 4/4 to the end.

Throughout the session Jackson's drumming is hyperactive, with a bass-drum beat on either every strong beat (like the drumming in marching and disco bands) or on every beat in each measure, and he sometimes uses both approaches in the same track ("Macho Woman"). Abandoning standard ideas of percussion interplay, he instead offers repeated snare patterns that sound like marching-band drums but that are often less mobile imitations of Ornette's alto phrases. It's a less swinging kind of drumming than Ornette's earlier drummers offered and, in the fast tempos the quintet plays throughout the date (even in the ballad "Fou Amour"), it tends to leave a two-beat feeling. The two guitarists also accent the strong beats, and though the recording balance leaves their role somewhat in the background, they provide a steady chatter; there is a Bo Diddley rhythm for a guitars-drums backdrop in "Voice Poetry" that sounds stiff compared to the free way Charlie Haden played it in "Ramblin' " sixteen years earlier. The electric bass, however, breaks with the band's heavy rock accents to play even, unbroken lines, usually a note on every beat; McDaniel conceives of his lines in two-bar units and likes to play high notes, so in effect he provides a running commentary on Ornette's alto lines. Although Ornette's own phrasing is considerably more symmetrical than in the past, with a great many sequences and repeated licks—he gravitates naturally to three-note phrases that accent strong beats, and to longer phrases that begin and end on downbeats—his improvising is by far the most varied, mobile, and melodic of the group. The net effect of these recordings, then, is of an alto soloist of uncommon stamina accompanied by rhythm players who take their cues from him and whose strong-beat accenting affects his own rhythmic organization.

The principles of Ornette's 1975 quintet are similar to those of his fifties groups, then—melodies that move freely from chord to chord, key to key, rising or dropping most often in whole- or half-steps, and players who use Ornette's own lines for their inspiration. The regularity of rock-music accenting makes these musicians less rhythmically free than Ornette's early players, and their roles are in a sense more restricted. The longest pieces recorded at this session were two two-beat versions of *Skies of America*'s "The Good Life," retitled "Theme from a Symphony" in the album released first, *Dancing in Your Head*. The only other track on that LP is "Midnight Sunrise," from a tape that Steve Goldstein recorded of Ornette playing with the Master Musicians of Joujouka. Ornette's alto sound is in the foreground; behind him high treble raitas—they sound like a cross between oboes and bagpipes—play a melodic line over low, somber drums. Faster drums and a faster melodic line appear. Ornette's sound fits the context perfectly, and his lines appear to be a broken commentary on the raitas' melodies. The effect is of constant movement and, on Ornette's part, continual response to the Master Musicians. "See, when I went there and started performing with them, I was never informed on what they were going to play, how they were going to play it, when they were going to stop, when they were going to start, any form. . . . I wasn't prepared for anything at all. . . . Sounded as if I had rehearsed it with them. It wasn't true. Not at all."

John Snyder, who had attended both music school and law school, had been an assistant to jazz producer Creed Taylor before his CTI Records went out of business, and in 1975 Snyder began the Horizon label, a jazz subsidiary of the highly successful pop label A&M. One of Snyder's projects was *Closeness*, a collection of duets by Charlie Haden with Alice Coltrane, Keith Jarrett, drummer Paul Motian, and Ornette. In March 1976 Snyder met Ornette, wearing a mink coat, at a New York airport; he had flown from France to record two duets with Haden. A close, complicated friendship began then for Snyder: "I spent five years with Ornette Coleman every day, and it changed my life. Like, going to law school, it's not what you learn, it's how they teach you to think— it's a brainwashing, in a way. And the same thing about Ornette—if you're around Ornette enough, you'll change, you'll become more like him."

After the record date with Haden, Ornette needed Snyder's legal help in clearing up the Artists House confusion. When Ornette needed money, then, Snyder suggested that he sell some tapes to record companies. Ornette chose to sell the *Dancing in Your Head* material that his new band had recorded in France. Although Snyder was an employee of A&M, Ornette's idea was to have him sell the recording to Columbia, and Snyder was willing to try it. "He said, 'Now, John, there are 300 countries in the world, and I'm sure each one of them can buy a thousand records. That's 300,000 records. I want $300,000." Snyder conveyed the proposal to Columbia, and soon thereafter received a telephone call from an assistant to Columbia's president, Bruce Lundvall: "He screamed at me, 'Who the fuck do you think you are, asking for $300,000 for fucking Ornette Coleman?' I said, 'What, is that a no?' " after which Snyder fired off a letter to Lundvall complaining of the assistant's rudeness. "Ornette would put you in a position of fighting his battle, and his battle, the other side doesn't understand it—they think that it's nuts."

Snyder did subsequently persuade A&M to pay Ornette $75,000 to issue *Dancing in Your Head* on Horizon, after which "Ornette came back to me and said, 'That's not enough—I need $10,000 more.' " Jerry Moss, A&M's operator, agreed to the extra $10,000, "but it really kind of turned the tide against me," says Snyder. "Jerry started thinking I was working more for Ornette than working for A&M, which was pretty much the case. I left A&M and became Ornette's manager kind of at the same time." That was in 1977, after Snyder had had a brief but solid history with Horizon, including releasing albums by the Thad Jones-Mel Lewis band, the Revolutionary Ensemble, Dave Brubeck-Paul Desmond, Don Cherry, and two sets of Haden duets.

Nineteen seventy-six was the year that Ornette's mother died. At the end of the year he gathered his original New York quartet (Cherry, Haden, Higgins) together to record an album of new songs; that collection remains unissued. As for the two Haden duet projects of the year, the first collection, *Closeness*, has Ornette playing Haden's tune "O.C." on alto, and particularly in the last third of the track the wonderful closeness of feeling between the two is evident—Ornette's lines are especially delightful. Ornette's first solo in "O.C." also demonstrates how much Ornette's original conception had changed, for much of it is in sequences, a rather static way of improvising, whereas Haden's solo recalls the early Ornette by instead playing motivic variations, with his phrases changing shape as they move in changing keys. In *The Golden Number* Ornette plays trumpet in Haden's lovely title ballad, and once again blurred sound and imprecision of pitch enhances the freshness of emotion in his lines; on the same disc Haden and pianist Hampton Hawes play Ornette's "Turnaround" as a medium-slow bebop blues.

This led to an album of duets by Haden and Ornette that features more ballads than is customary from Ornette, from the weepy TV theme "Mary Hartman, Mary Hartman" to his melodic variations in "Sex Spy," with its two suddenly happy finishing notes in the theme, and "Some Day." The latter has him playing trumpet; the rest of the *Soapsuds, Soapsuds* LP features him playing tenor saxophone for the first time since 1961 and almost for the last time on record. Far from the heavy, more traditional tenor sound of

Ornette on Tenor, this 1977 LP has him playing largely in the alto ranges of his horn and achieving an altolike sound—even more than classic-period Lester Young, Ornette here exemplifies the idea of playing the tenor sax as if it were an alto. He is especially melodically inventive in faster tempos here. This relaxed session is more of an intimate view of two great artists than a self-conscious performance. There had been a famous set of tenor-bass duets by Don Byas and Slam Stewart in 1945, when their pianist and drummer failed to show up, but this kind of exposed intimacy was rare in jazz before the post-Coleman generations. The Chicagoans, their St. Louis friends, and a number of European musicians in particular continued to develop this idiom of improvised chamber music, with few or no rhythm-section instruments, in solo, duet, or small-group combinations, to the extent that these jazz artists joined with musicians from classical, rock, and other musical backgrounds in regular improvised music festivals. Thus *Soapsuds, Soapsuds*, which might have created a sensation a decade earlier, was accepted as a fine but late-blooming result of the revolution Ornette had begun.

Soapsuds, Soapsuds was released by the new label Snyder began in 1977, named after Ornette's Prince Street loft, Artists House. Attempting to start a record company and at the same time manage Ornette's career was no easy task; Snyder had ten employees, and he estimates that all of them worked on Ornette's problems, which didn't really leave enough time and energy for the record business. Composing, not performing, was Ornette's priority. "He performed when he had to, and always for top dollar," Snyder recalls. "Because of the demands he would place on the promoter, he turned down a lot of work." Ornette was full of ideas, however. One was to publish a songbook; another was to rent Madison Square Garden, which would have cost thirty thousand dollars, and put on a concert there. One of his most interesting ideas was to compose a song that he titled "The Ball Song," which he intended to be performed, like "The Star-Spangled Banner," at sporting events— "they could sing it in front of every game, not just basketball but every game that had a ball. He had me send it to every singer there was, from Frank Sinatra on down. It was a totally weird song— there was no way Frank Sinatra was going to sing this song, but just like Ornette didn't judge, I suspended my judgment."

The new Ornette Coleman group was something of a problem. It had been comparatively easier to find musicians with whom to play in the fifties, for Ornette was growing out of bop then and Blackwell, Bradford, Higgins, Cherry, Haden, et al. were bop specialists by the times he'd met them; they only had to overcome conventional notions of chord changes and instead let their senses of melodic flow guide their playing with him. But Ornette's Free jazz–rock fusion band members came from more varied back-grounds, and had to learn not only how to keep up with his shifting tonalities, but also how to integrate their accustomed styles of play-ing into a new, synthetic kind of music. If Ornette's experiences in Joujouka were one inspiration for his new band, his own *Free Jazz* of 1960 was another. That gathering of separate voices, at best expanding separately and complementing each other in joined ideas—a unity of feeling, Ornette's "unison"—was an ideal toward which his fusion band aspired.

It may have also troubled Ornette that his new band's personnel was in flux, with Denardo, Ulmer, and McDaniel, for instance, in and out. Nineteen months after that band first recorded, it ap-peared in public for the first time, in a concert at the Newport in New York jazz festival. That concert offered three groups, starting with an Ornette Coleman octet that included Cherry, Higgins, and Blackwell, from his *Free Jazz* double quartet; Redman, Ulmer, and Izenzon from his later groups; and bassist Buster Williams subbing for the advertised Haden; the material was five new Ornette Cole-man songs, of which one featured each player soloing unaccompa-nied. There was an interlude during which Ulmer fronted a quartet for one song. To close the concert Ornette played alto, trumpet, violin, and bassoon with his Free fusion band, now a sextet named Prime Time: Nix and Ellerbee, guitars; Denardo and Shannon Jackson, drums; and electric bassist Albert McDowell. Their per-formance included a new setting of "What Reason Could I Give?" and the first public appearance of "Song X"; Artists House re-corded the entire concert. *Down Beat* reviewer Scott Albin noted that Ornette had admitted to having formed Prime Time "in order to make enough money to present symphonic performances of his large-scale works" and called the group's music "at best, good in small doses. . . . This very basic format fails to sustain interest for very long, because the r&b backdrop is too predictable, unchang-ing, and one-dimensional to match or enhance Coleman's varie-gated extended improvisations."[4]

In fact, it was in this period when Ornette's published interviews began including the frequent theme of his desire to make large amounts of money. He was living in apartments on or near the Bowery, in those days; some investments were going bad, Ornette was losing money, and in general, for an artist whose discoveries had largely inspired the evolution of his art form, his financial situation was preposterous. If he'd been a native European, of course, he would undoubtedly have been rich with honors, an acknowledged aristocrat. As an American he had to virtually produce performances of his classical works himself if they were to be performed at all. His alternatives were unappealing. He could have played a steady, exhausting round of nightclubs and concerts for a living, as he'd done in 1960. He could possibly have retreated into the academy, filling out grant applications and composing music to fulfill grant obligations. Or he could continue as he'd been doing, rehearsing Prime Time and hoping for the best.

There is no way that Ornette's band could have made much money for him in 1977, for that appearance at the Newport in New York festival was its only one in public all year. Ornette's own next public appearance was not until almost a year later, when he and Denardo played in duet on the south lawn of the White House in Washington, D.C. It was an afternoon when around three dozen jazz artists, with families, were guests of President Carter at a minifestival. The players covered nearly all eras of jazz and pre-jazz, from ragtime pianist Eubie Blake and vocalist Katherine Handy Lewis, daughter of W. C. Handy, to the Colemans and Cecil Taylor; Charles Mingus, devastated by his final illness, watched the proceedings from a wheelchair. Ornette and Denardo were allotted only five minutes for their duet, but six days later they stretched out with the Ornette Coleman Septet at Carnegie Hall for the 1978 Newport Jazz Festival. This time Ornette used two bassists, Haden on amplified bass and McDaniel, who by now had changed his name to Jamaaladeen Tacuma, on electric bass. The band's performance was well received; what was offensive was the behavior of Carnegie Hall's stagehands and sound technicians, who insulted the musicians, distorted the band's sound for the audience, and stiffed Ornette $250 for the privilege of recording the concert for his own use. "The sound for amplified music at Carnegie Hall is hideous," wrote *Down Beat*'s Chip Stern. "It is an insult and a disgrace that an artist of Ornette's gentility and stature had to endure such racist insensitivity. . . . The crowd had wanted more

music, but the stagehands threatened Ornette with staggering over-
time if he went one second past 2:30. . . . The operation insults
audiences and musicians alike."[5]

Ornette, who charged fabulous amounts of money for his services, was continuing to live in run-down locations; for half a year
he stayed in a hotel. John Snyder told him, "You should have a
place where you can come and work," and set aside a room in the
Artists House Records offices where Ornette could compose and
take care of business. Ornette not only used the room for work—he
moved in. He had to take sponge baths, because the offices had no
hot water or showers. His art collection, hung from the record
company's walls, made the Artists House headquarters a major art
gallery, says Snyder, who used paintings from Ornette's collection
on the jackets of the *Body Meta* and *Soapsuds, Soapsuds* albums.

> I'd go down to work, and he'd come in my office and sit there and
> tell me the troubles of the world for a couple hours, and by the time
> noon came I was ready to go home and go to bed. Although it was
> always enlightening, it was always depressing. Ornette is not a sim-
> ple person, so when you're discussing any matters, the matters are
> always put into a much bigger context—a cosmic context. . . . I
> always found that Ornette was so ahead that the things he knew
> about, that he took me to see, always a few years afterwards would
> come into more popular use, or presence.

For instance, Ornette predicted to Snyder the present-day popularity of African popular music in America. Said Snyder, "He was
always ahead like that, in the sense of picking up on what was going
to be coming next in pop culture. . . . That's because he was ubiq-
uitous on the SoHo arts scene."

Ornette loaned Snyder money to keep Artists House Records in
business, once as much as twenty-five thousand dollars; at other
times Snyder loaned Ornette large sums, and in the end Snyder
reckons that Ornette had borrowed the most. Artists House had a
unique setup whereby instead of owning its recording sessions, as
is customary, it leased from its artists the rights to issue recordings
of their own material. Among those in the company's stable were
several who had worked with Snyder at A&M/Horizon, plus James
"Blood" Ulmer and Art Pepper; in fact, Ulmer cut his very first
album for Artists House, and Pepper himself made an important

LP. Knowing that Snyder and his employees were amateur musicians of various levels of proficiency, Ornette organized them into a band and instructed them in harmolodics, maintaining, wrote Snyder, that

> "if I can teach you guys how to do this, I can teach anybody how to do it." . . . This was not his way of making a "put down." He was serious. He wants to develop the technique of communicating his ideas so that the student will then be encouraged to communicate the *student*'s ideas. . . . [Ornette] believes in the "healing" power of music and that there are as many ways of making music as there are people. He objects to the idea that there are mutually exclusive ways of going about it (e.g., the "jazz" and "classical" traditions, to name two). This objection manifests itself in his "harmolodic" theory, which is his structure for people to express their emotions and *themselves* through music.[6]

Indeed, Ornette was aware that he had become a teacher, and an important one. The most lasting kind of education is less an education in facts and information than in basic ways of thinking. No one who has studied with Ornette has been able to summarize his harmolodic system or describe more of it than the blind men who tried to describe the fabled elephant; virtually all of his students, however, have been changed by his musical beliefs. There had been his original musicians in Los Angeles, and there had been John Coltrane; he'd taught Leroy Jenkins and Anthony Braxton and James "Blood" Ulmer while they had been living with him; he was teaching his young musicians in his new group, and for recreation he taught the Artists House band. One day as they rehearsed, Ornette stood in front of Snyder, playing trumpet, and after awhile stopped him: "I can see what you're doing, but you're just guessing at it. Try using the interval between G and B." Wrote Snyder,

> Friends, I'm telling you, it was like someone gave me the key to a locked door. It worked! Whereas before, I was skating, outside of the music, now I was *inside* the music. . . . And as soon as I had gotten that, Ornette said, "Now don't do that anymore, do something *like* that." . . . You don't use language to repeat yourself. Ornette doesn't want you to remember what you want to say.[7]

Ornette himself says, "I hadn't gotten into teaching because I didn't want to turn out lots of Ornette Colemans. But I did want someone to know what I knew."[8] His objective, then, was to encourage others to discover the unique musics within themselves. For instance, in 1978, he says,

> I was out at Margaret Mead's school, and was teaching some little kids how to play instantly. I asked the question "How many kids would like to play music and have fun?" And all the little kids raised up their hands. And I asked, "Well, how do you do that?" And one little girl said, "You just apply your feelings to sound." And I said come and show me. When she went to the piano to do it she tried to show me, but she had forgotten about what she said. So I tried to show her why all of a sudden her attention span had to go to another level, and after that she went ahead and did it. But she was right—if you apply your feelings to sound, regardless of what instrument you have, you'll probably make good music.[9]

He'd also had the formal experiences of lecturing in colleges and teaching at a Creative Music Studio seminar; by the eighties he was willing to take on a handful of private students. The sparkling Danish guitarist-composer Pierre Dorge had already made valuable recordings with John Tchicai and his own New Jungle Orchestra when he came to America in 1980 and studied briefly with Ornette. Dorge says that Ornette gave him some lessons and

> some philosophy about the music. I brought my guitar to his loft, then I played for him and he gave me some ideas to how I could improvise, and wrote some theoretical things down from his harmolodic system. But I think his system is not really a system or theory, it's more a collection of ideas that you can work on and use in your music. It's not so precise—the idea of the equality of melody, harmony, and rhythm, and that every instrument should play all of these things . . . the theory is more a kind of feeling, something you think about before you play.

Dorge's composition "254, Bowery," a twelve-tone blues, is in honor of Ornette Coleman, named for the address, across the street from Ornette's loft, where they'd first met.

Many people over the years have spoken of Ornette's generosity. Snyder says,

> That's why he made lots of money and never had it. Ornette's the kind of person who would see a derelict on the street, and take him

home, clean him up, and let him sleep in his bed. He did that—Ornette was telling me the story. He said the guy stayed there two months, and he said, "It was weird—I didn't know what to do." Finally one day the guy got out of bed and said, "I'm going to Brooklyn, now," and that was it—he walked out, never said good-bye, never said thank you. Ornette said, "I was cleaning up after he left, and all under the bed it was full of liquor bottles." He's a humanitarian—he'll give his money away, and people are hitting on him all the time, and he'll give them money—thousands of dollars.

The Ornette Coleman Sextet, which used one bassist, Fred Williams (playing electric bass), and, in place of Ellerbee, Ulmer, took a European tour that Snyder says "turned out to be an absolute disaster. Ornette works on instinct. If you instinctively trust somebody who then screws you, what good is your instinct?"

The promoter, who screwed a lot of people, including Gil Evans, she gave me a check for ten grand—I was collecting the money after each gig and saving it for Ornette—she skipped out the last two nights, and gave me a bad check. . . . The tour was fraught with problems, not the least of which, the band was superloud, and we emptied more halls than anyone on the circuit that year. I sat in the halls and listened, and it was almost intolerable. But Ornette was never concerned about that.

The first document to show how Ornette's Free fusion music had evolved since 1975 was not by his own group, but by Ulmer, using the pseudonym James Blood; it was the Artists House LP *Tales of Captain Black*, and the three sidemen in the quartet were from Ornette's band (indeed, it was Ornette who encouraged Ulmer to record the album). Perhaps the now-uncluttered textures and the new space for solos by guitar and Ornette on alto are misleading, but this LP sounds like a genuine advance. Once again Tacuma's bass lines are melodic and decorative rather than propulsive, so the essential rhythm section is contained within Denardo's largely paradelike rhythms, including bass-drum emphases on every strong beat. Amid the group's wood, metal, and electricity textures, Ornette's alto-sax sound is wonderfully warm, and each of his solos includes striking melodic playing—his plunging cries in "Revelation March" are especially vivid. Perhaps it is Ulmer that brings out the rich blues cry in Ornette here, for the guitarist is the foreground soloist and his lines are built on blues phrasing—his "Arena" solo, for instance, could with only a slight rearrangement of modulations and phrase locations fit perfectly within the Chicago blues-band idiom.

In March 1979 Ornette brought Prime Time—that's what he was consistently calling his band by then—into RCA's New York recording studios to make a direct-to-disc album, but mechanical problems with the recording apparatus made the session a waste of time and energy. In April Ornette brought Prime Time to play on one of the most popular television programs in America, *Saturday Night Live*, a weekly broadcast of Second City–style comedy sketches. Ornette's manager by then was Kunle Mwanga, a friend since the days of 131 Prince Street; Mwanga had managed Anthony Braxton, the Art Ensemble of Chicago, and David Murray, and would go on to manage other forward-looking jazz artists, including Edward Blackwell, in years to come. Ornette now wanted to set up his own record company, Phrase Text, named after his music-publishing company; the failed direct-to-disc session was a Phrase Text project, and Mwanga set up a Phrase Text session at CBS Studios, with nineteen-year-old Calvin Weston replacing Ronald Shannon Jackson as Denardo's drum partner. It was the first time an American label had recorded a digital album in New York City, and it made front-page news in *Billboard*. This session went off without any technical difficulties, and only a few weeks later Mwanga was in Japan completing arrangements to issue the album on the Phrase Text label, by Trio Records, whose previous jazz albums included a collection of Ornette Coleman performances in Paris in 1966 and 1971. While in Japan, Mwanga also arranged for Ornette to perform *Skies of America* with the NHK Symphony Orchestra, Japan's equivalent of the BBC Symphony and French National Radio-Television orchestras. In fact, Mwanga had delivered the record stamper to Trio, and production was ready to begin on the album, but "when I came back from Japan," says Mwanga, "Ornette canceled the agreements." With that, Mwanga resigned; he had worked for Ornette only about four months.

The Phrase Text date was at first titled *Fashion Faces*, and was later issued by the Antilles label as *Of Human Feelings*. Somewhat surprisingly, the album offers essentially no new insights. Without Shannon Jackson's ingenuity for extracting drum patterns from Ornette's melodic phrases, the music is now less distinctive. The drummers continue to accent strong beats and play marching-drum patterns. The two guitars remain background instruments while Ornette's alto solos and Tacuma's very busy electric bass responses are the foreground; if anything, Tacuma is more virtuosic than before, with nonstop lines virtually always in his highest ranges. Of Ornette's songs here, "What Is the Name of That Song?" is a particularly witty melody.

While Ornette himself was wholly committed to Prime Time's medium, there was a band committed to exploring his mainstream jazz innovations: Old And New Dreams, made up of Cherry, Redman, Haden, and Blackwell. This quartet in a sense had its beginnings in an early-1970s Coleman-like quartet date by Charles Brackeen, *Rhythm X*, with tenor saxophonist Brackeen in place of Redman. The first Old And New Dreams album appeared in 1976. Like the members of the Modern Jazz Quartet and the Art Ensemble of Chicago, the Old And New Dreams four pursued separate careers, joining on occasion to tour and record as a cooperative unit to which each player contributed music. Ornette's themes provided a large part of Old And New Dreams' repertoire, as well: It recorded previously undocumented Coleman songs—"Handwoven," "Open or Close," "New Dream"—and treated his standards such as "Lonely Woman" and "Broken Shadows" as dramatic showpieces. Each of these players had also been involved in musics of Africa, Asia, and Latin America, and contributed material reflecting these nonjazz musics. Of the quartet's early albums, the most remarkable is the third, *Playing*, a concert from 1980—it was one of those special occasions when musicians were at the peak of creativity both as individuals and as ensemble players, and the performances of Ornette's "Happy House" and "New Dream" reveal wonderfully close empathy. Six years after playing regularly in Ornette's groups, Redman had abandoned much of the expressive character of his earlier work for a "cleaner" sound and a less blues-driven choice of notes; if his concept of developing a musical line remains Ornette-like, he is not an Ornette surrogate. Incidentally, for those who harrumph at Haden's frequent titling of his compositions after his social-political concerns, Ornette once wrote, "Charlie Haden's music has its roots in Viva la humans. It is not Capitalistic, Communistic or Socialistic. His music does not dictate. . . . Charlie's music brings one stranger to another and they laugh, cry and help each other to stay happy."[10]

One of the most important contributors to Ornette's music—David Izenzon—died in 1979 of a heart attack while chasing a car thief. He'd stuck with Ornette through thick and thin from 1961 to 1968, and played in some of Ornette's 1970s engagements, too. He'd also worked with Archie Shepp, Sonny Rollins, and Mose Allison, and in 1969 led a band of ten bassists (including Jimmy Garrison, Dave Holland, Steve Swallow, and Buster Williams) and a drummer. After 1971, when Izenzon's son Solomon was born with severe brain damage, he spent much of his time caring for the boy, and dedicated his 1975 jazz opera *How Music Can Save the World* to the volunteers who had helped him. Izenzon also received a Ph.D. in psychotherapy and had a private practice in the 1970s; the year before his death he became one of the early members of Pot Smokers Anonymous.

The deaths of Louis Armstrong in 1971 and Kid Ory in 1973 were milestones in jazz. Up to their final illnesses there had been musicians from all eras of jazz history playing for live audiences. After the passing of these last two important figures from New Orleans's earliest, greatest generations—jazz's last living links to its origins—the deaths of Duke Ellington and Harry Carney in 1974 dramatized the declining number of important swing players. As for jazz's lost generations of the 1940s and 1950s, the toll had been steady and fearful; jazz, it was clear, was mortal. For younger jazz audiences, it became steadily more difficult to experience the jazz tradition from its primary players.

Fusion music in general was almost played out as an innovative force by the end of the 1970s. Most of the main figures in fusion music had been associates of Miles Davis in his 1968–1969 experiments, and had made their major impact shortly after leaving Davis, at the beginning of the decade; Davis himself had been in retirement since 1975. In general, the most popular kinds of fusion music were linked to the ECM Records style, itself a development of the 1950s Davis–Gil Evans collaborations: Typically, some players in the group play mobile lines while others are static, in long, held chords and repeated subsidiary rhythm section motions; blue notes are replaced by consonant, pastoral harmonies, and the harmonic structures are either modal or else built on cadences. Certainly Ornette's Free fusion music was the most vivid fusion development, with his free approach to harmony and lack of mood setting or programmatic content, and Prime Time's ongoing high activity.

As for the main lines of jazz development, they continued to descend from Ornette's innovations of the late 1950s. The inspirations of Coltrane and Ayler continued long after their deaths. The most prominent artists who developed Free jazz in the 1970s included Keith Jarrett, in his solo piano phase, when he improvised both inside and outside fixed harmonic structures, the St. Louisans and Californians who formed the World and ROVA Saxophone Quartets, the Chicagoans, and the Europeans. Anthony Braxton continued exploring on many saxophones and clarinets, from solo and free-improvisation works to quartets to an important blending of composition and improvisation in his *Creative Orchestra Music 1976*. The individual members of the Art Ensemble of Chicago continued to pursue separate careers, most remarkably Roscoe Mitchell, whose albums *Nonaah* and *L-R-G/The Maze/SII Examples* were landmarks of both third-stream music and unrestrained improvisation. Muhal Richard Abrams led both big bands and a highly influential sextet. One of his sextet members, Henry Threadgill, formed the trio Air to play, first, Scott Joplin rags, and then his own remarkable compositions. Violinist-composer Leroy Jenkins, with the Revolutionary Ensemble, and trumpeter Leo Smith had been important in introducing New York to the Chicagoans' new ideas of forms and sounds; by the end of the decade most of the Chicago pioneers had left home, more often than not to settle in New York. Some of the best post–Ornette Coleman musicians taught in the more enlightened colleges, universities, conservatories, and high school programs across the nation, from John Carter (who abandoned his saxophones to concentrate on clarinet and composing) and the wonderfully melodic trumpeter Bobby Bradford in Los Angeles to George Russell, Jimmy Giuffre, and pianist Ran Blake in Boston.

The first generations of "outside" European jazz artists made impressive advances in the 1970s. Among them were the theatrical Dutch, including the opera buffa Willem Breuker Kollektief; the volatile South African exiles, including bassist Johnny Dyani (whose valuable *Song for Biko* quartet included an inspired Don Cherry); the intense East and West Germans, including trombonists Gunther Christmann and Conrad Bauer and drummers Gunther Sommer and Paul Lovens; and the freely improvising British, among them saxophonists Trevor Watt and Evan Parker, trombonist Paul Rutherford, guitarist Derek Bailey, bassist Barry

Guy, and drummer Paul Lytton. In fact, free improvisation, which dispensed with not only fixed harmonic structures but also themes, fixed meter, and fixed tempo, attracted players from all nationalities. Evan Parker and American expatriate Steve Lacy both worked prolifically in this medium, and were among the major post-Ayler saxophone innovators.

Besides Ornette, a few others such as Jarrett, the Art Ensemble, and Braxton toured the major concert-hall and festival circuit in America, Europe, and Japan, seldom playing in nightclubs. The majority of Free jazz artists played in smaller concert venues, and following the example of Ornette's Artists House, jazz lofts and storefront music spaces appeared in New York; throughout the rest of America small concert locations and college venues were where Free jazz was played. Just as the bop era replaced ballrooms with nightclubs as the primary jazz venues, the Ornette Coleman era made concert rooms the primary jazz venues.

The vengeful national mood that had begun the decade had not abated by the end. With school integration enforced by law, an antitax revolt had advanced in many areas around America, directed specifically against funding public schools—music-education programs in particular had been cut as a result. Homeless people began to appear in large numbers in American cities, large and small; it was an antiprogressive time during which Free jazz struggled and grew. Jazz audiences in general diminished, and the "outside" players felt the economic pinch. One healthy phenomenon that had grown progressively in import since it had begun in the sixties was the support for artistic endeavors by state and local arts councils and the National Endowment for the Arts. Jazz artists were included among those supported, and "outside" musicians received composition and performance grants, too.

By the 1980s Ornette was deliberately "more or less trying to place what I've found and done in the mass public. . . . I mean, I really think of it as playing at the Madison Square Garden instead of the Vanguard." The most popular rock acts had played the Garden. Was it reasonable to expect that a jazz artist could achieve such popularity? Ornette seemed to think so:

When I was in Germany in 1965 and I was playing something just out of the blue, there was over twenty-one thousand people there and they started clapping and applauding. And it wasn't any big song I had written or any particular thing I was trying to design, and they got the same sensation the way that people are supposed to do something they already know—and I said, then it *can* be done.

The Berlin audience, then, had responded to some unfamiliar music. Ornette wanted to get millions of additional listeners to respond, too.

But how to go about getting such a massive response? If Ornette had steadily maintained, over a period of years, a busy schedule of performing and recording like Miles Davis, John Coltrane, and very few other modern-jazz performers, he may have become wealthy like them (and then again, he may not). His stated aim, however, was to become far more popularly successful than them, despite lacking two essential elements for becoming a fabulous entertainment commodity—he was not a vocalist, and his musical ideas were not trivial. Since producing trivial art requires time, energy, and concentrated attention, just like producing valuable acts of communication, we can sympathize with Ornette's choice of the latter. Certainly a desire for great fame and fortune is harmless enough, provided we don't gamble all our resources on the lottery.

Did playing trivial music at all tempt him? "There is a music that satisfies the physical and sexual instincts . . . and they'll ask the performer: 'Let's see you go out there and move the people like that.' . . . There must be some music that doesn't have the problem of sex. It's true that the American music, the real million-sellers, is a sex music. I didn't have in my mind, 'I'm gonna write *Skies of America* and everybody gonna start screwing.' "[11]Ornette "always wanted" to be part of popular culture, "but I didn't want to sacrifice what I was doing to get there."[12]

By the 1980s, after three decades of playing jazz, Ornette was being accepted as one of the art form's elder statesmen. As a consequence, he began to show up in, for him, rather unique places: He went to a political rally for the Carter-Mondale presidential campaign, along with nearly four dozen other distinguished jazz artists from Jabbo Smith and Sonny Greer to Sam Rivers and Elvin Jones. He attended a ceremony at which a block of New York's Fifty-second Street was renamed Swing Street and plaques honoring leading jazz artists were installed in the sidewalk. During Ornette's early days in New York, his clothes attracted attention, and his first quartet had performed in waistcoats that he had designed himself. From "extravagantly colored suits" that he wore while performing in the 1970s, Ornette went on to clothe Prime Time in suits that were "unabashedly *show biz*. His outrageously neon suits became a trade mark . . . ," according to McRae.[13] John Snyder described a suit that Ornette wore for a concert "that looked like an out of focus color TV test pattern: the color hues were not aligned but they tended to be, so your eyes had difficulty focusing. It was a true performance suit, if not a performing suit."[14] In a *Village Voice* article devoted to Ornette's performing attire, he said that "the clothes make the performer feel stronger before he even gets to the stage. The clothes enlighten the person to feel good. And with the playing and the music, they both have this good positive effect on people."[15] In other words, he dresses colorfully because he and his audiences enjoy it.

The now largely forgotten Peter Frampton was one of several modestly successful rock-music performers who suddenly, in 1976, the year of a massive, unprecedented record-sales explosion, had albums that sold six, ten, and twelve million copies each. "I was telling someone I wish I had a manager like Dee Anthony—look what he did for Peter Frampton," Ornette said. "And the guy said, yeah, but Peter really worked very hard to get where he got, so they made a combination. I don't think there are only two people who have the capacity to do that."[16] In 1981 Ornette said, "I like John Snyder, I believe in his ideas. I worked with him for four years, and then woke up and realized I'd put too much of my time and trust in his philosophy, and we could no longer grow."[17] And Snyder felt that "our fortunes were so intertwined, it was not healthy. I had great respect for him—I loved him, and I would do what he wanted. He was never totally happy with the results I got for him, because I had one hand tied behind my back."

Ornette heard that Sid Bernstein was booking acts at Radio City Music Hall. In the early 1960s Bernstein had operated a well-known Hollywood nightclub, the Purple Onion, before moving to New York and booking jazz and popular-music events. His best-known success was bringing the Beatles to America for the first time, shortly after they'd become the most popular of sixties rock bands, to play at Shea Stadium, where the New York Mets played; Bernstein had also booked country-music shows at the Copacabana. Ornette had been attempting to shop the digital 1979 *Fashion Faces* recording session to several record companies without success, reportedly because of the prohibitively high price tag he had put on it, and he also wanted to present Prime Time with a laser light show at Radio City Music Hall. Sid Bernstein introduced his brother and partner Stan to Ornette, and the two had a serious conversation. Said Ornette,

> I was really turned off from the way he was—"Well, of course everybody knows you, but what does that mean? You're still not doing, you know, who do you think you are?" So, me not having that kind of ego to say, "Well, if you don't think I'm like this, I'm just going to walk out." Finally it dawned on me that the only thing that I was doing, again, was trusting what I wanted from a person, as opposed to trusting what they was trying to get me to do.
>
> So Stan, he never said anything different than what he wanted me to do. He said, "Well, you've done this, and this is wrong, and you have to do—I've *done* all of that—I sat here with tears in my eyes, I was just—I decided that the one thing that I wanted to do was not to be against myself.
>
> Being in New York City, I had met all of the people that I'm supposed to be trying to get approval—this doesn't make sense, that I know everybody and I can't get arrested. . . .
>
> What I really wanted was to find out how an American person had a value with the Establishment, what the Establishment represents, right? When I realized that I could not have that, no one knew how to do that for me, I realized I was coming off as some kind of racist problem, or whatever. I could go out and sell a tape and pay the rent, and then complain that no one ever paid me royalties. I didn't want to do that. I kept trying to figure out, how can I find a way to grow and not let the past be in my way?
>
> I realized that these two in this office was only interested in the job that they felt they could do for me. Stan said, "Don't do anything that you don't want to do—but please tell us *what* you're doing."[18]

In November 1980 Ornette made Sid Bernstein Associates his personal managers.

And now Ornette seemed to rediscover the delight of making music. He took Prime Time on another European tour, and he also brought the band to four concerts at the Public Theater in June 1981, their first New York appearance since 1978. He was also actively composing, and one of his projects was a composition that would include Cecil Taylor and Prime Time. Two other compositional projects were foremost in his mind in those days: the soundtrack music for a feature film, *Box Office*, and a symphonic work, *The Oldest Language*. Josef Bogdanovich produced *Box Office*, Michael Alston directed it, the cast included Eddie Constantine, Carol Cortne, Edie Adams, and Aldo Ray, and in the movie Cortne sang three songs by the fine songwriter-jazz pianist Freddie Redd. Ornette composed the soundtrack music during the winter of 1981 for a forty-piece orchestra, Prime Time, an opera singer, and a pop singer. "Basically, the film tells a very human story, about a young woman expressing a desire to be an individual; at the same time, there's the inner plight about the truly human condition of caste and quality of living," said Ornette. Said Bogdanovich, "The reason why Ornette and I have a good working relationship is that I think of him more as a classical musician."[19] *Box Office* appears to have had only a limited release, or perhaps none at all.

As for the symphony *The Oldest Language*, Ornette said, "I'm going to try to get two guys from each state of America to make up the orchestra and about twelve or twenty musicians from around outside of America that play nontempered instruments. I'm writing their [the nontempered instrumentalists'] parts in color." Would these nontempered instrument players include, perhaps, musicians from Joujouka?

> I would like to have a few of those. I would like to have some Siamese musicians, Russian, Jewish, Arabs, Africans, Chinese—as many different varieties of nontempered instruments, and playing with tempered instruments, you know—saxophones, violas, bassoons, clarinet, trumpet, French horn. . . .
>
> What I'd like to do with this piece of music is to try and get in touch with what brought music to people to know what they were playing—I mean, undoubtedly real music, whatever real music was or whatever it is, played a different role than the role it's playing now. And I want to find out how close I can get to that role, which undoubtedly must have something to do with the healing and preservation of the person's emotion that would make them feel more creative . . . whether they play or not. To stimulate the audience [so that] whatever you do, you would leave there inspired on a much more pure level about yourself.

The 1981 tours by Ornette and Prime Time continued into 1982, including, in May, a benefit for the National Urban League held at Constitution Hall in Washington, D.C. There, after Prime Time

played a set, Ornette returned to the stage with pianist McCoy
Tyner and altoist Arthur Blythe—a skillful, prolific musician,
Blythe had recently become a popular attraction—and the trio of
two altoists and pianist played Ornette's song "Straight Line and a
Circle." Heavy touring, however, was taking a toll on Ornette. One
of the ongoing problems was Prime Time's extremely loud volume
levels, which Ornette apparently regarded as a problem of balance:
"That problem is coming from the fact that everywhere I've been,
the engineers have been so virgin in this particular music that when
they start mixing the sound in the house and the sound in the dance
band, they get confused. . . . They don't have any idea of how the
dynamics are going. If I get soft, they turn someone else down or
someone else up. . . . And if you don't have time for a sound check,
you just get destroyed."[20] As for the physical effects of playing
one-nighters, Ornette said,

> I'm very tired right now from getting up at six o'clock in the morning
> to play to two in the evening. I was telling the agent that he has to,
> I have to at least get in town one day. I have to change my sched-
> ule—I thought slavery was over, at my age, especially. I don't get
> excited about getting up this early as I used to, because I feel too
> tired.[21]

Worst of all, in a sense, touring didn't leave much time to compose:

> I really consider myself a composer that performs. . . . But usually
> what I try to do is constantly stay in the state I was in when I wasn't
> performing, when I was writing, always picking up where I left off.
> Like, I know exactly where I am right now in the compositional
> concept of what I write, but I haven't spent my time trying to do
> that.[22]

The responsibility of leading Prime Time weighed on Ornette,
too, "because I need to support them as well as they need to support
me."[23] Most had grown up, from late teenage years, playing music
with him; in fact, most of Prime Time lived with him and ate at his
table, and inevitably imbibed much of his viewpoint and his phi-
losophies. Ornette paid them well; in return, they continually made
themselves available for his musical projects. Sun Ra has said, "I
tell my Arkestra that all humanity is in some kind of restricted

limitation, but they're in the Ra jail, and it's the best in the world."[24] John Snyder says, "That's the God's honest truth. There's a psychological jail as well as a musical. Now, it's a musical jail that maybe has a lot of advantages to it, but it's very much 'I'm the boss, you do what I say.' " While Ornette is hardly like Sun Ra in his attitudes or operations, "the result is the same. The musicians were always with [Ornette] and at his call. Their lives revolved around him. He was always very solicitous of his musicians, and he treated them as a great teacher, a loving, kind teacher, would treat a student. It was a very deep relationship."

Ornette's electric Free fusion music definitely inspired others in the 1980s: Altoist Oliver Lake formed Jump Up, a jazz-reggae group; Roscoe Mitchell and some former students formed his Sound Ensemble, which moved from Free jazz to jazz-rock; and a New York fusion band, James Chance and the Contortions, included the excellent, liberated saxophonist Henry Threadgill. More in Ornette's direct line of succession were the Free fusion groups led by James "Blood" Ulmer and Ronald Shannon Jackson. Jackson was proving a prolific, colorful composer, and especially his earliest records with his Decoding Society combined free improvising over multiple rhythm patterns, with the objective of joining lines and rhythms from many cultures and idioms—his principles, in fact, were quite like Ornette's own. And Jamaaladeen Tacuma, Ornette's antic bassist, would soon develop his own conception of Free fusion and begin leading recording sessions; in time Albert McDowell, Prime Time's other bassist throughout most of the eighties, would do likewise.

VII

On Rivington Street, in a dark, bleak, decaying neighborhood on the Lower East Side of Manhattan, stood an abandoned New York City school building. When the building was put up for public auction, Ornette purchased it, and moved in in 1982. He took over a classroom on the top floor for his living quarters; as usual, he traveled light, and his furniture, art collection, and possessions did not fill his classroom-apartment. He also set aside another room in the school as a rehearsal space for Prime Time. It was an old, cold building with very high ceilings, and though the water in the rest rooms ran, at least, it lacked heat. Ornette installed large warm-air units, suspended from the ceiling, to keep the winter's chill off in part of the building. As for the rest of the structure, he nursed a dream: to make it into an "art embassy" for international musicians and others—what he called "a multi-expression center, which involves space, artists, dramatics, and science."[1] Denardo, too, was enthusiastic about the building's possibilities, mentioning a music school, art galleries, and performances. But he also pointed out, "This is a dangerous area. At one point it was known as the most heavily drug-trafficked area on the Lower East Side. You always have people who are going to mug you, or rob you, or take your money or anything—a lot of junkies, a lot of poor people, also." Until the building could be developed, Denardo worried about his father's being there: "He's not necessarily going to stay here or live here, but just being in this area will be dangerous."[2]

Denardo said this after the attacks on his father. In September 1982 two teenagers looking for property to steal broke into the building while Ornette was there. They tied him up and hit him on the head with a hammer—"which they didn't have to do, but they were scared, and they were trying to take his equipment, take his money," said Denardo. "Someone saw them on the way out, and they had to drop everything, but they got away." They'd left Ornette believing he was dead. Still tied up, he managed to crawl across the floor and telephone Denardo at about seven o'clock in the morning. Denardo called the police, and his father was taken to the hospital with a concussion.

Around six months later Ornette needed to move some heavy sound equipment up the five flights of stairs to his classroom-apartment, and hired two neighborhood teenagers to help him. After they were done, Ornette went out for the evening. He and Denardo returned together, and as they were climbing the stairs in the dark the same teenagers, who had broken in, attacked them. One boy hit Ornette with a crowbar; Denardo managed to grab another and hit him with a board that had been lying nearby. Ornette was taken to a hospital and released the same evening. "But during the next day he had a lot of trouble breathing," Denardo said. Back in the hospital, it was discovered that the crowbar attack had punctured one of Ornette's lungs; he could not play for the next six months—"and all because he was just trying to do his work here in this building, where he could be peaceful, and people wouldn't have to bother him and he wouldn't have to bother other people. . . ."[3]

Meanwhile, the high hopes with which he had begun his relationship with Sid Bernstein Associates had turned sour. They had at last sold his 1979 digital album to Island Records "for less money than it had cost me to make it," according to Ornette, "and I never saw a penny of the royalties."[4] The twenty-five thousand dollars that Ornette was paid for the album was a high price for a jazz release. "The figure was based on what we realistically thought we could sell, not what it had cost Ornette to record the album," said Ron Goldstein, who ran Island's jazz label, Antilles.[5] Ornette was also given another twenty-five thousand dollars to record a follow-up album; the sum was to cover recording costs, and any money left over was Ornette's to keep. While recording the second Antilles album, then, Ornette went over budget; he asked for more money, was turned down, and as a result the recording project was never completed. Antilles did not pick up its option on Ornette, either, so the label released only the 1979 *Of Human Feelings.*

As an example of Ornette's other problems with his handlers, Ornette and Prime Time were booked to play a concert at the first University of Illinois-Chicago Jazz Festival. For this event they were paid six thousand dollars plus travel and lodging expenses—rather on the high end of the pay scale for a jazz group, but by no means in the rock-star range of fees. Either the booking agency or the Bernstein office or both told the festival's sponsors that Ornette was "distrustful" of presenters, "and had been known to cancel performances with very little notice." Indeed, the sponsoring committee's report to the university's financial department began, "Our experience with last-minute contract changes on the Ornette Coleman program placed in doubt whether Mr. Coleman would ultimately keep his appearance date with us." It proved to be not the Bernsteins or the booking agency but Denardo Coleman who cleared away the clutter of contract demands and logistical arrangements. When Prime Time arrived, the festival presenters found no evidence of Ornette's purported "mistrust"—on the contrary, says jazz department chairman Richard Wang, he and Prime Time were in "good spirits," and stretched out in what I recall was an exciting concert most notable for the fertile invention in Ornette's virtually nonstop alto lines.

Of course, that business about Ornette's "mistrust" and alleged history of canceling performances was hardly calculated to encourage concert presenters to engage Ornette Coleman and Prime Time. Were other music presenters in 1981–1982 confronted with similar obstacles, and was Denardo again called upon to take care of the band's business? Was something Ornette had said to the Bernsteins the source of some of the problems? "Nothing is simple for Ornette when it comes to money," Stan Bernstein has said. "He made demands that are unrealistic in this business unless you're Michael Jackson."[6] Clearly the Bernstein agency was not about to turn Ornette into a sudden, fabulous star, and the relationship between it and Ornette came to an end at the end of 1982 amid a tangle of legal countercharges.

Along with the old schoolhouse and the rise and fall of Ornette's association with the Bernsteins, Ornette was contending with the Internal Revenue Service. There had been a time, when he was still associated with Artists House Records, that he had not filed income-tax returns for two years, and now the IRS was demanding money: "They hated him, they wanted him. They were very vicious," according to John Snyder. After Artists House had run out of money, Snyder was broke; his wife had moved to North Carolina, and Snyder hung on for a year in New York before joining her. There a gun-toting tax investigator visited him to ask about Ornette's finances. IRS investigators also questioned John's brother Ray Snyder, who had also been a friend of Ornette's as well as president of the company. It happened that John Snyder had kept meticulous books about his financial dealings with Ornette. "They subpoenaed all my stuff and ended up calling me in front of the grand jury to talk about Ornette's finances," he says. The problem was that the IRS thought that Ornette was trying to evade paying taxes: "Ornette was not trying to cheat anybody. He wouldn't know how—it's just beyond him to think that way." After Ornette and Snyder went over the investigators' heads and talked with the federal prosecutor, the harassment ended and a settlement was worked out. There was no trial—"They saw he didn't cheat anybody—it's not because he kept money and spent it on himself. At the same time he's making $100,000 or $200,000 a year, he's living in my back office, taking sponge baths with cold water. I don't know where it all went—it didn't go for drugs, it didn't go for liquor, it didn't go for girls. It went for music, that's all I can say."

Ornette's life seemed to be a cycle of highs and lows, and it was fluctuating between ever more distant extremes by the early 1980s. Only intermittently during his career was he able to reconcile the humanity of his art with his viability as a commodity that competed with other commodities in arts-and-entertainment commerce. Ornette thought in grand terms. He gave or loaned large sums of money, he borrowed large sums, he conceived of vast projects, and he sought outlandish popular success. Despair—at being misunderstood, at the lack of opportunity to fulfill the creative projects that were his calling, at his endlessly boom-or-bust physical circumstances—would suddenly rise to extravagant hopes and plans; the crushing of those hopes and plans would lead to deeper despair. At this low point Ornette made a decision and was forming a new relationship, both of which would revive his spirits and change his life. The decision was to make Denardo his manager; Denardo was practical, businesslike, efficient, and most of all he could be trusted to look out for Ornette's best interests.

As for the new relationship—in downtown Fort Worth, Texas, a major project was taking shape. It was a three-story performance center that would include a 400-seat nightclub-restaurant, a 212-seat theater that would double as a recording studio (with 24-track digital equipment), a martial arts-dance studio, and atop the building a grotto bar and geodesic dome housing a collection of more than 300 species of rare cacti and succulents from the United States and Africa. The place was called Caravan of Dreams, after the final tale in *Arabian Nights*, about the poor cobbler Ma'aruf who dreamed of a caravan that was on its way to bring him great riches, and for whom, after a series of adventures, the dream came true, and he acquired a kingdom. The Caravan of Dreams cost $5.5 million to build; the money came from Ed Bass, the youngest of four brothers who, with their father, shared what was, at the time, the largest private fortune in the United States, estimated at $3 billion. The Bass family, heirs to Sid Richardson's oil wealth, were major figures both in Fort Worth cultural affairs and the development of the city's downtown, a place of gleaming, tall buildings that visitors view from the neon-lit dome of the Caravan of Dreams. Kathelin Hoffman, artistic director of the Caravan, wanted to stage a historic event for the opening of the performance center. Her friend John Rockwell, the music critic, played the *Skies of America* recording for her and pointed out that this would be an opportunity for Ornette, a native son who had been desperately anxious to leave Fort Worth in 1949, to make a glorious return. Hoffman, a playwright and drama producer—her Theater of All Possibilities had performed classic and original plays around the world—had made a good many contacts in creative circles. Two of them were writer William Burroughs and painter-writer Brian Gysin, whom she also contacted to appear at the Caravan of Dreams opening.

Hoffman also introduced Ornette to Buckminster Fuller, in France in 1982. Architect-mathematician-philosopher Fuller had for many years taught that humankind, faced with extinction on the one hand by war, probably nuclear, and on the other by suffocation in its own wastes, nevertheless had the capability to provide a full life, without hunger, for everyone on this highly populated planet.

Nationalism, racism, political ideologies stand in the way of human survival; replacing the internal-combustion engine is a prime necessity; yet human will, education, and technology, unencumbered by dogma, can provide. Fuller's was an optimistic vision, and his optimism is at least in part proving justified—witness the steady progress in the development of viable alternative energy sources in the 1990s. Ornette had heard Fuller lecture back in 1954, at Hollywood High School in California. When the two finally met, Fuller demonstrated for Ornette "his model of the tetrahedron, a geometric figure at the basis of the structural design of the universe. He manipulated the model, turned it inside out, made it dance—but the corners never touched. I said to myself, 'that's just like my music.' "[7] To Hoffman, Ornette said, "I've got to write some music for him."

For the Caravan of Dreams opening Ornette wanted to perform *Skies of America* with Prime Time and a symphony orchestra playing together. The Fort Worth Symphony was engaged; its conductor was John Giordano, another native son who in his own youth, in the 1950s, had played saxophone with Ornette in local jam sessions. Right away a problem with the music arose. There had been some confusion between Ornette and the original orchestrator of *Skies* that had led to an inaccurate transcription, and Ornette and Giordano had to do some corrective surgery. Ornette also worked on a new piece of music for string quartet plus drummer Denardo Coleman that was dedicated to Buckminster Fuller and titled *Prime Design*. Meanwhile, Hoffman wanted the opening of Caravan of Dreams documented on film, and since Shirley Clarke had already worked on her projected movie documentary about Ornette, beginning in the late 1960s, Clarke was the obvious choice to do the job. Ornette himself wanted his performances at the event to be professionally recorded. Since the Caravan of Dreams people were seriously thinking of forming a record company, too, Ornette's request "jump-started" their label, says Hoffman.

The mayor proclaimed Thursday, September 29, 1983, Ornette Coleman Day in Fort Worth and gave Ornette the key to the city. That night Ornette, Prime Time, and the Fort Worth Symphony, conducted by Giordano, performed *Skies of America* at the Tarrant County Convention Center. Reviewing the concert for *The New York Times*, John Rockwell noted that *Skies* had turned into a "rambling, 90-minute suite in which jazz ensemble passages and symphonic interludes mostly alternate." The 1972 recording "sounded more of a unity. . . . Now Mr. Coleman thinks of the two forces, jazz group and symphony orchestra, as dramatically opposed forces that attempt but fail to merge. But if the marriage must fail, why try to make art out of a doomed union? Still, the orchestral portions, full of grittily polytonal, hymnlike string chords and piercing brass writing, had a real personality, and the Prime Time sections sounded positively inspired."[8] That night, after the concert, the Caravan held a grand "black-tie or costume" party in the new building. On Friday and Saturday nights Ornette and Prime Time played two sets each at the nightclub. On Sunday afternoon the Gregory Gelman Ensemble, a string quartet from New York's Juilliard School of Music, and Denardo performed the world premiere of *Prime Design* at the Caravan.

The Ornette–Prime Time album recorded that weekend, *Opening the Caravan of Dreams*, offers the most enthusiastic of the band's albums. The guitarists, Nix and Ellerbee, are more prominent than previously; Tacuma and McDowell are the bassists, and Denardo and Sabir Kamal are now the drummers. "Compute" has bleeping, whirring electronic sounds in its intro and then fading in and out during the performance; the central section features Ornette's wild violin bowing in duet with Tacuma. "See-Thru" is a weepy torch-song theme played mostly as a ballad. The 1977 "Sex Spy" theme had concluded with two perfect notes that had mocked the rest of the melody while encapsulating Ornette's unique ironic whimsy; that marvelous finishing touch is absent in the revised version here, which is now built upon the Willie Dixon–Sam Lay bass-drums ostinato of Howling Wolf's 1961 "Shake for Me." As in the past, Prime Time again features heavy bass-drum accents on the first and third beats of each bar, and much of Ornette's soloing is in evenly spaced phrases and purely rhythmic figures.

Prime Design, issued on record as *Prime Design/Time Design*, begins with a long-noted theme intoned by each of the four string players (the opening notes recall Henry Mancini's song "Moon River"), after which the strings separate into four-part, pantonal counterpoint. Initially the strings are very busy, but via greater variety of texture and note values Denardo's drum accompaniment soon becomes the focus of the listener's attention. In passages where Denardo lays out, the listener realizes the music's momentum slows progressively, though never to any great degree—apart from the beginning and ending *Prime Design* is a ceaseless flow of musical line. Eventually Denardo and a violinist duet alone, and the conclusion is the strings playing a line in unison. Altogether the recording suggests a classical-music counterpart, consisting of angular melodic line with drum accompaniment, to the flux and interplay of improvised voices in the rhythm-rooted works of Prime Time. Writing in *The Wire*, critic Max Harrison wonders whether *Prime Design/Time Design* is an attempt

to mirror the flux of impressions that constantly bombards us? This rather than to select from it, to subject the chosen elements to a personal, and therefore arbitrary, order?

Does this staunchless flow of notes imply that art should not seek to organize the experience that life offers but just to absorb it all? Is one missing the point completely by suggesting that such encyclopaedic breadth is opposed to aesthetic value, and is merely a vain (in both senses) imitation of the world's immensity? . . . The image repeatedly suggested as one again and again plays this record of two violins, viola, and cello sawing away apparently without pattern, climax or relief is of a jigsaw puzzle in which *none* of the pieces fits together. Gertrude Stein's "clarity is of no importance because nobody listens" seems uncomfortably relevant, too. . . . Is *Prime Design/Time Design* a revolt, conscious or otherwise, against style, the concept which shapes so much of the talk about jazz and indeed other contemporary music? . . . Is the very directness of Coleman's non-stop assault on our nerves and emotions in this long piece an attempt . . . to evade completely the shaping influence of any style, even his own?

Harrison concludes with a quote from a Vaclav Havel play *The Garden Party:* " 'He who fusses over a mosquito net can never hope to dance with a goat.' That might serve as an epigraph for *Prime Design/Time Design.*"⁹

After the Caravan of Dreams opening, conductor Giordano began a major project: studying Ornette's "concepts of melody, counterpoint, and freedom of rhythm," and then completely re-orchestrating *Skies of America*, starting "with page one, working like a ghost writer on an autobiography, checking everything back with him. It's still Ornette's composition, though, in every sense. . . . As it was scored before, the piece literally irritated the symphony players. A violinist who's spent his whole life polishing the sort of tone you need to play Debussy doesn't necessarily like being told to scrape his $20,000 instrument with the wrong side of the bow."[10]

As for the Caravan of Dreams itself, it certainly became the major cultural center that had been intended. The Caravan's own troupe of actors presented original plays, and poetry readings and dance performances also were held in the theater. A wide range of blues and especially jazz and pop-jazz singers and players performed in the nightclub, among them Ellis, Wynton, and Branford Marsalis, the Art Ensemble of Chicago, saxophonists Dewey Redman, David Newman, James Clay, and Kirk Whalum, and pianists Ahmad Jamal and McCoy Tyner. Ornette maintained friendships with the Caravan crew, and wrote music that Prime Time performed for Kathelin Hoffman's play *Celestial Navigation*. This drama is the ancient Greek myth of Perseus and Medusa retold not only in mythological terms, but also as archaeological and personal history. Perseus, it seems, once actually lived in Mycenae, where he met Dionysius, the leader of a wandering troupe of actors, and built the first theater for them. "The music at the time was Dionysian," says Hoffman, and we can only wonder about what Dionysian music Ornette composed for the play. Ornette also became friends with John Allen, a.k.a. Johnny Dolphin, leader of the group that formed and operated Caravan of Dreams. Out of this friendship came a 1984 Ornette work for two trumpets, percussion, and strings titled *The Sacred Mind of Johnny Dolphin*.

One of the most remarkable performances that Ornette documented in the 1980s was his appearance as a sideman in Jamaaladeen Tacuma's rearrangement of "Dancing in Your Head" ("Theme from a Symphony," "The Good Life"). Tacuma's resetting offers underlying harmonies so distant that Ornette's alto now sounds emotionally isolated; over the chunky bass lines and funky electric-band sound there's great pain in the sax lines and strained tone, pain exacerbated when Charlie Ellerbee, after a passage of high sax squeaks and squeals, suddenly interpolates a reprise of the theme. The track ends with the raw cry of saxophone over electronic percussion; a once-happy song has now turned nearly desperate. "Dancing in Your Head" is in Tacuma's *Renaissance Man* album, which also features the Ornette-influenced altoist James R. Watkins and an extended composition, *The Battle of Images*, for string quartet and improvising electric bass and drums; far from Ornette-like complexity and angularity, this piece is centered around the movement of a single, direct melodic line and the improvisers' commentary—despite Tacuma's long importance to Prime Time, his sensibility is at heart dissimilar to Coleman's.

Despite the pain that informed this "Dancing in Your Head" solo, Ornette's fortunes were improving considerably. As his father's manager, Denardo Coleman proved astute and thorough in taking care of business, and Ornette seemed to be composing and performing as much as he wished. In mid-1985 the Hartford-based organization Real Art Ways presented an Ornette Coleman festival. This time, not only did the mayor present Ornette with the key to the city, but the governor also declared Ornette Coleman Week in Connecticut with a proclamation that stated, "Coleman changed the face of modern jazz through the development of harmolodic music. A contraction of harmony, movement, and melody, harmolodics carries the improvisational nature of jazz to the ultimate degree."[11] Prime Time played at midday in a downtown park; the film *Ornette: Made in America* was shown, in a preview; and three of Ornette's chamber works were performed: *Dedication to Poets and Writers, Time Design*, and *The Sacred Mind of Johnny Dolphin*. That fall the movie had its official East Coast premiere at the New York Film Festival.

At the end of 1985 came the recording with Pat Metheny, a collaboration that Charlie Haden had been urging on Ornette for years. Like Denardo, Metheny had been a musical prodigy; in his teens he'd joined Gary Burton's popular jazz groups, and he went on to become the most popular of fusion-music guitar virtuosos. He played a basically consonant, cadence-built, often decorative, sometimes ponderous music in pastoral harmonies, occasionally taking time for more straight-ahead jazz experiences, with artists such as Redman, Haden, Higgins, Sonny Rollins, Julius Hemphill, in which he occasionally played Ornette Coleman themes ("to me, you can sing them all, and they've got *hooks*"[12]). Ornette and Metheny rehearsed for three weeks, then recorded, joined by Haden, Denardo, and drummer Jack DeJohnette. On New Year's Eve, then, the group, minus DeJohnette, played at Caravan of Dreams, Ornette in purple cowboy hat and blue suit, using the group name Endangered Species.

The album was released as Pat Metheny/Ornette Coleman *Song X* in the spring of 1986, and the quintet went on tour. Their concert at Northwestern University, in Evanston, Illinois, was rewarding for the variety of combinations they offered, among other features. It began with a long, stunning electric drum solo by Denardo and included trios of soloist-bass-drums, quartets, duets by Ornette/ Metheny and Metheny/Denardo, as well as full quintet pieces. Quite the happiest surprise was the playing of Denardo Coleman, who previously had stayed largely in his father's shadow despite occasional appearances over the years in other contexts. (Those other contexts include several recordings accompanying his mother. Jayne Cortez, "the red pepper poet," had settled in New York and been enjoying a reputation as a vivid reader of her own poetry in the 1970s and 1980s.)

As for the album itself, the very fast title piece, which Ornette had played since at least 1977, is largely a wailing collective improvisation with nonstop, hyperactive guitar; a "Song X Duo" of alto and guitar is also included. "Kathelin Gray" is a ballad duet two choruses long and largely in alto-guitar unison; "Video Games" features excellent alto, and "Trigonometry," fine, complex guitar; "Endangered Species" has a frenzied, flapping, screaming theme and then wild collective improvisation, the alto largely in the background behind harsh guitar, and dense, powerfully propulsive drumming by Denardo, who also plays a melodic coda. Ornette's attractive melodic improvising throughout the album is free of the regular rhythmic shapes and emphases that characterize his Prime Time work. Metheny uses a guitar synthesizer that almost manages to simulate Ornette's saxophone sound—in some passages it is difficult to tell him and Ornette apart, or even to determine whether Ornette is playing—and his often hornlike lines develop motives in Ornette-like ways. Actually, Metheny had long had an affinity for playing in sequences, and the harmonic stringency in *Song X* is not new to him, either. What is new is that his phrases now sound quite like the slightly longer Ornette Coleman phrases, with similar modulations and responses to Haden's driving bass. The differences are rather subtle: Ornette conceives in strictly melodic lines and his phrases are full of blues, whereas Metheny does not naturally gravitate toward blue notes, despite his quick harmonic responsiveness and the pretty, bluesy chords with which he accompanies the sweet alto in "Mob Job," and often in the album he conceives of his role as that of an orchestrator, lending further variety to the album's textures and enhancing a sense that he's Ornette's alter ego here.

Ornette's next recording project, early in 1987, featured something his longtime admirers had long urged: a reunion of the original 1959 Ornette Coleman Quartet, on one LP of a two-LP set, titled *In All Languages*. The material is all new songs by Ornette, but, though the quartet's playing is quite fine, the performances are rather brief—in that, at least, the album is a disappointment. He plays tenor in "Feet Music," and there is great vitality in his "Word for Bird" alto improvisation. The quartet "In All Languages" has Ornette's vivid solo in several sections: a sequenced three-note lick over a bass ostinato, then fast lines, then a happy slow section, and he concludes in a slowed version of his opening sequences. The other LP in the set is by Prime Time, which also plays some of the same themes the quartet played. "Feet Music" has a shuffle rhythm added, and "Latin Genetics," which the quartet played as a calypso, now features an oompah rhythm. The album also includes an occasional added echo that, apart from detracting from the music's clarity, also adds an unwelcome portentous air to what is otherwise direct, straightforward playing—this problem is especially evident in the two versions of "Space Church (Continuous Services)." *Down Beat* reviewer Bill Shoemaker reaffirmed a primary value of Ornette's art when he wrote that "Track after track, the program brings home the point that Coleman's revolution was, and remains, a revolution of unrestricted melody."[13]

It would be the last Ornette Coleman recording released by the Caravan of Dreams label, though producer Kathelin Hoffman holds out hope that it may return in the 1990s. According to Ornette,

> The people in the Caravan, they're all artists in their own way. They're the kind of artists that are pure in their minds, they're not seeking publicity to be an artist. . . . I haven't had a major campaign to bring me to millions of people, like if I was Bruce Springsteen. Sound is all people hear in their ears, whether it's Bruce Springsteen or me. It's who's behind me that has to do with success. I'm not displeased at all with what Caravan has done for me and with me. It's just that they're not really trying to get behind me and make me millions of dollars. But I'm trying to get them to think that way.[14]

The possibility of Caravan of Dreams Records making millions of dollars on the sales of any album was unlikely indeed. This was a time when six major CD-tape-record distributors wholesaled more than 90 percent of the recordings sold in America. Regional independent distributors divided the rest of the recording sales, and these dedicated independents and the "small labels" that they peddle have for decades been the main force of the jazz recording business. Caravan of Dreams albums were distributed by a handful of independents who were in no way geared for the kind of fabulous sales that Ornette desired.

Moreover, Caravan of Dreams, despite its artistic success, has had an alarming undercurrent, described in recurring journalists' exposés, beginning in 1985 with the *Fort Worth Star-Telegram* and *Dallas Morning News*. Quite the longest chapter of historian Laurence Veysey's 1973 study *The Communal Experience*[15] describes the New Mexico commune out of which Caravan of Dreams eventually grew; he later described it as a "Jonestown-like" cult. (Ironically, William S. Burroughs, who, like Ornette, performed for the Caravan, once wrote an essay, "Sects and Death,"[16] telling how to form a cult. His description resembles Veysey's chapter, no doubt unknowingly.) Meanwhile, in the 1980s the Allen/Dolphin group was also building Biosphere 2, a project in the Arizona desert that would attempt to sustain eight people and four thousand species of plants and animals in an environment closed from the earth's atmosphere for two years. The project, which cost at least $150 million, was sealed off in the latter part of 1991; as I write in early 1992, the Associated Press and ABC-TV report that Biosphere 2 is already being charged with fraud and deception.

Between *Song X* and *In All Languages* Ornette sold the old school building on Rivington Street; a real estate speculator shelled out more than three million dollars for it. Nevertheless, considering Ornette's ongoing desire for "millions of dollars," his profits were not sufficient for the projects he had in mind. Nineteen eighty-seven continued to be a rewarding year for Ornette Coleman, in any case. After recording *In All Languages*, Prime Time went on tour; in Boston they were joined by the quartet, and the two groups together played an extended work by Ornette, *DNA Meets $E = MC^2$*. In New York, at Weill Hall (formerly Carnegie Recital Hall), oboist Joseph Celli presented a two-night retrospective of Ornette's works for chamber ensembles with soloists; the popular Kronos Quartet were among the performers. John Giordano's reorchestration of *Skies of America*, with Ornette and Prime Time added to a full symphony orchestra, was at last presented in Verona, Italy.

"I've tried to rewrite it in such a way that any orchestra can play it without resentment," said Giordano, "and with only minimal rehearsal, provided that they're conducted by someone completely in tune with Ornette's thinking. It seems to be working. The Verona orchestra plays nothing but Puccini and Verdi, and they loved it."[17] Also in Italy, the First International Conference on Jazz Studies, held at the University of Bologna, was devoted to the music and career of Ornette Coleman. Ornette had been in the *Down Beat* Hall of Fame since 1969; at the end of 1987 the magazine's readers voted him "Jazz Musician of the Year."

The next year Ornette, Prime Time, Giordano, and the Philharmonia Orchestra offered a London performance of *Skies of America*. Ornette also recorded his *Virgin Beauty* album, the stimulus for which had been, at least in part, a concert that he and Cecil Taylor had attended at Madison Square Garden, by the rock band The Grateful Dead. Ornette had been awed by the enthusiasm and dedication of the Dead's legions of fans: "They could have done anything up there and those people would have screamed. . . . I thought, 'Well, we could be friends here.' Because if these people here could be into this, they could dig what *we're* doing." Jerry Garcia, who stretches out in the Dead's guitar solos, joined Prime Time for three of *Virgin Beauty*'s songs; though he contributes some Django Reinhardt–like phrases to "Desert Players," he's primarily a third guitar voice in the improvising ensembles. "*Virgin Beauty* is Prime Time's best," reviewed Kevin Whitehead, who maintained that "Prime Time sounds more conservative but more focused. . . ."[18] Indeed, the nature of the group seemed to be changing. Some of the complex rhythmic excitement was now replaced by a no less infectious pop-music spirit, and Ornette's playing is for the most part especially lighthearted. "Bourgeois Boogie" hints at Charles Mingus's "Boogie Stop Shuffle"; the bubbly "Three Wishes" has a middle eastern theme over an exotic rhythm pattern; "Spelling the Alphabet" and "Happy Hour" offer clever Ornette; and the latter is a fast country music piece. Two tracks, "Virgin Beauty" and "Chanting," are ballads played by Ornette over darker-colored variations of ECM harmonies. Loveliest of these performances is the ballad "Unknown Artist," which begins with Ornette's alto, alone, in a sorrowing theme. *Virgin Beauty* is the most varied of Prime Time albums, and perhaps for that reason it sold more copies in the first year of its release than any of Ornette's other recordings.

Jamaaladeen Tacuma was absent from the disc, replaced by the more conservative Chris Walker. Prime Time's personnel had remained fairly steady for many years—Tacuma and guitarists Bern Nix and Charlie Ellerbee had been with Ornette since 1975, Denardo had joined soon after, and Calvin Weston had usually been the second drummer since 1979; most of them had lived with Ornette for extended periods and had devoted their adult careers to playing his music. In 1988, however, Ornette decided to make some changes. After he improvised on a Bach cello suite with guitarist Chris Rosenberg, he hired Rosenberg and his friend Ken Wessel, who'd been accompanying singer Arthur Prysock, to replace Nix and Ellerbee; to replace Weston he hired tablaist Badal Roy, who'd played in an early-seventies Miles Davis troupe. Denardo had contributed some electric-keyboard passages to *Virgin Beauty*, and then in 1990 Ornette made a breakthrough of sorts by hiring his first keyboard specialist since Walter Norris in 1958: David Bryant, player of synthesizers and organ.

Prime Time continues to tour, mostly in Europe and Japan, where jazz is better subsidized than in the United States and where, therefore, concert presenters can afford Ornette's high fees. He plays, reckons Denardo, from a handful to a few dozen appearances a year. "In America, I can't get arrested," Ornette says. "I don't have any idea why I have such a hard time in America. It's not because I personally have any enemies, because I don't."[19] Along with their own repertoire they have also on occasion played *Skies in America* (the mid-eighties reorchestrated version has been performed at least four times by now). Further reunions with old partners are not beyond the realm of possibility—in 1990, in Los Angeles, Ornette, Haden, and Higgins gave a concert of old and new songs (Don Cherry, scheduled to join them, was ill), and Herbie Hancock, introducing Ornette, said, "He is a man of great conviction, a pioneer always moving forward down the path he has chosen, a can opener who opens all of us up as musicians. I could not play what I play had it not been for Ornette Coleman."[20] And Ornette continues to compose. His chamber work for seventeen musicians, *The Country That Gave the Freedom Symbol to America*, was commissioned by the French government and played for the bicentennial of the French Revolution. The La Scala Opera, in Milan, Italy, has asked Ornette to compose an opera for it, and negotiations are continuing.

In 1991 the film *Naked Lunch* appeared. It was based largely on the William Burroughs novel of that name, and the soundtrack, composed mostly by Howard Shore, includes five Ornette Coleman themes and a bounty of Ornette's alto saxophone. In fact, Ornette's playing is brilliant on the soundtrack album. The ponderous, brooding chords of Shore's score, played by the London Philharmonic, appear to inspire Ornette as Gil Evans inspired Miles Davis, or Duke Ellington inspired Cootie Williams. He plays wonderful, crying lines in "Mujahaddin" and an impressionist revision of Thelonious Monk in "Misterioso"; he offers stunning, elongated Charlie Parker–like playing in the album's title track. His very mobile alto in "Welcome to Annexia" concludes in an incredible gasping, yearning cry. In general the great value of the orchestral pieces lies in Ornette's soloing, while four of the high points in the soundtrack are Ornette Coleman songs played by himself, accompanied by Denardo and bassist Barre Phillips. There is enormous power in their fire-breathing "Bugpowder," while the great contrasts of emotions in turmoil in his fast "Writeman" solo, over the complex, rumbling bass and drums, make it one of his most emotionally compelling works ever. Of the two ballads he composed for the film, the sweet "Intersong" (a cousin of "Unknown Artist") is a long line of thwarted cadences and crushed emotions. The disc demonstrates conclusively that after playing saxophones for nearly five decades and being one of the great jazz artists for more than thirty years, there has been no diminution of his immense powers of creativity.

Jazz in general has been attracting a growing audience in recent years, and while the main beneficiaries have been young players who choose to persist within the harmonic-rhythmic boundaries established in the bop era—most famously, the sons of Ornette's old friend from New Orleans, Ellis Marsalis—there are also plenty of young listeners discovering the other realms of jazz, including the artists who continue to advance the revolution that Ornette began. "Outside" jazz composers have continued to reassess and discover new balances of improvisation and composition: There are, for instance, pianist Anthony Davis's opera *X*, based on the life of Malcolm X; John Carter's *Roots and Folklore*, a series of suites tracing, musically, the African-American experience from its African origins; and the most monumental of jazz recording projects, *Cecil Taylor in Berlin '88*, ranging from utterly free improvisation to complex big band composition. Some composer-improviser-leaders find the little big bands—larger than a combo, smaller than a big band—the ideal medium for projecting solo expression and ensemble weight, as well as both traditional and Free concepts. Their projects include Edward Wilkerson's Eight Bold Souls, David Murray's Octet, and Henry Threadgill's groups. In Europe bands such as Pierre Dorge's New Jungle Orchestra and Trevor Watt's Moire Music fuse jazz and African musics, while in America bands such as Hal Russell's NRG Ensemble (which began by playing Ornette's songs) and the ones led by John Zorn (who recorded a tribute to Ornette, *Spy vs. Spy*) mingle the excitement of energy music with original composition. Free jazz and free improvisation, in their many guises, are the content of such annual festivals as those in Moers and Berlin (the Total Music Meeting), Germany; Victoria-ville, Quebec, Canada; and Derek Bailey's Company Weeks, usually in London. These genres make regular appearances at the more traditional jazz festivals around the world as well.

As for the artists who were important to Ornette in the early stages of the revolution he brought about in jazz values, Bobby Bradford continues to teach and perform in the Los Angeles area; he was a recurring partner of John Carter up to Carter's death in 1991. Don Cherry, now playing trumpet and African stringed instruments, continues to seek to fuse jazz with traditional musics from around the world; he likes to conclude performances by playing piano, in free-floating medleys of Thelonious Monk themes, sometimes ending in a Monk-like rearrangement of Johnny Dyani's "Song for Biko." A most stimulating Cherry album from 1988, *Art Deco*, is a quartet with James Clay, Charlie Haden, and Billy Higgins, and includes three of Ornette's songs. Higgins continues to be in great demand among hard-bop leaders, while Haden, in 1982 and again in 1990, produced important Liberation Music Orchestra collections, using Carla Bley's arrangements of mostly Latin American folk music. One especially rewarding evening featured Haden in sensitive collaborations with the bold, blues-crying tenor saxophonist Fred Anderson (whose own early career had been inspired by Ornette) and drummer Hamid Drake, in a Chicago benefit for the Committee in Support of People of El Salvador. Edward Black-well taught at Wesleyan University in Middletown, Connecticut, and despite recurrent kidney problems, has worked with Old And New Dreams in their irregular reunions; with them and with his old New Orleans mates the American Jazz Quintet, he played in an Edward Blackwell tribute at the Atlanta Jazz Festival. In 1992, after a kidney operation, he formed a new band, the Ed Blackwell Project. But in October he died—and jazz lost one of its few genuinely great percussionists. Charles Moffett continued as a dedicated teacher in New York. Among his talented musical family, bassist Charnett and drummer Cody have been enjoying active careers. Dewey Redman was himself feted with a tribute night in 1991 at New York's Lincoln Center; his son Joshua is a rising young tenor saxophonist himself.

So Ornette Coleman, like a benign parent, can survey a large, active jazz scene that he fathered through his persistence and dedication. A couple of years ago a friend of John Snyder's told him he wanted to meet Ornette. So back in New York, Snyder, a very busy independent record producer, one day drove his ten-year-old son Benjie and the friend over to Ornette's home, an apartment on 125th Street in Harlem. In the first room Ornette's musicians were scattered on the floor, asleep; in the back was Ornette. "We sat and talked awhile," said Snyder, "and he asked Benjie if he was going to play an instrument. He said, yeah, he was going to be in the fifth grade and he was going to play saxophone. Ornette said, 'Oh, yeah?' He pulls out his saxophone and hands it to Benjie and said, 'Play it.' Benjie says, 'I've never held a saxophone before.' 'There's nothing to it—just play it.' For the next two and a half hours he gave Benjie a saxophone lesson. My friend, who had his own agenda, couldn't believe it. It was incredible—at the end of those two hours and a half Benjie was playing saxophone like Ornette. After that lesson, Ornette gave Benjie the saxophone—he said, 'Just keep it, and someday you can give it back to me.' I told you he was generous."

"Free"—An Ornette Coleman Solo
From *Change of the Century*
(Atlantic 1327)
Recorded October 9, 1959
Transcribed by David Wild

FREE

Ornette Coleman
October 9, 1959

½ Time Feel

(Tempo I)

SOLO

DAW
30 XI 92

Transcriber David Wild appends these comments:

(1) Although the solo is annotated throughout in 4/4 time, drummer Billy Higgins begins in a strong 3/4 (with a snare accent every three beats). Bassist Charlie Haden accentuates this pattern by playing on every third beat for the first few measures. Haden begins walking at measure 14 (initially still with a 3/4 feel, although after one or two measures the feeling is 4/4). Higgins gradually de-emphasizes the feeling of three. However, the 4/4 time is not locked in until about measure 38. Until that point, Coleman's lines tend to float over the tempo.

(2) Although the tempo is essentially a very fast 4/4, there is a two-beat feeling at measure 105, and at measure 118 Coleman's line leads the rhythm into a half-time feeling for a few measures.

(3) The rhythm section ceases playing at measure 131. Coleman continues in tempo but gradually ritards into measure 143.

(4) The question marks in measure 143 denote a "hit" (trumpet, bass, and drum accent) which covers up Coleman's notes at that point.

(5) The tonality of the solo is generally F. However, Coleman successively emphasizes and obscures the tonality throughout the solo. Although the first part of the solo is generally centered around F, Coleman does not establish it strongly until measure 33; the long notes from measure 38 emphasize both the F tonal center and the fast 4/4 tempo. The line at measure 52, however, destroys the sense of tonality, followed by the seconds and ninths at measure 54 and much freer lines at 62. This builds to a long, almost atonal section at measures 72 through 86. The F tonality is again established starting at measure 87, and continues through 96. The two ascending lines at measures 97–99 and 101–103 obscure the tonality, but at measure 105 Coleman pulls back into F and changes the tempo. From measure 123 through 129 tonality is again obscured, and tonality at the end of the solo is quite ambiguous.

—David Wild

There is surely no such thing as a "typical" Ornette Coleman alto saxophone solo during his early, greatest period; "Free" is among his very best, for its construction and for its great fire, which sounds surely enough to melt down his alto altogether. The theme (in F) of "Free" is arpeggios rising and falling over two whole octaves, in eighth notes; trumpet and alto play it unaccompanied, which prepares for the rhythmic ambiguity that opens the bass-and-drums accompaniment to Ornette's solo. In a sense the opening alto phrases may be taken as a contrast to the theme's regularity, for these solo phrases are also in contours of rising and falling eighth notes—but now phrases begin and end irregularly, and the phrases are rising sheets of sound and angular tumbles rather than even drops. A crucial development begins in measure 38: A four-note motive appears, cradle-rocking in long tones that distill the rising-tumbling contours that initiate the solo; that cell is quickly atomized into a three-note motive, and that new motive becomes embedded in the repetitive passages of measures 52–62.

The unity of this solo results from the rising-falling contours that recur throughout, usually in the form of eighth-note lines; there's a further sequencing of a two-note motive in measures 87–96—within two years Ornette would begin expending particular energy on the direct statement and variation of small motives—and then the longer note values of measures 105–114 suggest the completion of the solo's main line of development, especially since the next seven measures are new material. But the conclusion of the accompanied portion of this solo not only returns to its initiating contours, it transforms the emotional content: In place of the fiery exultation that had heretofore ruled, measures 123–129 are a single phrase that rises five times and drops precipitously, as much as an entire octave, as though battering against a barrier. And when the alto is suspended, finally, without bass-drums support, the result is the frustration expressed in a four-note trill, before the tumbling angularities of the concluding measures.

For too many jazz soloists in this period, including some of the best, the only element of formal unity in their solos was their adherence to recurring chord changes. So the formal unity of Ornette Coleman solos such as "Free," only a minute and a half in length but shattering in its power, was a particularly remarkable achievement—clearly, "free form" meant, not "free from form," but "free *to create* form," and that remains true of the best post-Coleman musicians right up to the present.

—J.L.

Discography

(12) Atlantic SD1364, *1364-2* (Ornette Coleman Double Quartet *Free Jazz*)

(13) Atlantic SD1378 (Ornette Coleman *Ornette!*)

(14) Atlantic SD1394 (Ornette Coleman *Ornette on Tenor*)

(15) ESP-Disk 1006, *1006-2* (Ornette Coleman *Town Hall Concert 1962*)

(16) CBS (France) 62 896/62 897 (Ornette Coleman *Chappaqua Suite*)

(17) Polydor (England) 623246/247 (*An Evening with Ornette Coleman*); Arista-Freedom AL1900 (Ornette Coleman *The Great London Concert*)

(18) Atmosphere (France) IRI 5006 (Ornette Coleman *Who's Crazy? 1*)

(19) Atmosphere (France) IRI 5007 (Ornette Coleman *Who's Crazy? 2*)

(20) Blue Note 84224, *CDP-84224* (The Ornette Coleman Trio *At the "Golden Circle," Stockholm, Volume 1*)

(21) Blue Note 84225, *CDP-84225* (The Ornette Coleman Trio *At the "Golden Circle," Stockholm, Volume 2*)

(22) Trio PA7169/7170 (Japan) (Ornette Coleman *Paris Concert*)

(23) Blue Note 84246 (Ornette Coleman *The Empty Foxhole*)

(24) RCA Victor LSC 2892, Bluebird, *6561-2RB* (*The Music of Ornette Coleman*)

(25) Blue Note 84262 (Jackie McLean *New and Old Gospel*)

(26) Joker (Italy) UPS-2061-KR (*The Unprecedented Music of Ornette Coleman*)*

(27) Apple SW3373 (Yoko Ono *The Plastic Ono Band*)

(28) Blue Note 84287 (Ornette Coleman *New York Is Now!*)

(29) Blue Note 84356 (Ornette Coleman *Love Call*)

(30) Blue Note (France?) (*History of Blue Note*)

(31) Impulse 9178 (Ornette Coleman *Ornette at 12*)

(32) Impulse 9187 (Ornette Coleman *Crisis*)

(33) Flying Dutchman FDS-123 (*Friends and Neighbors: Ornette Live at Prince Street*)

(34) Amsterdam 12009 (*Louis Armstrong and His Friends*)

(35) Impulse AS9210 (Alice Coltrane *Universal Consciousness*)

(36) Columbia KC31061 (Ornette Coleman *Science Fiction*)

(37) Columbia FC38029 (Ornette Coleman *Broken Shadows*)

(38) Unique Jazz UJ13 (Italy) (Ornette Coleman Quartet *European Concert*)*

(39) Columbia KC31562 (Ornette Coleman *Skies of America*)

(40) Jazz Anthology 5248 (Ornette Coleman *Stating the Case*), also issued as JforJazz JFJ 803*

(41) A&M/Horizon SP-722 (Ornette Coleman *Dancing in Your Head*)

(42) Craws (unnumbered) (Ornette Coleman *In Concert*)*

(43) Barclay 90 025 (Claude Nougaro *Femmes et Famines*)

---

* Bootleg recording

(44) Artists House AH-1 (Ornette Coleman *Body Meta*)
(45) A&M/Horizon SP-710 (Charlie Haden *Closeness*)
(46) A&M Horizon SP-727 (Charlie Haden *The Golden Number*)
(47) Artists House AH-6 (Ornette Coleman-Charlie Haden *Soapsuds, Soapsuds*)
(48) Artists House AH-7 (James Blood *Tales of Captain Black*)
(49) Antilles AN-2001 (Ornette Coleman *Of Human Feelings*)
(50) Gramavision GR8308, *GRCD8308* (Jamaaladeen Tacuma *Renaissance Man*)
(51) Caravan of Dreams *CDP85001* (Ornette Coleman & Prime Time *Opening the Caravan of Dreams*)
(52) Caravan of Dreams *CDP85002* (Ornette Coleman (*Prime Design/Time Design*)
(53) Geffen GHS24096, *24096-2* (Pat Metheny-Ornette Coleman *Song X*)
(54) Caravan of Dreams CDP85008, *CDPCD-85008* (Ornette Coleman *In All Languages*)
(55) Bola Press 8601 (Jayne Cortez *Maintain Control*)
(56) Portrait 44301 (Ornette Coleman and Prime Time *Virgin Beauty*)
(57) Repertoire RR4905CC (Ornette Coleman and Prime Time *Jazz-buhne Berlin '88*)*
(58) Milan *73138 35614-2* (*Naked Lunch: Music from the Original Soundtrack*)
(59) Flying Dutchman FDS-104 (Bob Thiele *Head Start*)

Ornette Coleman compositions recorded by other artists, but not by Ornette Coleman:

A Girl Named Rainbow	(Jocque and Le Scott *The Ornette Coleman Songbook*, TEA-100)
Handwoven	(*Old and New Dreams*, Black Saint BSR 0013, *BSR-0013CD PSI*)
O.C.	(*New York Contemporary Five*, Sonet SLP 36)
Open or Close	(*Old and New Dreams*, ECM-1-1154, *829379-2*)
Ornette Tune	(Don Cherry *Live in Ankara*, Sonet SNTF 669)
Ornette's Concept	— — — — —
Perfection	(Frank Lowe Quintet *Exotic Heartbeat*, Soul Note SN 1032)
Play It Straight	(Marzette Watts, in anthology album *New Music, Second Wave*, Savoy 2235)
Race Face	(Don Cherry-Collin Walcott-Nana Vasconcelos *Codona*, ECM-1-1132, *829371-2*)

Sortie*	—	—	—	—	—

Tacuma Song   (Jamaaladeen Tacuma *Show Stopper*, Gram-
avision GR8301, *GRCD8301*)
Untitled   (Bobo Stenson, ECM)
War Ophans   (Charlie Haden *Liberation Music Orchestra*,
Impulse AS9183)
Without Name or Number   (Bob Degan-Teramasu Hino, Enja 3027)

DISCOGRAPHY

This is a summary of Ornette Coleman's recorded material, not
including most noncommercial recordings (unless they are of unusual historical importance). One original catalog number is shown
for each title, except in the case of simultaneous mono and stereo
releases; these entries are cross-referenced to an index of currently
available releases (with catalog numbers) wherever applicable. This
discography is based on the far more complete research of David
Wild and Michael Cuscuna in their *Ornette Coleman 1958–1979: A
Discography*, revised and supplemented by David Wild in *disc'ribe*,
issues 1, 2, and 3, all published by Wildmusic, GPO 362566, San
Juan, Puerto Rico 00936. These works thoroughly document Coleman's recording career through 1982; Mr. Wild has very kindly
edited my additions, which cover the period from 1983 to 1991.

Where a song has been given more than one title, by Coleman or
by a record company, the new title is shown first and the previous
title or titles shown in parentheses. Compositions are by Ornette
Coleman, unless indicated otherwise. Asterisks (*) indicate artists
who performed in specific compositions. In the key, then, vinyl-LP
catalog numbers are shown first, and compact-disc catalog numbers, where applicable, are shown in italics.

---

* "Sortie" is a later title for a Latin version of "The Jungle Is a Skyscraper."

These abbreviations are also used:

arr	arranger	fl	flute
as	alto saxophone	fr-h	french horn
b	bass	g	guitar
bcl	bass clarinet	p	piano
bn	bassoon	perc	percussion
cl	clarinet	ss	soprano saxophone
cond	conductor	tb	trombone
d	drums	tp	trumpet
dir	director	ts	tenor saxophone
el	electric	vcl	vocal
eng-h	english horn	vla	viola
		vln	violin

1949 Natchez, Mississippi	Ornette Coleman Ornette Coleman (ts); unknown instrumentalists unknown titles unknown label (unissued) Note: The other musicians were probably members of the Clarence Samuels band, as was Coleman, who wrote "eight or nine songs" that were recorded at this session.
December 1957 Cellar Club Vancouver, British Columbia	Don Cherry Group Don Cherry (tp); Ornette Coleman (as); Don Friedman (p); Ben Tucker (b); unknown d unknown titles radio station CFUN Note: Two or more sets by the Cherry group were recorded and later broadcast.
February 10, 1958 Los Angeles	Ornette Coleman Quintet Don Cherry (tp); Ornette Coleman (as); Walter Norris (p); Don Payne (b); Billy Higgins (d) Alpha (1) Con C3551 Jayne (1) — — Chippie (1) — — Note: Two unissued works were also recorded at this session.
February 22, 1958 Los Angeles	Ornette Coleman Quintet Personnel same as for February 10 The Blessing (1) Con C3551 The Sphinx (1) — — Invisible (1) — —

Angel Voice (1) — —
The Disguise (1) — —
Note: Unissued performances of "Embraceable You" (Gershwin) and "When Will the Blues Leave?" were also recorded at this session.

March 24, 1958	Ornette Coleman Quartet	
Los Angeles	Personnel same as for February 10 and 22	

When Will the
 Blues Leave?   (1) Con C3551
Note: Two unissued performances were also recorded at this session.

Oct.–Nov. 1958	Paul Bley Quintet
Hillcrest Club	Don Cherry (tp); Ornette Coleman (as); Paul
Los Angeles	Bley (p); Charlie Haden (b); Billy Higgins (d)

Klactoveedsedstene (2) Inner City 1007
I Remember Harlem (2) —   —
The Blessing   (2) —   —
Free   (2) —   —
When Will the Blues
 Leave?   (3) IAI 37.38.52
Crossroads   (3) —   —
Ramblin'   (3) —   —
How Deep Is the
 Ocean?   (3) —   —
Note: Bley evidently recorded several nights during the six weeks his quintet with Coleman appeared at the Hillcrest, and reportedly more material from these sets is extant.

January 16, 1959	Ornette Coleman Quartet
Los Angeles	Don Cherry (tp, pocket tp); Ornette Coleman
	(as); Red Mitchell (b); Shelly Manne (d)

Lorraine (4) Con M3569

February 23, 1959	Ornette Coleman Quartet
Los Angeles	Personnel same as for January 16

Turnaround (4) Con M3569
Endless   (4) — —

March 9–10, 1959 Los Angeles	Ornette Coleman Quartet Percy Heath (b) replaces Mitchell Tears Inside (4) Con M3569 Tomorrow Is the Question (4) — — Compassion (4) — — Giggin' (4) — — Rejoicing (4) — — Mind and Time (4) — —
May 22, 1959 Hollywood, California	Ornette Coleman Quartet Focus on Sanity (5) Atl SD1317 Chronology (5) — — Peace (5) — — Congeniality (5) — — Lonely Woman (5) — — Monk and the Nun (6) Atl SD1588 Just for You (7) Atl SD1572 Eventually (5) Atl SD1317
August 29, 1959 Berkshire Music Barn School of Jazz Lenox, Massachusetts	Lenox Student Small Group #4 Don Cherry, (pocket tp); Kent McGarity (tb, bass tp); Ornette Coleman (as); Steve Kuhn or Ron Brown (p); Larry Ridley (b); Barry Greenspan (d) The Sphinx S.O.J. #1/2 Inn Tune (Margo Guryan) — — Note: S.O.J. #1/2 was a privately pressed record of excerpts from the School of Jazz's 1959 benefit concert. This group, which was the fourth on the concert, included "students" who had worked with Max Roach and John Lewis, and also performed Coleman's songs "Compassion" and "Giggin'."
August 29, 1959 Berkshire Music Barn School of Jazz Lenox, Massachusetts	Lenox Student Large Ensemble Tony Greenwald (tp); Herb Gardner (tb); David Baker (bass tb), Ornette Coleman, Lenny Popkin (as); Ian Underwood (fl, as); Ted Casher (ts); David Mackay (p); John Keyser (b); Paul Cohen (d); possibly others; Herb Pomeroy (cond) To Thee, O Asphodel (Bobby Freedman) S.O.J. #1/2

Paul's Pal (Rollins)   —   —
Blue Grass (Danny Kent)   —   —
Note: This band also performed three other
works at the same concert. Presumably the entire concert was recorded.

October 8, 1959   Ornette Coleman Quartet
Hollywood,   Don Cherry (tp); Ornette Coleman (as); Charlie
California   Haden (b); Billy Higgins (d)
                   Una Muy Bonita   (8) Atl SD1327
                   Bird Food   (8) —   —
                   Change of the Century (8) —   —
                   Music Always   (9) Atl (Japan)
                                              P-10085A
                   The Face of the Bass   (8) Atl SD1327

October 9, 1959   Ornette Coleman Quartet
Hollywood,   Personnel same as for October 8
California   Forerunner   (8) Atl SD1327
                   Free   (8) —   —
                   The Circle with a Hole
                     in the Middle
                     (Crossroads)   (7) Atl SD1572
                   Ramblin'   (8) Atl SD1327
                   Note: Three unissued works were also recorded
                   at this session.

July 19, 1960   Ornette Coleman Quartet
New York City   Don Cherry (pocket tp); Ornette Coleman (as);
                   Charlie Haden (b); Edward Blackwell (d)
                   Little Symphony   (6) Atl SD1588
                   Kaleidoscope   (10) Atl SD1353
                   Blues Connotation   (10) —   —
                   P.S. Unless One Has
                     (Blues Connotation) (9) Atl (Japan)
                                              P-10085A
                   Brings Goodness   (9) —   —
                   Note: Four untitled originals recorded at this
                   session have not been released.

July 26, 1960   Ornette Coleman Quartet
New York City   Personnel same as for July 19
                   Joy of a Toy   (6) Atl SD1588

To Us	(6) Atl	(Japan) P-10085A
The Fifth of Beethoven	(7) Atl	SD1572
Humpty Dumpty	(10) Atl	SD1353
Motive for Its Use	(9) Atl	(Japan) P-10085A
Moon Inhabitants	(7) Atl	SD1572
The Legend of Bebop	(7) —	—
Some Other	(9) Atl	(Japan) P-10085A
Embraceable You (Gershwin)	(10) Atl	SD1353
Dawn		unissued
All (Cherryco) (Cherry?)	(9) Atl	(Japan) P-10085A

August 2, 1960
New York City

Ornette Coleman Quartet
Personnel same as for July 19 and 26

Folk Tale	(10) Atl	SD1353
Poise	(10) —	—
Beauty Is a Rare Thing	(10) —	—

Note: Thirteen other works recorded at this session have not been released.

December 19, 1960
New York City

Gunther Schuller Orchestra
Ornette Coleman (as); Jim Hall (g); Alvin Brehm, Scott LaFaro (b); Sticks Evans (d); The Contemporary String Quartet: Charles Libove, Roland Vamos (vln); Harry Zaratzian (vla); Joseph Tekula (cello); Gunther Schuller (cond)
Abstraction (Schuller)   (11) Atl SD1365
Note: This ensemble, minus Ornette Coleman, recorded Jim Hall's "Piece for Guitar and Strings" at the same session.

December 20, 1960
New York City

Gunther Schuller Orchestra
George Duvivier replaces Brehm; add Eric Dolphy (as, fl, bcl); Robert DiDomenica (fl); Eddie Costa (vib); Bill Evans (p)
Variants on a Theme of Thelonious Monk (Criss Cross) (Schuller)   (11) Atl SD1365
Note: This ensemble, minus Coleman, recorded

Schuller's "Variants on a Theme of John Lewis (Django)" at the same session.

December 21, 1960 New York City	Ornette Coleman Double Quartet Don Cherry (pocket tp); Freddie Hubbard (tp); Ornette Coleman (as); Eric Dolphy (bcl); Charlie Haden, Scott LaFaro (b); Billy Higgins, Edward Blackwell (d)

| First Take (Free Jazz) | (6) Atl SD1588 |
| Free Jazz | (12) Atl SD1364 |

January 31, 1961 New York City	Ornette Coleman Quartet Don Cherry (pocket tp); Ornette Coleman (as); Scott LaFaro (b); Edward Blackwell (d)

W.R.U.	(13) Atl SD1378
Check Up	(6) Atl SD1588
T. & T.	(13) Atl SD1378
C. & D.	(13) — —
R.P.D.D.	(13) — —
The Alchemy of Scott LaFaro	(7) Atl SD1572

March 22, 1961 New York City	Ornette Coleman Quartet Don Cherry (tp, pocket tp); Ornette Coleman (ts); Jimmy Garrison (b); Edward Blackwell (d)

Eos	unissued
Ecars	unissued
Cross Breeding	unissued

Note: Two untitled originals, both unissued, were also recorded at this session.

March 27, 1961 New York City	Ornette Coleman Quartet Personnel same as for March 22

Enfant	(14) Atl SD1394
Ecars	(14) — —
Eos	(14) — —
Cross Breeding	(14) — —
Harlem's Manhattan	(7) Atl SD1572
Mapa	(14) Atl SD1394

Note: One untitled original recorded at this session has not been released.

June, 1961 New York City	Ornette Coleman Octet Bobby Bradford, Don Cherry (tp); Steve Lacy (ss); Ornette Coleman (as); Jimmy Garrison, Art Davis (b); Edward Blackwell, Charles Moffett (d)

Unknown titles   Atlantic unissued

Other recording sessions may have taken place in this period; a studio photograph pictures only Coleman, Bradford, Garrison, and Moffett—the "working" Coleman Quartet of June 1961. This session is not listed in Atlantic's files.

December 21, 1962
Town Hall
New York City

Ornette Coleman Groups
String Quartet: Selwart Clarke, Nathan Goldstein (vln); Julian Barber (vla); Kermit Moore (cello)
Dedication to Poets
  and Writers   (15) ESP-Disk 1006
Ornette Coleman Trio: Coleman (as); David Izenzon (b); Charles Moffett (d)

Story Teller	unissued
Sadness	(15) ESP-Disk 1006
The Ark	(15) — —
Taurus (bass solo)	unissued
I Don't Love You	unissued
Children's Books	unissued

Add Nappy Allen (g); Chris Towns (p); Barney Richardson (b)

Blues Misused	unissued

Trio: Coleman, Izenzon, Moffett

Architect	unissued
Play It Straight	unissued
Doughnut	(15) ESP-Disk 1006

December 1963
New York City

Ornette Coleman
Ornette Coleman (tp); Charles Tyler (C melody sax); Albert Ayler (ts); Norman Butler (cello, as); Fred Lyman (g); Earle Henderson (b)
unknown titles   private tape

1963

Ornette Coleman
Ornette Coleman (as); others unidentified
unknown titles   soundtrack

Note: This is the soundtrack for the short subject film *Soundtrack for Improvisations*, Stefan Sharp, director.

June 15, 16, and
17, 1965

Ornette Coleman Group
Ornette Coleman (as); Pharoah Sanders (ts); David Izenzon (b); Charles Moffett (d); eleven other unidentified musicians; Joseph Tekula (cond)
Chappaqua Suite:
    Parts I–IV   soundtrack
Note: Though commissioned as soundtrack music for Conrad Rooks's film *Chappaqua*, this music was never used in the film. A partial version of "Chappaqua Suite," edited to include little more than Ornette Coleman's improvisations, appeared on (16) CBS (France) 62 896/62 897.

August 29, 1965
Fairfield Hall
Croydon, England

Ornette Coleman
Trio: Ornette Coleman (as, tp, vln); David Izenon (b); Charles Moffett (d)
Sadness (as)   (17) Polydor (England) 623246/
                                            623247
The Clergyman's
    Dream (as)   (17)   —   —
Falling Stars
    (tp, vln)   (17)   —   —
Silence (as)   (17)   —   —
Happy Fool (as)   (17)   —   —
Ballad (as)   (17)   —   —
Doughnut (as)   (17)   —   —
Virtuoso Ensemble: Edward Walker (fl); Derek Wickens (oboe); Sidney Fell (cl); Cecil James (bn); John Burden (fr-h); replace Coleman, Izenzon, Moffet.
Forms and Sounds
    for Wind
    Quintet   (17) Polydor (England) 62346/
                                            62347
Note: The "Doughnut" performed here is not the same theme as the "Doughnut" performed December 21, 1962, at Town Hall. But "The Clergyman's Dream" shares a crucial phrase with the Town Hall "Doughnut."

November 1965 Paris, France	Ornette Coleman Trio Ornette Coleman (as, tp, vln); David Izenzon (b); Charles Moffett (d)		
	January (vl, tp, as)	(18) Atmosphere IRI 5006	
	Sortie le Co- quard (as)	(18) —	—
	Dans la Neige (as, vln, tp)	(18) —	—
	The Changes (as, vln, tp)	(18) —	—

	Better Get Your-
	    self Another
	    Self (as, vln, tp)
		(18) —	—

	The Duel, Two
	    Psychic Lovers,
	    and Eating Time
	    (vln, as, tp)
		(18) —	—

	The Misused Blues
	    (The Lovers and
	    the Alchemist)
	    (as)
		(19) Atmosphere IRI 5007	

	The Poet (vln, tp)	(19) —	—
	Wedding Day and Fuzz (as)	(19) —	—

	Fuzz, Feast, Break-
	    out, European
	    Echoes, Alone,
	    and the Arrest
	    (as, vln)
		(19) —	—

Note: This music was recorded for the sound-track of the film *Who's Crazy?*; most of the titles are probably not Ornette Coleman's.

December 3, 1965 Gyllene Cirkeln Stockholm, Sweden	Ornette Coleman Trio Ornette Coleman (as); David Izenzon (b); Charles Moffett (d)		
	Antiques	(21) Blue Note 4225	
	Morning Song	(21) —	—
	Dawn	(20) Blue Note 4224	

December 4, 1965 Gyllene Cirkeln Stockholm, Sweden	Ornette Coleman Trio Personnel same as for December 3, except Ornette Coleman plays as, tp, and vln.		
	European Echoes (as)	(20)	Blue Note 4224
	The Riddle (as)	(21)	Blue Note 4225
	Snowflakes and Sunshine (vln, tp)	(21) —	—
	Dee Dee (as)	(20)	Blue Note 4224
	Faces and Places (as)	(20) —	—

February 1966 Paris, France	Ornette Coleman Trio Ornette Coleman (as, tp, vln); David Izenzon (b); Charles Moffett (d)	
	Doughnut (Doo Nut)	(22) Trio PA7169/ 7170
	unknown title (14 Juillet)	(22) — —
	unknown title (Reminiscence)	(22) — —
	Note: These three works may be mistitled performances of "The Clergyman's Dream," "European Echoes," and "Doughnut," all with Ornette Coleman playing as.	

August 1966	Ornette Coleman Trio Personnel same as for February 1966
	unknown titles soundtrack
	Note: Soundtrack for Pierre Herbert's fourteen-minute animated cartoon *Population Explosion*, produced by the Canadian Film Board.

September 9, 1966 Englewood, New Jersey	Ornette Coleman Trio Ornette Coleman (as, tp, vln); Charlie Haden (b); Ornette Denardo Coleman (d)		
	The Empty Foxhole (tp)	(23)	Blue Note 4246
	Freeway Express (tp)	(23) —	—
	Zig Zag (as)	(23) —	—
	Faithful (as)	(23) —	—
	Sound Gravitation (vln)	(23) —	—
	Good Old Days (as)	(23) —	—

| March 17, 1967
The Village
Theater
New York City | Ornette Coleman/Philadelphia Woodwind
Quintet
Ornette Coleman (tp); Philadelphia Woodwind
Quintet: John DeLancie (eng-h, oboe); Murray
Panitz, (piccolo, fl); Anthony Gigliotti (cl, bcl);
Bernard Garfield (bn); Mason Jones (fr-h)
Forms and Sounds (24) RCA LM/LSC 2982 |

March 24, 1967
Englewood Cliffs,
New Jersey

Jackie McLean Quintet
Ornette Coleman (tp); Jackie McLean (as); La-
mont Johnson (p); Scotty Holt (b); Billy Hig-
gins (d)
Old Gospel   (25) Blue Note BST 84262
Strange as It
  Seems   (25) —   —
Lifeline (McLean) (25) —   —
    Offspring
    Midway
    Vernzone
    The Inevitable End

March 31, 1967
New York City

Chamber Symphony of Philadelphia Quartet
Stuart Canin, William Steck (vln); Carlton
Cooley (vla); Willem Stokking (cello)
Space Flight   (24) RCA LM/LSC-2982
Saints and
  Soldiers   (24) —   —

July 21, 1967
St. Peter's
Lutheran Church
New York City
(John Coltrane
funeral)

Ornette Coleman Quartet
Ornette Coleman (as); David Izenzon, Charlie
Haden (b); Charles Moffett (d)
Holiday for a
  Graveyard   (59) FD DS-104

February 8, 1968
RAI radio
broadcast
Rome, Italy

Ornette Coleman Quartet
Ornette Coleman (as, tp, musette); David Izen-
zon, Charlie Haden (b); Edward Blackwell (d)
Lonely Woman (as) (26) Joker UPS -2061-KR
unknown title
  (Monsieur le
  Prince) (as)   (26) —   —
Let's Play (Forgotten
  Children) (tp)   (26) —   —

                              Buddah's Blues
                                (musette)   (26) —   —

February 29, 1968   Ornette Coleman Quartet with Yoko Ono
Royal Albert Hall   Ornette Coleman (tp); David Izenzon, Charlie
London, England   Haden (b); Edward Blackwell (d); Yoko Ono
                        (vcl)
                        Aos (Ono)   (27) Apple SW3373
                        Note: A tape made at an afternoon rehearsal is
                        the source of this performance.

April 29, 1968   Ornette Coleman Quartet
New York City   Ornette Coleman (as, vln); Dewey Redman (ts);
                        Jimmy Garrison (b); Elvin Jones (d)
                        We Now Interrupt
                          for a Commercial
                          (vln)   (28) Blue Note BST84287
                        The Garden of
                          Souls (as)   (28) —   —
                        Open to the
                          Public (as)   (29) Blue Note BST84356
                        Toy Dance (as)   (28) Blue Note BST84287
                        Check-Out
                          Time (as)   (29) Blue Note BST84356
                        Airborne (as)   (29) —   —
                        Broadway
                          Blues (as)   (28) Blue Note BST84287
                        Note: Mel Fuhrman, announcer, added for "We
                        Now Interrupt for a Commercial."

May 7, 1968   Ornette Coleman Quartet
New York City   Personnel same as for April 29, except for Or-
                        nette Coleman (as, tp)
                        Love Call (tp)   (29) Blue Note BST84356
                        Just for You (tp)   (30) Blue Note
                        Broadway Blues
                          (as) (insert)   (28) Blue Note BST84287
                        The Garden of
                          Souls (as) (insert) (28) —   —
                        Round Trip (as)   (28) —   —
                        Note: The "Broadway Blues" and "The Garden
                        of Souls" inserts recorded at this session were

edited onto the performances of these songs recorded April 29.

August 11, 1968 Hearst Greek Amphitheatre University of California Berkeley, California	Ornette Coleman

Quartet: Ornette Coleman (as, vln, tp); Dewey Redman (ts); Charlie Haden (b); Ornette Denardo Coleman (d)

C.O.D. (as)	(31) Impulse	9178
Rainbows (tp)	(31) —	—
New York (as)	(31) —	—
Bells and Chimes (vln)	(31) —	—

Add twenty-five-piece orchestra conducted by Coleman, including Bobby Bradford (solo tp); Allan Smith (tp); John Mosher (b); Jerry Granelli (solo perc); and members of the San Francisco Symphony
Sun Suite of San Francisco   unissued

March 22, 1969 Loeb Student Center New York University New York City	Ornette Coleman Quintet

Don Cherry (tp, cornet, Indian fl); Ornette Coleman (as, vln); Dewey Redman (ts, cl); Charlie Haden (b); Ornette Denardo Coleman (d)

Broken Shadows (as)	(32) Impulse	AS9187
Comme Il Faut (as)	(32) —	—
Song for Che (Haden) (as)	(32) —	—
Space Jungle (Trouble in the East?) (as)	(32) —	—
Trouble in the East (Space Jungle?) (vln)	(32) —	—

Note: The titles for the last two tracks are given as they appear on the record; a review of this concert by Martin Williams in *Down Beat*, May 15, 1969, suggests that Impluse Records may have reversed these two titles.

June 7, 1969 New Jersey	Ornette Coleman Quartet

Ornette Coleman (as); Dewey Redman (ts); Charlie Haden (b); Edward Blackwell (d); Emmanuel Ghent (synthesizer)*

Man on the Moon* (Ghent)	Impulse 45-275

Growing Up   —   —
Note: Ornette Coleman overdubbed tp on
"Growing Up."

February 14, 1970   Ornette Coleman Quartet
Ornette Coleman's   Ornette Coleman (as,.tp, vln); Dewey Redman
Prince Street loft   (ts); Charlie Haden (b); Edward Blackwell (d)
New York City   Friends and Neighbors
                            (vocal version) (vln)   (33) FD FDS-123
                         Friends and Neighbors
                            (instrumental version)
                            (vln)   (33) — —
                         Long Time No See (as)   (33) — —
                         Let's Play (tp)   (33) — —
                         Forgotten Songs (as)   (33) — —
                         Tomorrow (as)   (33) — —
                         Note: The singers in the vocal version of
                         "Friends and Neighbors" are the concert audi-
                         ence.

late May 1970   Louis Armstrong and Friends
New York City   Louis Armstrong (vcl); chorus: Carl Hall, Janice
                         Bell, Tasha Thomas, Ila Govan, Matthew Led-
                         better, Ornette Coleman (vcl); big band, Oliver
                         Nelson (arr, cond)
                         We Shall Over-
                            come (traditional) (34) FD FDC/AMS 12009
                         Give Peace a
                            Chance (Lennon) (34) —   —
                         Note: Ornette Coleman sat in with an amateur
                         "chorus" at the last of three sessions featuring
                         singer Louis Armstrong. The accompanists in-
                         cluded, at various sessions, such players as Thad
                         Jones, Jimmy Owens, Ernie Royal, Marvin
                         Stamm (tp, flugelhorn); Garnett Brown, Bill
                         Campbell, Al Grey, Quentin Jackson (tb); Rob-
                         ert Ashton, Danny Bank, Jerry Dodgion, Billy
                         Harper, James Spaulding (reeds); Frank Owens
                         (p); Sam Brown, Kenny Burrell (g); Richard
                         Davis, George Duvivier, Chuck Rainey (b); Ber-
                         nard "Pretty" Purdie (d); and string orchestra.

April 6, 1971	Alice Coltrane Orchestra
Coltrane Studios	John Blair, Leroy Jenkins, Julius Brand,
Dix Hills,	Joan Kalish (vln); Alice Coltrane (org, harp, arr);
New York	Jimmy Garrison (b); Jack DeJohnette (d); Or-
	nette Coleman (orchestrator)

Universal Conscious-
ness (A. Coltrane)   (35) Impulse AS9210
Oh Allah
(A. Coltrane)   (35) —   —
Hare Krishna[1]
(traditional)   (35) —   —

[1]Inserts recorded on May 14, 1971, by Alice Coltrane, Jimmy Garrison, Tulsi (tamboura), and Clifford Jarvis (d) were edited onto the original take of "Hare Krishna" for release.

Note: This album's liner credits read: "String arrangements by Alice Coltrane, transcriptions by Ornette Coleman." Presumably Coleman orchestrated the violin parts from Alice Coltrane's drafts.

September 9, 1971	Ornette Coleman Groups
New York City	Don Cherry, Bobby Bradford (tp); Ornette
	Coleman (as); Dewey Redman (ts); Charlie
	Haden (b); Billy Higgins, Edward Blackwell (d)

Happy House   (37) Columbia FC38029
Broken Shadows   (37) —   —
Elizabeth   (37) —   —
Quartet: Cherry, Coleman, Haden, Higgins
Civilization Day   (36) Columbia KC31061
Country Town
Blues   (37) Columbia FC38029
Steet Woman   (36) Columbia KC31061
Quintet: Bradford, Coleman, Redman, Haden,
BlackwellSchool Work
(The Good Life[1])   (37) Columbia FC38029
The Jungle Is a
Skyscraper   (36) Columbia KC31061
Law Years   (36) —   —

[1]Besides "School Work" and "The Good Life" (in the symphony *Skies of America*), this theme is also known as "Theme from a Symphony" and "Dancing in Your Head."

September 10, 1971   Ornette Coleman Group
New York City   Don Cherry (pocket tp); Bobby Bradford (tp);
                     Ornette Coleman (as); Dewey Redman (ts);
                     Charlie Haden (b); Billy Higgins, Edward
                     Blackwell (d); David Henderson (narrator)
                     Science Fiction   (36) Columbia KC31061

September 13, 1971   Ornette Coleman Groups
New York City   Gerard Schwarg, Carmon Fornaroto (tp); Or-
                     nette Coleman (as); Dewey Redman (ts); Charlie
                     Haden (b); Billy Higgins, Edward Blackwell (d);
                     Asha Puthli (vcl)
                     What Reason
                       Could I Give?   (36) Columbia KC31061
                     All My Life   (36) —   —
                     Quartet: Ornette Coleman (tp, vln); Dewey
                     Redman (ts, musette); Charlie Haden (b); Ed-
                     ward Blackwell (d)
                     Rock the Clock   (36) Columbia KC31061

November 5, 1971   Ornette Coleman Quartet
Philharmonic,   Ornette Coleman (as, tp, vln); Dewey Redman
Berlin, Germany   (ts, musette); Charlie Haden (b); Edward Black-
                     well (d)
                     Who Do You Work
                       For? (as)   (38) Unique Jazz UJ13
                     Street Woman (as)   (38) —   —
                     Song for Che
                       (Haden) (as)   (38) —   —
                     Rock the Clock
                       (tp, vln)   (38) —   —
                     Happy House
                       (Written Word) (as) (38) —   —
                     Note: The source of this recording is a private
                     tape.

Nov. 20, 1971   Ornette Coleman Quartet
Cascais Jazz   Ornette Coleman (as); Dewey Redman (ts);
Festival   Charlie Haden (b); Edward Blackwell (d)
Cascais, Portugal   Street Woman   private tape
                     Dedication by Charlie Haden
                     Song for Che (Haden)   —   —
                     Note: Haden played this tape on WKCR-FM,

New York City, while a broadcast guest in 1972. The source of the tape was Ornette Coleman's cassette recording of the concert.

November 22–
24, 1971
London, England

Ornette Coleman Group
Ornette Coleman (as, tp, vln); Dewey Redman (ts); Edward Blackwell (d); probably Jeff Clyne (b); others unidentified
unknown titles   soundtrack
Note: Soundtrack for the Stefan Sharp film *Run*. Haden missed this recording because he was still detained in Portugal at the time.

Probably same
period
Probably Paris,
France

Ornette Coleman Quartet
Ornette Coleman (as, tp, vln); Dewey Redman (ts, musette); Charlie Haden (b); Edward Black-well (d)

Street Woman (Second Fiction) (as)	(22) Trio	PA7169/7170
unknown title (Summer Thang) (as)	(22) —	—
unknown title (Silhouette) (as)	(22) —	—
Rock the Clock (Fantasy 77) (tp, vln)	(22) —	—

April 17–20, 1972
London, England

Ornette Coleman with the London Symphony Orchestra
London Symphony Orchestra; unidentified drummer; Ornette Coleman (as)*

Skies of America	(39) Columbia	KC31562
Native Americans	(39) —	—
The Good Life[1]	(39) —	—
Birthdays and Funerals	(39) —	—
Dreams	(39) —	—
Sounds of Sculpture	(39) —	—
Holiday for Heroes[2]	(39) —	—

[1]See note to "School Work" under September 9, 1971 session.
[2]Similar to "Forgotten Songs."

All of My Life	(39) —	—
Dancers	(39) —	—
The Soul Within Woman[3]	(39) —	—
The Artist in America*	(39) —	—
The New Anthem	(39) —	—
Place in Space	(39) —	—
Foreigner in a Free Land*	(39) —	—
Silver Screen*	(39) —	—
Poetry*	(39) —	—
The Men Who Live in the White House*	(39) —	—
Love Life*	(39) —	—
The Military	(39) —	—
Jam Session	(39) —	—
Sunday in America	(39) —	—

[3]Similar to "Street Woman"

Note: These titles, in order, make up the symphony *Skies of America*.

Probably
September 22,
1972
Artists House
New York City

Ornette Coleman Group
Don Cherry (tp); Ornette Coleman (as); Dewey Redman (ts); Charlie Haden (b); Edward Blackwell (d)

The Word Became Music	(40) JforJazz JFJ 803	
Unknown Races	(40) —	—
Love Eyes	(40) —	—
The Good Life	(40) —	—
Skies of America	(40) —	—

Note: Judging from the sound quality of this album, its source is likely a cassette tape recorded by a member of the audience.

September 1972
New York City

Ornette Coleman
Ornette Coleman (as); Dewey Redman (ts); Cedar Walton (p); Jim Hall (g); Charlie Haden (b);

Edward Blackwell (d); unidentified woodwind
quintet (oboe, bn, fr-h, fl, cl)
Good Girl Blues (37) Columbia FC38029
Is It Forever (37) — —
Coleman, Redman, Haden, Blackwell only
Rubber Gloves (37) Columbia FC38029

January 1973 Joujouka, Morocco	Ornette Coleman and the Master Musicians of Joujouka Ornette Coleman (as, tp, el vln); Robert Palmer (cl); the Master Musicians of Joujouka: pipes players, flutists, three lutanists, violinist, drummers

Midnight Sun-
rise (as) (41) A&M/Horizon SP-722
Music from the
Cave (tp) unissued
unknown titles unissued
Note: According to Palmer, these recording sessions spanned three days and employed varying combinations of Joujouka musicians. Enough material for three albums was recorded.

May 4, 1974 Teatro S. Pio X Padua, Italy	Ornette Coleman Quartet Ornette Coleman (as, tp, vln); James "Blood" Ulmer (g); Sirone (Norris Jones) (b); Billy Higgins (d)

Tutti[1] (42) Craws unnumbered
Love Call (tp) (42) — —
What Reason Could
I Give? (as) (42) — —
The Story of the
King and
Queen (as) (42) — —
Harloff (as) (42) — —
Comme Il Faut (as) (42) — —
Bells and Chimes
(vln) (42) — —
Something to Lis-
ten To (as) (42) — —
[1]Same as "The Good Life," "School Days," etc.

December 10, 1975 Paris, France	Claude Nougaro		
	Claude Nougaro (vcl); Ornette Coleman (as); Maurice Vander (p); Luigi Turssardi (b); Charles Bellonzi (d)		
	Gloria (unknown)	(43)	Barclay 90 025

December 28, 1975 Paris, France	Ornette Coleman Group		
	Ornette Coleman (as); Bern Nix, Charlie Ellerbee (g); Rudy MacDaniel (Jamaaladeen Tacuma) (el-b); Ronald Shannon Jackson (d)		
	Fou Amour	(44)	Artists House AH-1
	Voice Poetry	(44) —	—
	Home Grown	(44) —	—
	Macho Woman	(44) —	—
	European Echoes	(44) —	—
	Theme from a Symphony: Variation One[1]	(41)	A&M/Horizon SP-722
	Theme from a Symphony: Variation Two[1]	(41) —	—
	Ghetto Kid		Artists House (unissued)

[1]Same as "Tutti," "The Good Life," "School Days," etc.

March 21, 1976 New York City	Charlie Haden		
	Ornette Coleman (as); Charlie Haden (b)		
	O.C. (Haden)	(45)	A&M/Horizon SP-710
	Law Years		unissued

December 19, 1976 New York City	Charlie Haden		
	Ornette Coleman (tp); Charlie Haden (b)		
	The Golden Number	(46)	A&M/Horizon SP-727

December 21–22, 1976 New York City	Ornette Coleman Quartet		
	Don Cherry (tp); Ornette Coleman (as); Charlie Haden (b); Billy Higgins (d)		
	The Adjuster		Artists House (unissued)
	Energy, Mind and Matter	—	—
	Without Name or Number	—	—

Don't Know — —
Night Worker — —

January 30, 1977 Ornette Coleman-Charlie Haden
New York City Ornette Coleman (tp, ts); Charlie Haden (b)
Mary Hartman,
   Mary Hartman
   (S. Shafer) (ts) (47) Artists House AH-6
Human Being
   (Haden) (ts) (47) — —
Soap Suds (ts) (47) — —
Sex Spy (ts) (47) — —
Some Day (tp) (47) — —

June 30, 1977 Ornette Coleman Groups
Newport in Don Cherry (tp); Ornette Coleman (as); Dewey
New York Redman (ts); James "Blood" Ulmer (g); Buster
Avery Fisher Hall Williams, David Izenzon (b); Edward Blackwell,
New York City Billy Higgins (d)
Name Brain Artists House (unissued)
The Black House — —
Mr. and Mrs.
   Dream — —
Race Face — —
Sound Amoeba — —
Ornette Coleman and Prime Time: Ornette
Coleman (as, tp, vln, bn); Bern Nix, Charlie
Ellerbee (g); Albert McDowell (b); Ronald Shan-
non Jackson, Ornette Denardo Coleman (d)
Writing in the
   Streets Artists House (unissued)
Mukami — —
Sleep Talking — —
What Reason
   Could I Give? — —
Song X — —

December 5, 1978 James Blood (Ulmer)
New York City Ornette Coleman (as); James "Blood" Ulmer (g);
Jamaaladeen Tacuma (el-b); Ornette Denardo
Coleman (d)
Theme from Cap-
   tain Black
   (Blood) (48) Artists House AH-7

Moons Shines
   (Blood)   (48) —   —
Morning Bride
   (Blood)   (48) —   —
Revelation March
   (Blood)   (48) —   —
Woman Coming
   (Blood)   (48) —   —
Nothing to Say
   (Blood)   (48) —   —
Arena (Blood)   (48) —   —
Revealing (Blood) (48) —   —

March 1979	Ornette Coleman and Prime Time
New York City	Ornette Coleman (as); Bern Nix, Charlie Ellerbee (g); Jamaaladeen Tacuma (b); Ronald Shannon Jackson, Ornette Denardo Coleman (d)
	unknown titles Artists House unissued

April 25, 1979	Ornette Coleman and Prime Time
New York City	Ornette Coleman (as); Charlie Ellerbee, Bern Nix (g); Jamaaladeen Tacuma (b-g); Ornette Denardo Coleman, Calvin Weston (d)

Sleep Talk (Dream
   Talking)   (49) Antilles AN-2001
Jump Street   (49) —   —
Him and Her   (49) —   —
Air Ship   (49) —   —
What Is the Name of
   That Song? (incl.
   "Forgotten Songs,"
   a.k.a. "Holiday for
   Heroes")   (49) —   —
Job Mob   (49) —   —
Love Words   (49) —   —
Times Square (Writ-
   ing in the Streets) (49) —   —

April 1980	Ornette Coleman Group
New York City	Probably Ornette Coleman (as, tp, vln); Charlie Ellerbee, Bern Nix (g); Jamaaladeen Tacuma (el-b); Ronald Shannon Jackson, Ornette Denardo Coleman (d)

unknown titles   unissued
Note: Ornette Coleman produced this digital recording session.

March 1981
New York City

Ornette Coleman
Ornette Coleman (as, tp, vln, arr, cond); probably Bern Nix, Charlie Ellerbee (g); Albert MacDowell, Jamaaladeen Tacuma (el-b); Ornette Denardo Coleman, D. Michael Alston (d); forty-piece symphony orchestra; "classical" and "pop" vocalist
unknown titles   soundtrack
Note: this is the recording of Coleman's score for the Josef Bogdanovich film *Box Office*.

January 24, 1982
New York City

Ornette Coleman and Prime Time
Probably Ornette Coleman (as, tp, vln); Bern Nix, Charlie Ellerbee (g); Jamaaladeen Tacuma, Albert MacDowell (el-b); Denardo Coleman, James Jones (d)

Title	Label	Status
Straight Line in a Circle	Antilles	unissued
Latin Genetics	—	—
News Item	—	—
In All Languages	—	—
Song X	—	—
Kartham Place	—	—
Script Trip	—	—
Be with Me	—	—
Compute	—	—
To Know What to Know	—	—
A Minor Augment	—	—
Asia	—	—
Sex Spy II	—	—
Old Wives Tales	—	—
Police People	—	—
City Living	—	—

Note: This single recording session was designed to result in two Antilles albums. Some earlier songs may have been retitled here.

1984   Jamaaladeen Tacuma
New York City   Ornette Coleman (as); Charles Ellerbee (g); Ja-
                            maaladeen Tacuma (el-b, arr); Ron Howerton
                            (perc, el perc); Jamaaladeen Tacuma, Greg
                            Mann (DMX, d programming)
                            Dancing in Your
                              Head (The Good
                              Life, Theme
                              from a
                              Symphony, etc.) (50) Gramavision GR8308

September 30, 1983   Ornette Coleman and Prime Time
Caravan of Dreams   Ornette Coleman (as); Bern Nix, Charles Eller-
Fort Worth, Texas   bee (g); Jamaaladeen Tacuma, Albert MacDow-
                            ell (b); Denardo Coleman, Sabir Kamal (d)
                            To Know What to
                              Know   (51) CofD CDP85001
                            Harmolodic Bebop   (51) —   —
                            Sex Spy   (51) —   —
                            City Living   (51) —   —
                            See-Thru   (51) —   —
                            Compute   (51) —   —

October 1, 1983   Ornette Coleman
Caravan of Dreams   Gregory Gelman Ensemble: Gregory Gelman
Fort Worth, Texas   (1st vln); Larissa Blitz (2nd vln); Alex Deych
                           (vla); Matthew Meister (cello); Denardo Coleman
                           (perc)
                           Prime Design/Time
                             Design   (52) CofD CDP85002

December 12–14,   Pat Metheny-Ornette Coleman
1985   Ornette Coleman (as, vln); Pat Metheny (g, g-
New York City   synthesizer); Charlie Haden (b); Jack DeJohnette
                           (d); Denardo Coleman (d, perc)
                           Song X (as)   (53) Geffen GHS24096
                           Mob Job (vln)   (53) —   —
                           Endangered Species
                             (Coleman-Metheny) (53) —   —
                           Video Games   (53) —   —
                           Kathelin Gray
                             (Coleman-Metheny) (53) —   —

Trigonometry
  (Coleman-Metheny) (53) —   —
Song X Duo
  (Coleman-Metheny) (53) —   —
Long Time No See   (53) —   —

September 10,
1986
Sound Ideas
Studio
New York City

Jayne Cortez
Jayne Cortez (voice); Ornette Coleman (as);
Charles Moffett, Jr. (ts); Bern Nix (g); Al Mac-
Dowell (b); Denardo Coleman (d)
No Simple Explanations
  (Collective
  composition)   (55) Bola Press 8601
Ornette and Abdul Wadud (cello) added for one
track each on this session; the balance of the LP
features only Cortez and the quartet. Denardo
Coleman assembled the band.

February 1987
New York City

Ornette Coleman
Quartet: Don Cherry (tp); Ornette Coleman (as,
ts); Charlie Haden (b); Billy Higgins (d)
Peace
  Warriors   (54) CofD CDP85008
Feet Music   (54) —   —
Africa Is the Mirror
  of All Colors   (54) —   —
Word for Bird   (54) —   —
Space Church
  (Continuous
  Services)   (54) —   —
Latin Genetics   (54) —   —
In All Languages   (54) —   —
Sound Manual   (54) —   —
Mothers of the Veil   (54) —   —
Cloning   (54) —   —
Prime Time: Ornette Coleman (as, tp); Bern
Nix, Charles Ellerbee (g); Al MacDowell, Ja-
maaladeen Tacuma (el-b); Denardo Coleman,
Calvin Weston (d)
Music News   (54) CofD CDP85008
Mothers of the Veil   (54) —   —
The Art of Love
  Is Happiness   (54) —   —

Latin Genetics	(54) —	—
Today, Yesterday and Tomorrow	(54) —	—
Listen Up	(54) —	—
Feet Music	(54) —	—
Space Church (Continuous Services)	(54) —	—
Cloning	(54) —	—
In All Languages	(54) —	—
Biosphere	(54) —	—
Story Tellers	(54) —	—
Peace Warriors	(54) —	—

Fall 1987– Spring 1988	Ornette Coleman and Prime Time Ornette Coleman (as, tp, vln); Bern Nix, Charlee Ellerbe (g); Al MacDowell, Chris Walker (b-g), Denardo Coleman, (d, keyboards, perc); Calvin Weston (d)	
	Bourgeois Boogie	(56) Portrait 44301
	Happy Hour	(56) — —
	Virgin Beauty	(56) — —
	Healing the Feeling	(56) — —
	Honeymooners	(56) — —
	Chanting	(56) — —
	Spelling the Alphabet	(56) — —
	Unknown Artist	(56) — —
	add Jerry Garcia (g)	
	3 Wishes	(56) — —
	Singing in the Shower	(56) — —
	Desert Players	(56) — —

1988 East Berlin, East Germany	Ornette Coleman and Prime Time Ornette Coleman (as, tp, vln); Ken Wessel, Chris Rosenberg (g); Chris Walker, Al MacDowell (b); Denardo Coleman (d, perc); Badal Roy, tablas	
	Song X	(57) Repertoire RR49905CC
	Music News	(57) — —
	Chanting	(57) — —
	Honeymoon	(57) — —
	Realing the Feeling	(57) — —

Singing in the
　Shower　　　　　(57) —　　　　　—
Dancing in
　Your Head　　　(57) —　　　　　—
Bourgeoise
　Blues　　　　　(57) —　　　　　—

August 12, 13, 17,
1991
London, England

Howard Shore/Ornette Coleman/London
Philharmonic Orchestra
Ornette Coleman (as); London Philharmonic Or-
chestra, Howard Shore (cond)
Naked Lunch
　(Shore)　　　　(58) Milan　73138 35614-2
Centipede (Shore)　(58) —　　　　　—
Mujahaddin
　(Shore)　　　　(58) —　　　　　—
Dr. Benway
　(Shore)　　　　(58) —　　　　　—
add Denardo Coleman (d)
Welcome to Annex-
　ia (Shore)　　　(58) —　　　　　—
David Hartley (p) replaces Denardo Coleman
Simpatico (Shore)/
　Misterioso
　(Monk)　　　　(58) —　　　　　—
Coleman (as); LPO, Shore (cond); Barre Phillips
(b); Denardo Coleman (d)
Hauser and O'Brien
　(Shore)/
　Bugpowder　　　(58) —　　　　　—
Ornette Coleman (as); Barre Phillips (b); De-
nardo Coleman (d)
Intersong　　　　(58) —　　　　　—
Ballad/Joan　　　(58) —　　　　　—
Writeman　　　　(58) —　　　　　—
add double-reed instrument, perc
Interzone Suite
　(Shore)　　　　(58) —　　　　　—

Notes

(Quotations without footnotes are from the author's interviews.)

PROLOGUE

1. Nat Hentoff, liner notes to Ornette Coleman: *Something Else!* (Contemporary 3551).
2. David Fricke, "Ornette Coleman's Time," *Rolling Stone*, March 9, 1989.
3. Ornette Coleman, liner notes to *This Is Our Music* (Atlantic 1353).
4. Ornette Coleman, interview with Bob Blumenthal, November 21, 1981.

CHAPTER I

1. Whitney Balliett, *American Musicians* (New York: Oxford University Press, 1986); originally published as "Jazz: Ornette," *The New Yorker*, August 30, 1982.
2. Ibid.
3. David Grogan, "Ornette Coleman," *People*, October 13, 1986.
4. Joe Goldberg, *Jazz Masters of the 50s* (New York: Macmillan, 1963; New York: Da Capo Press).

5. Nat Hentoff, "Ornette Coleman: Biggest Noise in Jazz," *Esquire*, March 1961, reprinted in Hentoff, *The Jazz Life* (New York: Da Capo Press, 1975).
6. Ibid.
7. Ibid.
8. Ibid.
9. Valerie Wilmer, *As Serious as Your Life*, rev. ed. (Westport, Conn.: Lawrence Hill, 1980).
10. Program notes to *Jimmy Liggins and His Drops of Joy* (Specialty CD 7005).
11. A. B. Spellman, *Black Music: Four Lives* (New York: Schocken Books, 1970) (First published as *Four Lives in the Bebop Business* [New York: Pantheon, 1966].)
12. Balliett, *American Musicians*.
13. Grogan, "Ornette Coleman."
14. Peter Watrous, "The Return of Jazz's Greatest Eccentric," *The New York Times*, June 23, 1991.
15. Spellman, *Black Music: Four Lives*.
16. Watrous, "Jazz's Greatest Eccentric."
17. John Rockwell, *All American Music* (New York: Knopf, 1983).
18. John Morphland, "Roots & Branches," *High Fidelity*, October 1984.
19. Spellman, *Black Music: Four Lives*.
20. Goldberg, *Jazz Masters*.
21. Ibid.
22. Ibid.
23. Ibid.
24. Balliett, *American Musicians*.
25. Watrous, "Jazz's Greatest Eccentric."
26. Howard Mandel, "Ornette Coleman: The Creator as Harmolodic Magician," *Down Beat*, October 5, 1978.
27. Eileen Southern, *The Music of Black Americans: A History* (New York: Norton, 1971).
28. Spellman, *Black Music: Four Lives*.
29. Ibid.
30. Jason Berry, Jonathan Foose, and Tad Jones, *Up from the Cradle of Jazz* (Athens: University of Georgia Press, 1986).
31. Valerie Wilmer, "Edward Blackwell," *Down Beat*, October 3, 1968.

CHAPTER II

1. Valerie Wilmer, *As Serious as Your Life*, rev. ed. (Westport, Conn.: Lawrence Hill, 1980).

2. Nat Hentoff, "Ornette Coleman: Biggest Noise in Jazz," *Esquire*, March 1961, reprinted in Hentoff, *The Jazz Life* (New York: Da Capo Press, 1975).

3. Valerie Wilmer, "Edward Blackwell," *Down Beat*, October 3, 1968.

4. Valerie Wilmer, "Alvin Batiste and Ellis Marsalis," *Coda* 173 (June 1980).

5. Wilmer, "Edward Blackwell."

6. Hentoff, "Biggest Noise."

7. Richard Williams, "Memories of Ornette," *Melody Maker*, July 17, 1971, quoted in Wilmer, *As Serious*.

8. Martin Williams, "Introducing Eric Dolphy," *Jazz Review*, June 1960, reprinted in Williams, ed., *Jazz Panorama* (New York: Collier Books, 1964).

9. A. B. Spellman, *Black Music: Four Lives* (New York: Schocken Books, 1970). First published as *Four Lives in the Bebop Business* (New York: Pantheon, 1966).

10. Wilmer, "Edward Blackwell."

11. Spellman, *Black Music: Four Lives.*

12. Ornette Coleman, interview with Bob Blumenthal, November 21, 1981.

13. Rick Senger, "Judgment of Freedom, Freedom of Judgment," *WHPK Program Guide*, Fall 1988.

14. Howard Mandel, "Ornette Coleman: The Creator as Harmolodic Magician," *Down Beat*, October 5, 1978.

15. Spellman, *Black Music: Four Lives.*

16. Wilmer, "Batiste and Marsalis."

17. Ibid.

18. Marc Cobb, "Billy Higgins," *Be-Bop and Beyond*, May–June 1984.

19. Don Cherry, from a lecture delivered in Ann Arbor, Michigan, March 28, 1980; quoted in David Wild, "Biography," in David Wild and Michael Cuscuna, *Ornette Coleman 1958–1979: A Discography* (Ann Arbor, Mich.: Wildmusic, 1980).

20. Tim Schuller, "James Clay," *Coda* 178 (April 1981).

21. Ibid.

22. Lester Koenig, interview with John Tynan, quoted in Hentoff, "Biggest Noise."

23. Nat Hentoff, liner notes to Ornette Coleman: *Something Else!* (Contemporary 3551).

24. Ibid.

25. Ibid.

26. Keith Raether, "Ornette: Bobby Bradford's Portrait of an Emerging Giant," *Jazz*, Spring 1977.

27. Hentoff, liner notes, *Something Else!*

28. Hentoff, "Biggest Noise."
29. John Tynan, "Critics Poll," *Down Beat*, August 21, 1958.
30. John Tynan, record review of *Something Else!* in *Down Beat*, October 30, 1958.
31. Bill Smith, "Paul Bley Interview," *Coda* 166 (April 1979).
32. Ibid.
33. Spellman, *Black Music: Four Lives*.
34. Richard Williams, "Ornette and the Pipes of Joujouka," *Melody Maker*, March 17, 1973, quoted in Wilmer, *As Serious*.
35. John Lewis, interview with Fran Thorne in *Jazz di ieri e di oggi*, quoted by Nat Hentoff, liner notes to Ornette Coleman: *Tomorrow Is the Question!* (Contemporary 3569).
36. Hentoff, "Biggest Noise."
37. Gunther Schuller, "Two Reports on the School of Jazz," *Jazz Review*, November 1960.
38. Lorin Stephens, "Jimmy Giuffre: The Passionate Conviction," *Jazz Review*, February 1960.
39. Dick Hadlock, "Monterey Outside," *Jazz Review*, December 1959.
40. Gene Lees, "The Monterey Festival," *Down Beat*, November 12, 1959.
41. Hsio Wen Shih, record review of *Change of the Century*, *Jazz Review*, November 1960.
42. T. E. Martin, "The Plastic Muse, Part 1," *Jazz Monthly*, May 1964.
43. Ibid.
44. Ibid.
45. Gunther Schuller, liner notes to Ornette Coleman: *Ornette!* (Atlantic 1378).
46. Martin, "Plastic Muse, Part 1."
47. Ibid.
48. Martin Williams, record review of *Tomorrow Is the Question! Jazz Review*, November 1960.

CHAPTER III

1. George Hoefer, "Caught in the Act," *Down Beat*, January 7, 1960.
2. Whitney Balliett, "Jazz Concerts: Historic," *New Yorker*, December 5, 1959; reprinted in Balliett, *Dinosaurs in the Morning* (New York: Lippincott, 1959).
3. Nat Hentoff, "Ornette Coleman: Biggest Noise in Jazz," *Esquire*, March 1961, reprinted in Hentoff, *The Jazz Life* (New York: Da Capo Press, 1975).
4. Ibid.

5. Joe Goldberg, *Jazz Masters of the 50s* (New York: Macmillan, 1963; New York: Da Capo Press).

6. Larry Kart, "Ornette Coleman travels the long road, making up the rules as he goes along," *Chicago Tribune*, May 11, 1986.

7. John Snyder, "Ornette Coleman" (unpublished essay).

8. George Crater (Ed Sherman): *Out of My Head* (Riverside LP 841).

9. Bob Abel, "The Man with the White Plastic Alto Saxophone," *HiFi/Stereo Review*, August 1960.

10. Charles Mingus, "Mingus on Ornette Coleman, *Down Beat*, May 26, 1960.

11. Stanley Dance, "Lightly and Politely," *Jazz Journal*, 1960.

12. Francis Newton in *New Statesman*, quoted in Nat Hentoff, "Jazz in Print," *Jazz Review*, November 1960.

13. T. E. Martin, "The Plastic Muse, Part 2," *Jazz Monthly*, June 1964.

14. George Russell and Martin Williams, "Ornette Coleman and Tonality," *Jazz Review*, June 1960.

15. Martin, "Plastic Muse, Part 2."

16. Ibid.

17. Ibid.

18. Ibid.

19. Kenneth Rexroth, "What's Wrong with the Clubs?" in Rexroth, *Assays* (New York: New Directions, 1961).

20. Robert Palmer, "Charlie Haden's Creed," *Down Beat*, July 20, 1972.

21. Buell Neidlinger, program notes to *The Complete Candid Recordings of Cecil Taylor and Buell Neidlinger* (Mosaic MR6-127).

22. Nat Hentoff, "Ornette Coleman: Biggest Noise in Jazz," *Esquire*, March 1961, reprinted in Hentoff, *The Jazz Life* (New York: Da Capo Press, 1975).

23. "The Talk of the Town: The True Essence," *New Yorker*, June 4, 1960.

24. Buell Neidlinger, program notes, *Complete Candid Recordings of Taylor and Neidlinger*.

25. Ibid.

26. John Tynan, "The Monterey Festival," *Down Beat*, November 10, 1960.

27. Gunther Schuller, preface to *A Collection of the Composition of Ornette Coleman* (New York: MJQ Music, 1961).

28. Gunther Schuller, liner notes to Schuller-Jim Hall: *John Lewis Presents Jazz Abstractions* (Atlantic 1365).

29. A. B. Spellman, *Black Music: Four Lives* (New York: Schocken Books, 1970). First published as *Four Lives in the Bebop Business* (New York: Pantheon, 1966).

30. Howard Mandel, "Charlie Haden's Search for Freedom," *Down Beat*, September 1987.

31. Gunther Schuller, liner notes to Ornette Coleman: *Ornette!* (Atlantic 1378).
32. T. E. Martin, "The Plastic Muse, Part 3," *Jazz Monthly*, August 1964.
33. A. B. Spellman, liner notes to Ornette Coleman: *Ornette on Tenor* (Atlantic 1394).
34. Valerie Wilmer, *As Serious as Your Life*, rev. ed. (Westport, Conn.: Lawrence Hill, 1980).
35. Kenny Mathieson, "Edward Blackwell: Tap, March and Dance," *The Wire*, June 1988.
36. Don Heckman, "Jimmy Garrison," *Down Beat*, March 9, 1967.
37. Spellman, *Black Music: Four Lives*.
38. Richard Williams, "Memories of Ornette," *Melody Maker*, July 17, 1971, quoted in Wilmer, *As Serious as Your Life*, rev. ed. (Westport, Conn.: Lawrence Hill, 1980).
39. George Coppens, "Charles Moffett," *Coda* 191 (1983).
40. Spellman, *Back Music: Four Lives*.
41. "News," *Down Beat*, January 3, 1963.
42. John Morphland, "Roots & Branches," *High Fidelity*, October 1984.
43. Frederic Ramsey, Jr., and Charles Edward Smith, *Jazzmen* (New York: Harcourt, Brace & Co., 1939).

CHAPTER IV

1. Michael Bourne, "Ornette's Innerview," *Down Beat*, November 22, 1973.
2. Robert Seidenberg, "Made in America," *Horizon*, November 1986.
3. John Tynan, "Take Five," *Down Beat*, April 11, 1963.
4. "Ad Lib," *Down Beat*, October 24, 1963.
5. Barry McRae, *Ornette Coleman* (London: Apollo Press, 1988).
6. Ornette Coleman, in the film *Ornette: Made in America*, Shirley Clarke, director.
7. Joachim Berendt, "Caught in the Act," *Down Beat*, January 14, 1965.
8. Alan Bates, "Caught in the Act," *Down Beat*, October 8, 1964.
9. Martin Williams, "Two Views of the Avant Garde," *Down Beat*, November 19, 1964.
10. Dan Morgenstern, "Caught in the Act," February 25, 1965.
11. J. B. Figi, "Ornette Coleman: A Surviving Elder in the Universal Brotherhood of Those Who Make Music," (Chicago) *Reader*, June 22, 1973.
12. Max Harrison, *A Jazz Retrospect* (London: Quartet Books, 1992).
13. Ibid.
14. Ornette Coleman, liner notes to Coleman: *The Empty Foxhole* (Blue Note 8246).

15. Dan Morgenstern, "Charlie Haden—From Hillbilly to Avant Garde— A Rocky Road," *Down Beat*, March 9, 1967.
16. Ibid.
17. Shelly Manne and Julian "Cannonball" Adderley, " 'Round the Empty Foxhole," *Down Beat*, November 2, 1967.
18. Leonard Feather, "Blindfold Test: Freddie Hubbard," *Down Beat*, April 18, 1968.
19. Pete Welding and Ornette Coleman, " 'Round the Empty Foxhole," *Down Beat*, November 2, 1967.
20. Ornette Coleman, liner notes, *Empty Foxhole*.
21. McRae, *Ornette Coleman*.
22. Jackie McLean, liner notes to McLean: *Let Freedom Ring* (Blue Note 84106).
23. Nat Hentoff, liner notes in Jackie McLean: *New and Old Gospel* (Blue Note 84262).
24. Ibid.
25. McRae, *Ornette Coleman*.
26. Harrison, *A Jazz Retrospect*.
27. Dewey Redman, interview with Kevin Whitehead, March 3, 1982.
28. Ornette Coleman, liner notes to *The Music of Ornette Coleman* (RCA LSC2982).
29. Harrison, *A Jazz Retrospect*.
30. Spellman, *Black Music: Four Lives*.
31. Arthur Taylor, *Notes and Tones* (New York: Perigee Books, 1982).
32. Ibid.
33. Ibid.
34. Ibid.
35. Ibid.

Chapter V

1. Valerie Wilmer, *As Serious as Your Life*, rev. ed. (Westport, Conn.: Lawrence Hill, 1980).
2. Mark Weber, "Bobby Bradford," *Coda*, October 1977.
3. Jim Roberts, "Charlie Haden," *Bass Player*, July/August 1991.
4. Michael Zipkin, "Charlie Haden: Struggling Idealist," *Down Beat*, July 13, 1978.
5. Ibid.
6. "News: Haden Gets Lesson in Portuguese Politics," *Down Beat*, January 20, 1972.
7. John Rockwell, *All American Music* (New York: Knopf, 1983).
8. Richard Williams, "Music of the Sky," *The Times* of London, June 3, 1988.

9. David Grogan, "Ornette Coleman," *People*, October 13, 1986.

10. Ornette Coleman, interview with David Wild, July 1982.

11. Michael Bourne, "Ornette's Innerview," *Down Beat*, November 22, 1973.

12. Rockwell, *All American Music.*

13. J. B. Figi, "Ornette Coleman: A Surviving Elder in the Universal Brotherhood of Those Who Make Music," (Chicago) *Reader*, June 22, 1973.

14. Rockwell, *All American Music.*

15. Jim Szantor, "Newport in New York," *Down Beat*, September 14, 1972.

16. Ornette Coleman, liner notes to Coleman: *Skies of America* (Columbia 31562).

17. Ornette Coleman, "Prime Time for Harmolodics," *Down Beat*, July 1983.

18. Ornette Coleman, "Harmolodic—Highest Instinct: Something to Think About," in Paul Buhle et al., eds., *Free Spirits: The Insurgent Imagination* (San Francisco: City Lights, 1982).

19. Howard Mandel, "Ornette Coleman: The Creator as Harmolodic Magician," *Down Beat*, October 5, 1978.

20. Conrad Silvert, "Old and New Dreams," *Down Beat*, June 1980.

21. Don Cherry, from a lecture delivered in Ann Arbor, Michigan, March 28, 1980; quoted in David Wild and Angelyn Wild, "A Note on the Harmolodic Theory," in David Wild and Michael Cuscuna, *Ornette Coleman 1958–1979: A Discography* (Ann Arbor, Mich.: Wildmusic, 1980).

22. Robert Palmer, "Charlie Haden's Creed," *Down Beat*, July 20, 1972.

23. Rick Senger, "Judgement of Freedom, Freedom of Judgement," *WHPK Program Guide*, Fall 1988.

24. Peter Watrous, "The Return of Jazz's Greatest Eccentric," *New York Times*, June 23, 1991.

25. *Oxford English Dictionary*, compact edition.

26. Wilbur Ware, interview with Ted Panken.

27. Figi, "Surviving Elder."

28. William S. Burroughs, "Face to Face with the Goat God," *Oui*, August 1973, quoted in Burroughs, program notes to *The Master Musicians of Jajouka Featuring Bachir Attar* (Axiom 314–510 857–2).

29. Drew Franklin, "Playing in the Register of Light," in "Jazz Special: Ornette Coleman" section, (New York) *Village Voice*, June 23, 1987.

30. Burroughs, "Face to Face."

31. Brion Gysin, "The Pipes of Pan," *Gnaoua*, Spring 1964, quoted in Burroughs, program notes, *Master Musicians of Jajouka*.

32. Franklin, "Register of Light."

33. Figi, "Surviving Elder."
34. Barry McRae, *Ornette Coleman* (London: Apollo Press, 1988).

Chapter VI

1. Clifford Jay Safane, "The Harmolodic Diatonic Funk of James 'Blood' Ulmer," *Down Beat*, October 1980.
2. Cliff Tinder, "Jamaaladeen Tacuma: Electric Bass in the Harmolodic Pocket," *Down Beat*, April 1982.
3. Ibid.
4. Scott Albin, "Newport '77: Farewell to the Apple," *Down Beat*, October 6, 1977.
5. Chip Stern, "Newport Turns 25," *Down Beat*, September 7, 1978.
6. John Snyder, "Ornette Coleman" (unpublished essay).
7. Ibid.
8. Ornette Coleman, interview with Bob Blumenthal, November 21, 1981.
9. Howard Mandel, "Ornette Coleman: The Creator as Harmolodic Magician," *Down Beat*, October 5, 1978.
10. Ornette Coleman, in liner notes to Charlie Haden: *The Golden Number* (A&M/Horizon SP-727).
11. Michael Bourne, "Ornette's Interview," *Down Beat*, November 22, 1973.
12. David Fricke, "Ornette Coleman's Time," *Rolling Stone*, March 9, 1989.
13. Barry McRae, *Ornette Coleman* (London: Apollo Press, 1988).
14. John Snyder, "Ornette Coleman" (unpublished essay).
15. Greg Tate, "Change of the Century," in "Jazz Special: Ornette Coleman" section, (New York) *Village Voice*, June 23, 1987.
16. Mandel, "Harmolodic Magician."
17. Ornette Coleman, interview with Bob Blumenthal, November 21, 1981.
18. Ibid.
19. Leonard Feather, "Ornette Coleman: The Long, Winding Road Back to L.A.," *Los Angeles Times*, March 1, 1981.
20. Ornette Coleman, interview with David Wild, July 1982.
21. Ibid.
22. Ibid.
23. Ibid.
24. Bob Blumenthal, "The Sun Ra Show," *Boston Phoenix*, May 6, 1975.

CHAPTER VII

1. Ornette Coleman, in the film *Ornette: Made in America*, Shirley Clarke, director.
2. Denardo Coleman, in *Ornette: Made in America*.
3. Ibid.
4. Francis Davis, *In the Moment* (New York: Oxford University Press, 1986).
5. Ibid.
6. Ibid.
7. Ornette Coleman, liner notes to Coleman: *Prime Design/Time Design* (Caravan of Dreams 85002).
8. John Rockwell, "Jazz: Ornette Coleman Goes Home," *New York Times*, October 3, 1983.
9. Max Harrison, record review of *Prime Design/Time Design*, *The Wire*, April 1987.
10. Richard Williams, "Music of the Sky," *The Times* of London, June 3, 1988.
11. Joe Cohen, "Riffs: Ornette Coleman," *Down Beat*, October 1985.
12. Art Lange, "Ornette Coleman & Pat Metheny," *Down Beat*, June 1986.
13. Bill Shoemaker, record review of *In All Languages*, *Down Beat*, October 1987.
14. Howard Mandel, "Ornette Coleman: The Color of Music," *Down Beat*, August 1987.
15. Laurence Veysey, "New Mexico, 1971: Inside a 'New Age' Social Order," in Veysey, *The Communal Experience* (Chicago: University of Chicago Press, 1973).
16. Williams S. Burroughs, "Sects and Death," in Burroughs, *Roosevelt After Inauguration* (San Francisco: City Lights, 1979).
17. Williams, "Music of the Sky."
18. Kevin Whitehead, record review of *Virgin Beauty*, *Down Beat*, October 1988.
19. Peter Watrous, "Return of Jazz's Greatest Eccentric," *The New York Times*, June 23, 1991.
20. Larry Rohter, "Ornette Coleman Takes His Quartet Home," *The New York Times*, September 10, 1990.

Index